THE SIGN IN
THEORY AND
PRACTICE

An Introductory Reader
in Semiotics

edited by
Marcel Danesi, *University of Toronto*
and
Donato Santeramo, *Queen's University*

Canadian Scholars' Press   Toronto   1999

The Sign in Theory and Practice: An Introductory Reader in Semiotics
edited by Marcel Danesi and Donato Santeramo

First published in 1999 by
Canadian Scholars' Press Inc.
180 Bloor Street West, Ste. 1202
Toronto, Ontario
M5S 2V6

We acknowledge the financial support of the Government of Canada through the Book Publishing Industry Development Programme for our publishing activities.

Canadian Cataloguing in Publication Data

Main entry under title:
The sign in theory and practice

Previously published under the title: Introducing semiotics: an anthology of readings.
Includes bibliographical references.
ISBN 1-55130-111-3

1. Semiotics. I. Danesi, Marcel, 1946– . II. Santeramo, Donato, 1959– .
III. Title: Introducing semiotics: an anthology of readings

P99.I68 1999   401'.41   C98-933014-1

Page layout and cover design by Brad Horning

CONTENTS

CLOSING REMARKS

PREFACE

In 1992, the compilers of the present anthology decided to put together ten readings in a volume entitled *Introducing Semiotics: An Anthology of Readings* (published by Canadian Scholars' Press). Our intention at the time was to provide our own students at the University of Toronto with foundational readings in semiotic theory. *Introducing Semiotics* was envisaged, in other words, as a supplementary manual designed to give the student and the interested general reader a first-hand glimpse into some of the texts and/or figures that have helped to lay the foundation of the semiotic theoretical edifice. We had also hoped that as a spin-off the readings would spur our students on to pursue the study of semiotics on their own in a more in-depth way—i.e., we had hoped that by reading a little Peirce or a little Saussure students would welcome the challenge of reading more. We never thought for a moment that our anthology would be used by other university instructors in Canada, the United States, and abroad who also wanted to expose their own students to source texts in semiotic theory. This was both surprising and gratifying.

The comments, critiques, suggestions, and advice that the users of *Introducing Semiotics* have passed on to us over the years have guided every phase and aspect of the work of putting together this modified second edition, which is now entitled *The Sign in Theory and Practice: An Introductory*

Reader in Semiotics. We have attempted to make the present volume more pedagogically useful in the following three ways: (1) we have provided our own pre-reading synopses and historical notes to the eleven readings in an opening section (What Is Semiotics?); (2) we have appended a list at the end of ten classic works in semiotics to encourage students to pursue further reading in semiotics; and (3) we have drafted three follow-up activities and three questions for discussion per chapter that can be used as the basis for post-reading classroom work. We hope that this volume reflects both what instructors and students of semiotics have told us would be most useful to them.

Marcel Danesi
University of Toronto

Donato Santeramo
Queen's University

OPENING REMARKS

The third branch may be called *semiotike,* or the *Doctrine of Signs*,
the most influential whereof being Words, it is aptly enough termed
also *logike*; the business whereof, is to consider the Nature of Signs,
the Mind makes use of for the understanding of Things,
or conveying its Knowledge to others.

–John Locke (1632-1704)

WHAT IS SEMIOTICS?

Marcel Danesi
Donato Santeramo

INTRODUCTION

The perennial question that any instructor of semiotics gets, as students scan the list of courses their university makes available to them each fall, is "What is semiotics?" This question is symptomatic of the fact that semiotics has not yet worked its way into the everyday vocabulary of education, or social discourse generally. Every student seems to have some idea of what philosophy, culture studies, media studies, and other such disciplines are about, even though when questioned on what they purport to investigate, one gets as many different responses as there are respondents. But the very mention of the word semiotics, on the other hand, rarely fails to elicit quizzical looks. And if problems of recognizability were not enough, semiotics is also beset by jurisdictional uncertainties, defying, as it does, the traditional types of classificatory schemas that are found in university calendars. Semiotics cannot be easily accommodated within the established disciplinary categories of North American universities.

Yet, semiotics is all about the most remarkable attribute of the human brain—its innate capacity to produce, understand, and make use of *signs*. A *sign* is anything (a word, a gesture, a wink, a smile, etc.) that stands for something other than itself: a word such as *tree* does not stand for the sounds that comprise it *(t-r-ee)*, but rather for something else (a type of plant); and similarly, a finger pointing at something or someone does not stand for itself, the finger, but for the someone or something to which it calls attention. People and cultures everywhere intuitively grasp the crucial importance of signs to human life. This is why that very word is used in the make-up of certain words in English—*signification, significant, resign, consign, insignia, signature,* etc.—and in many expressions—"This is a *sign* of the times."

The modern-day practice of semiotics traces its origins to the writings of the Swiss linguist Ferdinand de Saussure and the American philosopher Charles S. Peirce. As an autonomous field of inquiry, it has been expanded and developed throughout the twentieth century by such scholars as Charles Morris, Roland Barthes, Louis Hjelmslev, A.J. Greimas, Thomas A. Sebeok, and Umberto Eco, to mention but a few. But like a spider's web, which entraps its prey in a network of interwoven strands, semiotics has been gradually luring more scientists, educators, and humanists working in other disciplinary realms into its intricate loom of insights into human mentality, behaviour, and culture. Indeed, today semiotics is being used more and more by scholars from many fields as an investigative framework for understanding the *raison d'être* of such phenomena as language, myths, works of art, narratives, and scientific theories. These scholars have obviously come to understand that signs are "windows" that open up into the landscape of human consciousness and the imagination.

The metaphor of the "web," which so colourfully, yet so accurately, captures the idea that the human arts and sciences spring from the same fundamental core of sign-based capacities in the brain, was chosen in 1986 by the Sebeoks—Thomas A. and Jane Umiker—to designate the interlacing and interfacing nature of semiotic theory and research with other disciplines. There is no doubt that a large part of the recent increase in the popularity of semiotics has been brought about by the publication in 1983 of a best-selling medieval detective novel, *The Name of the Rose*, written by one of the most distinguished practitioners of semiotics, Umberto Eco. Eco has since published two other best-sellers—*Foucault's Pendulum* and *The Island of the Day Before*. His three novels have certainly gone a long way towards putting semiotics on the world map of pop culture.

4

THE OBJECT OF SEMIOTICS

The world of Nature has no apparent interest in "saying something" about itself. Only humans feel an intrinsic need to do so. We insist on meaning. Indeed we can't help but to think of the world and of ourselves as meaningful entities. In our search for meaning and purpose, we are greatly aided by the remarkable ability to refer to the inner and outer dimensions of experience with signs. The primary object of semiotics is to understand how this comes about. The term used to refer to the innate capacity of human beings to produce and understand signs of all kinds, from simple physiological signals to those which reveal a highly complex symbolism, is semiosis (e.g., Sebeok, 1976, 1979, 1981, 1985a, 1986, 1991, 1994). The etymology of this term is traceable to the Greek word *semeion* "mark, sign." In its oldest usage (Nöth, 1990: 12-14), the term referred to an observable physiological symptom induced by a specific ailment or disease. It was used first by Hippocrates (460?-377? BC)—the founder of medical science—to alert medical practitioners to the value of knowing how to decipher bodily signs that are both observable on and/or reported by their patients. The science of *semeiotika* was thus established so that medical practitioners could carry out accurate diagnoses and formulate suitable prognoses. As Fisch (1978: 41) points out, it was soon after Hippocrates's utilization of the term *semeion* to refer to a symptom that it came to mean—by the time of Aristotle (384-322 BC)—the mental activity that involves knowledge of a sign itself, or the correlative act of sign interpretation. Ever since, the study of signs has focused on identifying what the main semiosic processes are, the types of signs that humans are capable of producing, their uses, how they make messages and texts of all kinds possible, how they underlie the capacity for art, performance, ritual, scientific theorizing, and so on, which make-up the unique world of human culture. This world is not inherited through genes by subsequent generations but through the very signs people acquire in social contexts.

The eleven chapters that comprise this reader will give you a broad overview of what semiotics is all about, from the early writings of St. Augustine to recent discussions of the relation between semiosis and thought. The basic axiom that undergirds all writing on semiotics is that the sign has a triadic reality. First, there is the physical sign itself, the sounds that comprise a word, the movements that define a gesture, the wave lengths that fix the limits of a colour,

5

etc.; this dimension of the sign is called vicariously as its signifier, representamen, or even just sign. Second, there is the sign's referent (also called object or signified); this is the entity (object, event, idea, being, etc.) to which the sign refers and thus calls attention. Finally, there is the sign's meaning, or signification, that results when the sign and the referent are linked together. The meaning is not coincident with the referent. Even a concrete sign like the word cat can have various meanings (personal, social, etc.). Indeed, ask yourself what the word cat means to you. A semiotician would say that the sign cat is: (1) a word made up of a specific combination of sounds, c-a-t; that (2) calls attention to a carnivorous mammal with retractile claws that kills mice and rats; and that (3) will evoke a system of mental meanings that are shaped, on one side, by previous experience with such mammals and, on the other side, by the cultural classification of such mammals.

The meaning that is created by a sign is really a sign itself, or as Charles Peirce called it, an *interpretant* of that meaning. The interpretant encompasses the specific designations, emotions, feelings, and ideas that the sign evokes for a person at a certain point in time. As Peirce (1931-58, vol. 2: 228) put it: "A sign addresses somebody, that is, creates in the mind of that person an equivalent sign, or perhaps a more developed sign." Charles Morris (1938) added a behavioural dimension to this basic model of the sign by emphasizing the physical as well as the purely cognitive responses that an interpretant elicits in the human being.

Some of the readings in this book deal more with human communicative behaviour than with semiosis. Semiotically speaking, *communication* can be defined as *bilateral semiosis:* (1) *unilateral semiosis* is the capacity of an organism to receive and process specific kinds of signals in isolation (Meyer-Eppler, 1959); (2) *bilateral semiosis* is the capacity to participate with other organisms in the reception and processing of specific kinds of signals. The systematic pattern of signal-responses in which organisms participate through bilateral semiosis defines the communication system for the species to which they belong. In the case of human beings, bilateral semiosis involves not only physical signals but all kinds of signs. As Ruesch (1972: 83) has appropriately pointed out, communication is the "organizing principle of nature."

CHAPTER 1

The opening chapter in this reader, written by the well-known semiotician Tzvetan Todorov, constitutes an important historical preface to this volume and to the entire field of semiotics. For Todorov, the true scientific study of signs starts with St. Augustine (354–430 AD), the philosopher and religious thinker who was among the first to distinguish clearly between natural (nonarbitrary) and conventional (arbitrary) signs, and to espouse the view that there is an inbuilt interpretive component to the whole process of representing the world with signs (foreshadowing the Peircean notion of interpretant).

Like most writings in theoretical semiotics, this is a difficult chapter. But its main points are straightforward and historically important for you to grasp before proceeding with the other readings. Todorov starts by tracing St. Augustine's theory to various ancient Greek sources. Prominent among these are the writings of Aristotle (384-322 BC)—the philosopher who surveyed and systematized nearly all the extant branches of knowledge of the ancient world, invented the field known as formal logic, and addressed virtually every major philosophical problem known during his time—and the Stoic school of philosophy, which emphasized ethics as the main field of knowledge. The Stoics developed theories of logic and natural science to support their ethical doctrines. Their most important contribution to logic was the discovery of the hypothetical syllogism, which has become the primary form of Western logical thinking (in mathematics, science, law, etc.). All syllogisms have the following form: (1) If all humans are mortal, and (2) Beatrice is human, then (3) she is mortal.

From Aristotle, St. Augustine adopted the idea that words are only special kinds of signs. But he challenged Aristotle's view that words referred to the world in arbitrary, conventional ways, i.e., without any attempt to reflect or refer to the perceivable properties (sound, sight, etc.) of the referent to which they call attention. Aristotle's "conventionalist" perspective contrasted with the "naturalist" views of other philosophers of his time that words were, in fact, originally reflective of such properties.

Both Aristotle and the Stoics saw signs as being part of the triadic relation described below: (1) the physical part of the sign itself; (2) its reference to something in the world; (3) its evocation of a meaning.

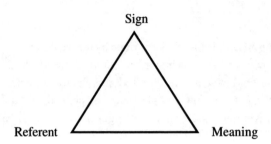

They also affirmed that the dimensions of this triadic relation occurred simultaneously. And it is indeed impossible to think of a word without thinking at the same time of the being, object, idea, or event to which it refers and to the meaning(s) that this entails. Another remarkable contribution by Aristotle to theories of meaning was his discovery of *metaphor.* Aristotle was fascinated by this unique signifying phenomenon, which he defined as "giving a thing a name that belongs to something else."

Among other influences that shaped St. Augustine's theory of signs, Todorov mentions the *hermeneutic* tradition of the ancient world: i.e., the study and interpretation of ancient texts, especially those of a religious or mythical nature. Among the first to study texts hermeneutically was Clement of Alexandria (150?-215? AD), the Greek theologian and early father of the church. Clement established the method of ascertaining as far as possible the meaning that a Biblical writer intended on the basis of linguistic considerations, sources, and historical background. Clement also maintained that the interpreter should not ignore the fact that the original meaning of the text developed in the course of history, and that the act of interpretation is bound to be coloured by cultural factors.

To the Aristotelian theory of the sign St. Augustine added the ideas that signs serve communication, that human learning occurs through signs, and that signs are visible tokens of our spiritual nature. St. Augustine also devised the first useful typology of signs. He classified signs according to:

(1) mode of transmission (primarily through visual and audio-oral channels of transmission);
(2) their origin and use, as both natural and conventional, intentional and nonintentional;

(3) their social function;

(4) the ways in which they refer to their objects (as proper or literal signs and as metaphors);

(5) the nature of the referent (natural signs tend to be associated with concrete objects and conventional ones with abstract referents).

CHAPTER 2

Although you might find this chapter by one of the modern-day founders of semiotics, Charles Sanders Peirce (1839-1914), rather difficult, it is worth the effort to get through it. We suggest first reading it over quickly once, without pausing to wrestle with its intricate ideas, doing the follow-up activities at the back of the book next, and then re-reading it several times.

Peirce defines semiotics, as the philosopher John Locke (1632-1704) did before him, as the "doctrine of signs." The word *doctrine* is used by Peirce in the sense of "set of principles," not in any religious sense. He then defines *sign*, which he also calls a *representamen* (literally something that does the representing), as "something that stands to somebody for something [which Peirce calls the *object*] in some respect or capacity [the mental *interpretant*]." Peirce then goes on to distinguish among three basic types of "trichotomies" of signs. The first is that all signs can be classified as *qualitative, singular,* and *conventional*. He calls these, respectively, *qualisigns, sinsigns,* and *legisigns*. These refer to the nature of the representamen itself:

- A *qualisign* is a representamen that refers to some quality of its referent. In language, an adjective is a qualisign since it refers to some object, being, idea, or event in terms of its qualities (colour, shape, size, etc.). In other media, qualisigns can be the colours used by painters, the harmonies or tones used by composers, and so on.
- A *sinsign* is a representamen that refers to some particular existent object, being, idea, or event.
- A *legisign* is a conventionalized representamen.

The second trichotomy refers to the kinds of interpretants associated with signs:

9

- *Rhemes* are interpretants of qualisigns that evoke the perceived "essences" of referents.
- *Dicisigns* are interpretants of sinsigns that refer to concrete referents.
- *Arguments* are interpretants of legisigns that refer to things, events, ideas, etc. by convention.

Peirce's third trichotomy, namely the classification of signs according to how they refer to their objects or referents as *icons*, *indexes*, and *symbols*, has become a foundational typology for the scientific study of signs that most semioticians have adopted today as basic to an understanding of semiosis:

- An *icon* is a sign that refers to something through some form of replication, simulation, or resemblance: a photo resembles its referent visually, a word such as *drip* (known technically as an onomatopoeic word), resembles its referent by attempting to replicate the sound it makes.
- An *index* is a sign that refers to the existence of something in space, time, or in relation to someone else: a pointing index finger is an indication of where an object is in space; smoke is an index of fire; the words *here* and *there* are indexes of relative location.
- A *symbol* is a sign that refers according to some conventional practice that is constrained culturally: a *rose* is a symbol of love in some cultures; words such as *love* and *hope* refer by convention to various emotions or concepts.

Peirce refers to icons as *Firstness* signs because they are tied, *first*, to sense-based semiosis. In a sense they are substitutes for the stimuli they refer to themselves. Since icons must also be understood in cultural context, Peirce uses the term *hypoicon* to acknowledge this fact. Nevertheless, icons refer to objects by similarity, so that even in cultural contexts many of these can be figured out by those who are not necessarily a part of the culture. For Peirce *iconicity* is the primary form of semiosis or representation: i.e., it is innate and natural for all of us to resort to iconic signing first and then to proceed on to other forms. *Indexicality* is defined by Peirce as a *Secondness* form of representation: i.e., one in which the sign directs attention to its referent by singling it out in time and/or space. Unlike icons, the sign is not a substitute for the stimuli. For instance, an arrow on a sheet of paper pointing out something in relation to a second referent is an example of an index. Perhaps the best known kinds of indexes are the pointing index finger and the indices used at the back of books. Finally, *symbols* reveal a *Thirdness* form of representation, says Peirce, because in this case the sign, the sign-user, and the referent are linked to each other by the forces of historical and social convention.

The relation of these trichotomies to each other can be summarized with the following diagram:

	Type of representamen	Relation of the sign to its referent (object)	Type of interpretant the sign evokes
Firstness form of semiosis	QUALISIGN	ICONIC	RHEME
Secondness form of semiosis	SINSIGN	INDEXICAL	DICISIGN
Thirdness form of semiosis	LEGISIGN	SYMBOLIC	ARGUMENT

CHAPTER 3

Unlike the previous two chapters, this chapter is a much easier one to follow, perhaps because it was originally designed to be part of a university course given by the author. Indeed, the *Cours de linguistique générale,* which has become a foundational text for both modern linguistics and semiotics, was compiled and put together from the notes taken by Saussure's students after his death.

Ferdinand de Saussure (1857-1913) was born in Geneva, and attended science classes for a year at the University of Geneva before turning to language studies at the University of Leipzig in 1876. As a student he published his only book, *Mémoire sur le système primitif des voyelles dans les langues indo-européennes* ("Memoir on the Original Vowel System in the Indo-European Languages," 1879), an important work on the vowel system of Proto-Indo-European languages, considered the parent language from which the Indo-European languages descended. Saussure taught at the École des Hautes Études in Paris from 1881 to 1891 and then became a professor of Sanskrit and Comparative Grammar at the University of Geneva. Although he never wrote another book, his teaching proved highly influential. After his death, two of his students compiled their lecture notes and other materials into the seminal work, *Cours de linguistique générale* (1916), that bears his name. The book explained Saussure's approach to language and established a series of theoretical notions that have become basic to the study of linguistics.

Saussure starts by distinguishing between language and speech, with the former referring to the system that underlies the utterances one makes, and the latter to the actual utterances themselves. The former is mental knowledge or competence; the latter physical and socio-pragmatic competence. Then he defines *semiology* as the science that aims to "study the life of signs within society." This term is still used extensively in France and in a few other parts of Europe, although the term *semiotics* is probably the more widespread one in general use today.

The important concepts for semiotics that Saussure goes on to discuss and illustrate can be summarized as follows:

- A *sign* is made up of two intrinsically inseparable components: the *signifier* and the *signified*. The former is the actual physical part of signs. In language, for instance, words are "sound-images." These are the signifiers that refer to something in phonic ways. The signifier is more or less equivalent to Peirce's *representamen*.
- Saussure calls what the sign refers to the *signified*. This makes the sign a two-sided mental entity: it is a combination of signifier

(sound-image) and signified (concept). The signified is roughly equivalent to Peirce's *object*.

- The relationship of the signifier to the signified is *arbitrary*, i.e., there is no physical or psychological reason for using one signifier, say *tree* or *arbre* (French), to designate "an arboreal plant." There are some instances whereby the signifier has some iconic connection with the signified, e.g., onomatopoeic words (*drip, plop, whack,* etc.) which attempt to reflect the sound properties of their referents. But for Saussure, unlike for Peirce, iconicity is a relatively isolated and infrequent phenomenon. Note that there is no concept of *interpretant* in Saussure's definition of the sign.

- The meaning of signs is fixed at a certain point in time by the society that uses them. Saussure refers to this as the *synchronic* or *immutable* aspect of semiosis. But he also points out that the signifiers and/or signifieds will change over time. He calls this the *diachronic* aspect of signs.

CHAPTER 4

This chapter by Rick Osborn deals with one of the most intriguing questions of all time: Do linguistic categories influence or determine how people view the world? This idea is called the Whorfian hypothesis, after the American anthropological linguist Benjamin Lee Whorf (1897–1941), even though versions can be found before Whorf. The Whorfian analysis of words starts by classifying lexical items according to a common range of meaning which is said to constitute a semantic domain. Such a domain is characterized by the distinctive features that differentiate individual items in the domain from one another, and also by features shared by all the items in the domain. For example, in the domain where "seat" occurs in English can be found the words "chair," "sofa," "loveseat," and "bench." These can be distinguished from one another according to how many people are accommodated and whether a back support is included. At the same time all these items share the common component, or feature, of meaning "something on which to sit."

Whorfian linguists pursuing such analysis hope to identify a universal set of such semantic features, from which are drawn the different sets of features that characterize different languages. This idea of universal semantic features has been applied to the analysis of systems of myth and kinship in various cultures by the French anthropologist Claude Lévi-Strauss (1908-), who has shown that people organize their societies and interpret their place in these societies in ways that, despite apparent differences, have remarkable underlying similarities. More importantly, such linguists claim that these features predispose an individual to attend to certain objects and events in the world. In a phrase, they influence or shape the individual's thinking.

The interesting thing about Osborn's treatment of the Whorfian hypothesis is his testing of it in the areas of computer programming and sexism in language. After going through some basic features of programming techniques, Osborn suggests that these very techniques have a structure which not only has an effect on what programs can do but also upon programmers, i.e., they actually shape the ways in which programmers approach a programming problem. Similarly, sexist terms like "chairman," and "spokesman" are often cited as examples of how language predisposes its users to view certain things, events, and people in terms of socially biased gender categories. Osborn concludes that both linguistic and social factors coexist in a language community to shape cognition and attitudes. What linguists and semioticians should be looking for, therefore, is not whether the Whorfian hypothesis is true or not, but how these factors interact.

CHAPTER 5

Although interest in metaphor is as old as Aristotle, the scientific study of its relation to cognition and communication is a relatively recent phenomenon. Since the 1970s, interest in metaphor on the part of behavioural, social, and cognitive scientists has become so intense that it is virtually impossible to skim even the surface of the data its investigation has generated. What stands out most from this pile of information is that metaphor is an intrinsic feature of language and cognition (e.g., Danesi, 1993; Gibbs, 1994; Goossens et al., 1995). It is the specific line of research initiated by Lakoff and Johnson's 1980 work, *Metaphors We Live By*, that has had truly intriguing implications for the study of how humans make meaning through language. This chapter constitutes the opening chapter of that pivotal book.

Lakoff and Johnson argue that our concepts reveal, typically, a metaphorical form, which permeates all of discourse, not just the poetic kind (Pollio, Barlow, Fine, and Pollio, 1977; Lakoff, 1987; Johnson, 1987; Hausman, 1989). Consider, for example, the following common portrayals of health by our culture (Lakoff and Johnson, 1980: 15, 50):

(1) Your at the *peak* of your health
(2) My health is *down.*
(3) You're in *top* shape.
(4) My body is in perfect *working order.*
(5) My body is *breaking down.*
(6) My health is going *down the drain.*
(7) His pain *went away.*
(8) I'm going to *flush out* my cold.

The first three sentences represent health in terms of an orientation metaphor, i.e., the state of being healthy is conceptualized as being oriented in an upwards direction, while the opposite state is conceptualized as being oriented in a downwards direction. This is probably because in our culture, as Lakoff and Johnson (1980: 15) point out, serious "illness forces us to lie down physically." Sentences (4) and (5) compare health, and its converse, to a machine. And in the last three sentences health and its converse are envisaged as being entities within a person. This is why they can *go away,* why they can be *flushed out,* and so on.

The upshot of the work of Lakoff and Johnson is that metaphor is one of the primary capacities of the human mind that underlies the representation of most of our abstract concepts, and that it structures the unconscious ways in which we perceive, think, and act.

CHAPTER 6

This chapter by Paul Perron presents the ideas of the influential French semiotician Algirdas Julien Greimas (1917-1992), the French semiotician who developed the branch of semiotics known as *narratology*, the study of how human beings in different cultures invent remarkably similar stories (myths, tales, etc.) with virtually the same stock of characters, motifs, themes, and actions. As an expository essay itself, it requires very little commentary here.

The main point made by Perron is that the work of Greimas has alerted semioticians and others to the idea that the mind has a narrative structure that manifests itself in the stories that all peoples and cultures invariably create. It is interesting to note that this notion is being taken rather seriously today by many psychologist, whose work has been showing that children develop concepts and world views primarily through the story formats to which they are exposed. As Wells (1986: 194) has put it, this is because in the human species "constructing stories in the mind is one of the most fundamental means of making meaning" and "as such it is an activity that pervades all aspects of learning." Psychological research has, in fact, been showing that children will grasp new concepts primarily if these are presented to them in the form of narratives (e.g., Vygotsky, 1961; Winner, 1982: 266-305). Stories provide the intelligible formats that mobilize the child's natural ability to learn from context (e.g., Miller and Gildea, 1991). The cognitive psychologist Jerome Bruner (1990) has persuasively argued, after reviewing a large body of research in this domain, that culturally shaped narrative thinking underlies how we come to understand ourselves and the social world in which we live. Beginning with the acquisition of language, narrative thinking brings the developing human organism into the arena of human culture. It is the form of thinking that gives pattern and continuity to human perception and experience.

According to Greimas, typical stories such as fairytales are subject to the rules of structure, which he calls the narrative grammar. Its "parts of speech" are: a subject (a lion, a hero) desires an object (the sun, a sought-after person), encounters an opponent (Mars, a villain, a false hero), finds a helper (the moon, a donor), gets an object from a sender (a dispatcher), gives it to a receiver (the earth), etc. In order to explain the passage from these categories (which he calls *actants*) to actual narrative discourse, Greimas posits a "generative trajectory" that maps these categories onto other constituents of a social interaction to produce the discourses that make up a large portion of human communication. An actant can be converted into various fundamental roles along a certain number of specified positions of its narrative trajectory. At the surface level, one actant can be represented by several actors, and several actants by one and the same actor. In a mystery novel, for instance, the subject, or hero, may have several enemies, all of whom function actantially as an opponent. In a love story, a male lover may function as both object and

16

sender. A simple example of how actantial theory might be applied to a novel such as *Madame Bovary* (1857) by Gustave Flaubert (1821-1880) goes somewhat like this: *subject* = Emma, *object* = happiness, *sender* = romantic literature, *receiver* = Emma, *helper* = Léon, Rodolphe, *opponent* = Charles, Yonville, Rodolphe, Homais, Lheureux.

CHAPTER 7

The American philosopher, Susanne K. Langer (1895-1985), who wrote extensively on aesthetics and on analytic and linguistic philosophy, has become highly influential in the development of modern aesthetic theory. This chapter is taken from her principal work, *Philosophy in a New Key: A Study of the Symbolism of Reason, Rite and Art* (1942), in which she showed that art and science are based on the same signifying characteristics. However, Langer makes an important distinction between the *presentational* symbols found in art, which allow a variety of interpretations, and *discursive, representational* symbols found in science and ordinary language, which have dictionary meanings.

Langer comes from the intellectual lineage initiated by the eighteenth-century German philosopher Immanuel Kant (1724-1804), who proposed that objects can be judged as beautiful when they satisfy a disinterested desire—one that does not involve personal interests or needs. Beautiful objects have no specific purpose, claimed Kant, and judgments of beauty are not expressions of mere personal preference but universal intuitions. Although one cannot be certain that others will be satisfied by the objects one judges to be beautiful, one can at least say that others ought to be satisfied. Art should give the same disinterested satisfaction as natural beauty does. Paradoxically, art can accomplish one thing Nature cannot. It can offer ugliness and beauty in one object—a fine painting of an ugly face is still beautiful aesthetically.

CHAPTER 8

In this chapter, Stanley J. Grenz comments upon the main cultural influences that have gone into the crystallization and development of what semioticians and philosophers call the "postmodern mind." As such, therefore, it requires no commentary here. It is interesting to note that the notion of *postmodernism* traces its roots to architecture. By the 1960s, it seemed to many architects as well as to the public that the initial purism of modernist architecture had degenerated into sterile and monotonous formulas. The architecture that developed in reaction to modernist orthodoxy became known as *postmodernist.* In general it called for greater individuality, complexity, and eccentricity in architectural design, while also demanding acknowledgment of historical precedent and continuity. To a large extent, this style was achieved through the innovative reinterpretation of traditional ornamental symbols and patterns.

By the 1980s, postmodernism had become prevalent among architects, especially in the United States. In keeping with its emphasis on individuality, its practitioners worked in highly diverse styles ranging from austere complexity to contrasting colours and historical allusions. The effect on the most visible form of urban architecture, the corporate office tower, was to give this once mostly anonymous building structure a high stylistic profile, as the AT&T building (1982) in New York City demonstrates.

In art and culture, the notion of postmodernism started to catch on around the mid 1970s. The term is now commonly used to refer to a state mind that has severed connections with the previous "truths" of history. Postmodernism has become a defining feature of the modern psyche which, like a character in Luigi Pirandello's (1867-1936) play *Six Characters in Search of an Author* (1921), is desperately seeking a *raison d'être* that will imbue life with a new meaningful "content."

CHAPTER 9

This chapter constitutes a brief commentary by Marcel Danesi on the effects of advertising on culture. Is the world under the influence of the "ad image"? Are the canons of discourse and aesthetics being more and more shaped by advertising textualities? These are the kinds of questions raised by this chapter.

CHAPTER 10

This chapter also requires little commentary. Rocco Capozzi simply gives us an interesting and in-depth critical reading of Umberto Eco's (1932-) novel *The Name of the Rose*, which was also made into a movie starring the actor Sean Connery. Eco is an Italian semiotician and novelist who claims that while the interpretation of a text may be influenced primarily by cultural trends, there is, nevertheless, an authorial purpose inherent in the text that cannot be ignored. Capozzi alludes to the rich *intertexuality* in Eco's novel. Intertextuality is the term used in semiotics to refer to the feature by which texts allude to other culturally defined or culturally institutionalized texts, especially mythical or Biblical narratives.

CHAPTER 11

This final chapter by Floyd Merrell provides a summing up and final commentary to this volume. As Merrell suggests, semiotics is the study of how we make meaning through signs. Semioticians try to answer the question "What is the meaning of x?" They do this by studying what signs are, as well as how signs possess meaning, that is, how they are intended by users, how they designate (make reference to things and ideas), and how they are interpreted by others. The goal of semiotics is to match the meanings of signs—what they stand for—with the process of assigning those meanings.

Merrell refers to the delightful book, *Flatland: A Romance of Many Dimensions*, written by the literary critic Edwin A. Abbott (1838-1926), to illustrate how we are easily constrained in our knowledge by biological and semiosic limitations. Living in a two-dimensional world, Flatlanders can only see each other as dots or lines. To see how this is so, imagine being a creature living in a plane—the flat surface of a table. There, you would only be able to see objects in one or two dimensions, i.e., as dots or lines depending on their orientation. If you look at a circle cut-out lying on a table with your eyes flush along the table's surface, you will see it as a line. The same applies to all the other geometrical figure cut-outs. The only way, then, to distinguish a "circle" from a "straight line," an "ellipse," and other figures is to view them from a vantage point above the plane. This third dimensional viewing of the figures

19

will give you a different understanding of Flatland and its inhabitants—literally a different world view. So too with all world views—they are conditioned by vantage points. The goal of semiotics is to locate and identify the various vantage points of human cognition.

CONCLUDING REMARKS

In conclusion, the question of "What is Semiotics?" with which we started off this preliminary exposition and commentary can now be answered simply as: "It is the science of meaning." Without going into what science and meaning imply, suffice it to say that, like any other science, semiotics has practitioners who differ in various ways, e.g., there are those who prefer to adopt a Peircean perspective, others a Saussurean one, and so on. And as in any other scientific domain, semiotics too has its debates, its controversies, its different theories. That is where the fun is! Semiotics is a dynamic, vibrant, ever-changing science. And it is indeed remarkable to note that with barely a handful of notions and concepts, it can be used so powerfully to describe and understand such things as art, advertising, language, clothing, buildings, and, indeed, anything that is "interesting in itself," as a fellow semiotician once anecdotally caricatured semiotics to us. Hopefully, the readings in the next eleven chapters will give you a glimpse into the theoretical heart of semiotics.

Today, semiotics is practiced primarily as a structuralist science based on theories developed by American and French linguists that languages and cultures are determined by immutable basic structures of the body and mind. To what extent are we "in the sign," as Merrell puts it? An intelligent search for that answer must start with a close study of the ideas of those who have made it their life's purpose to understand the sign.

REFERENCES

Black, M. (1962). *Models and Metaphors*. Ithaca: Cornell University Press.
Bruner, J. (1990). *Acts of Meaning*. Cambridge, Mass.: Harvard University Press.
Danesi, M. (1993). *Vico, Metaphor, and the Origin of Language*. Bloomington: Indiana University Press.

Fisch, M. H. (1978). Peirce's General Theory of Signs. In *Sight, Sound, and Sense*, ed. by Thomas A. Sebeok, 31-70. Bloomington: Indiana University Press.

Gibbs, R. W. (1994). *The Poetics of Mind: Figurative Thought, Language, and Understanding*. Cambridge: Cambridge University Press.

Goossens, L. et al. (1995). *By Word of Mouth: Metaphor, Metonymy and Linguistic Action in a Cognitive Perspective*. Berlin: Mouton de Gruyter.

Hausman, C. R. (1989). *Metaphor and Art*. Cambridge: Cambridge University Press.

Johnson, M. (1987). *The Body in the Mind: The Bodily Basis of Meaning, Imagination and Reason*. Chicago: University of Chicago Press.

Lakoff, G. (1987). *Women, Fire, and Dangerous Things: What Categories Reveal about the Mind*. Chicago: University of Chicago Press.

Lakoff, G. and Johnson, M. (1980). *Metaphors We Live By*. Chicago: Chicago University Press.

Meyer-Eppler, W. (1959). *Grundlagen und Anwendungen der Informationstheorie*. Berlin: Springer Verlag.

Miller, G. A. and Gildea, P. M. (1991). How Children Learn Words. In W. S-Y Wang, (ed.), *The Emergence of Language: Development and Evolution*, pp. 150-158. New York: W.H. Freeman.

Morris, C. W. (1938). *Foundations of the Theory of Signs*. Chicago: University of Chicago Press.

Nöth, W. (1990). *Handbook of Semiotics*. Bloomington: Indiana University Press.

Peirce, C. S. (1931-58). *Collected Papers* , Vols. 1-6. Cambridge, Mass.: Harvard University Press.

Pollio, H., Barlow, J., Fine, H., and Pollio, M. (1977). *The Poetics of Growth: Figurative Language in Psychology, Psychotherapy, and Education*. Hillsdale, N. J.: Lawrence Erlbaum Associates.

Richards, I. A. (1936). *The Philosophy of Rhetoric*. Oxford: Oxford University Press.

Ruesch, J. (1972). *Semiotic Approaches to Human Relations*. The Hague: Mouton.

Sebeok, T. A. (1976). *Contributions to the Doctrine of Signs*. Lanham, Maryland: University Press of America.

Sebeok, T. A. (1979). *The Sign and Its Masters*. Austin: University of Texas Press.

Sebeok, T. A. (1981). *The Play of Musement*. Bloomington: Indiana University Press.

Sebeok, T. A. (1985a). Pandora's Box: How and Why to Communicate 10,000 Years into the Future. In *On Signs*, ed. by M. Blonsky, pp. 448-466. Baltimore: Johns Hopkins University Press.

Sebeok, T. A. (1985b). On the Phylogenesis of Communication, Language and Speech. *Semiotic Inquiry* 5: 361-367.

Sebeok, T. A. (1986). *I Think I Am a Verb: More Contributions to the Doctrine of Signs*. New York: Plenum.

Sebeok, T. A. (1987). In What Sense is Language a "Primary Modeling System?" In *Proceedings of the 25th Symposium of the Tartu-Moscow School of Semiotics*, ed. by H. Broms and R. Kaufmann, pp. 67-80. Helsinki: Arator.

Sebeok, T. A. (1991). *A Sign is Just a Sign.* Bloomington: Indiana University Press.

Sebeok, T. A. (1994). *Signs.* Toronto: University of Toronto Press.

Vygotsky, L. S. (1961). *Thought and Language.* Cambridge: MIT Press.

Wells, G. (1986). *The Meaning Makers: Children Learning Language and Using Language to Learn.* Portsmouth: Heinemann.

Winner, E. (1982). *Invented Worlds: The Psychology of the Arts.* Cambridge, Mass.: Harvard University Press.

READINGS

A science that studies the life of signs within society is conceivable. It would be part of social psychology and consequently of general psychology; I shall call it *semiology* (from Greek *semeion* "sign"). Semiology would show what constitutes signs, what laws govern them.

–Ferdinand de Saussure (1857-1913)

1

THE BIRTH OF
WESTERN SEMIOTICS

Tzvetan Todorov

The ambitious title of this chapter obliges me to begin with a limitation. My starting point was a summary notion of semiotics, two components of which are important here: the fact that, with semiotics, we are dealing with a discourse whose objective is knowledge (not poetic beauty or pure speculation), and the fact that its object is constituted by signs of various types (not by words alone). These two conditions were fully met for the first time, it seems to me, by Augustine. But Augustine did not invent semiotics; it can even be said that, quite to the contrary, he invented virtually nothing, that he merely combined ideas and notions drawn from several horizons. Thus I had to go back to his "sources," as they are found in grammatical and rhetorical theory, in logic, and so forth. By no means, however, have I undertaken a complete historical survey of each of these disciplines up to Augustine's day—even though, at other times, they may have inspired new developments in semiotics. The pre-Augustinian tradition is thus taken into account here only to the extent that it seems to be encountered in Augustine's work, hence the impression (an illusory one) that all antiquity leads to Augustine. This is clearly false, and—to take

Todorov, Tzvetan. "The Birth of Western Semiotics." In Catherine Porter (trans.), *Tzvetan Todorov: Theories of the Symbol*. New York: Cornell University Press, 1982.

but one example—if the Epicurean philosophy of language is not dealt with here, this is simply because its relationship to Augustinian semiotics is not particularly significant.

These factors account for the way the chapter is organized. One of its sections is devoted to Augustine's predecessors, who are grouped in categories chosen more because of their logical coherence than because they represent genuinely separate traditions. The other section focuses on Augustinian semiotics itself.

PRE-AUGUSTINIAN DISCIPLINES

Semantics

I trust I shall be forgiven for beginning this overview with Aristotle; he will reappear under several headings. For the moment, I shall limit myself to his theory of language as it appears in particular in the early chapters of *On Interpretation*. The key passage is the following:

> Spoken words are the symbols of mental experience and written words are the symbols of spoken words. Just as all men have not the same writing, so all men have not the same speech sounds, but the mental experiences, which these directly symbolize, are the same for all, as also are those things of which our experiences are the images.

If we juxtapose this short paragraph with other parallel developments, we can distinguish several assertions.

(1) Aristotle speaks of *symbols*, among which words are a special case. This term should be noted. It is important that the term "sign" does not figure in the initial definition. As we shall see in a moment, "sign" has for Aristotle another, technical sense.

(2) The sort of symbol immediately taken up as an example is made up of words; these are defined as a relation among three terms: sounds, states of mind, and things. The second term serves as intermediary between the first and the third, which are not in direct communication with each other; this intermediate term thus participates in two relations that are different in nature,

as are the terms themselves. Things are identical to themselves, always and everywhere; so are states of mind; for they are independent of individuals. Thus things and states of mind are linked by a motivated relation in which, as Aristotle says, the one is the *image* of the other. On the other hand, sounds are not the same in different countries. Their relationship with states of mind is unmotivated: the one signifies the other, without being the image of it.

This argument draws us into the ancient controversy over the cognitive power of nouns, and, correlatively, over the origin of language (was it natural or conventional?), of which the most familiar discussion is found in Plato's *Cratylus.* This debate emphasizes problems of knowledge and origin that will not preoccupy us here, and it concerns only words, not all types of signs; we must, however, take note of its form, for it can (and will) be said that signs are either natural or conventional. This was already true of Aristotle, who adhered, in this controversy, to the conventionalist hypothesis. The affirmation recurs frequently in his work; it is used to justify, among other things, his distinction between language and animal cries, which are also vocal, also interpretable. "By noun we mean a sound significant by convention . . . . The limitation 'by convention' was introduced because nothing is by nature a noun or name—it is only so when it becomes a symbol; inarticulate sounds, such as those which brutes produce, are significant, yet none of these constitutes a noun" (*On Interpretation*, 16a). The symbols are thus subdivided into (conventional) "nouns" and (natural) "signs." Let us note in this regard that, in the *Poetics*, 1456b, Aristotle provides still another basis for the distinction between human and animal sound: the latter cannot combine into larger signifying units. This suggestion seems not to have been pursued further in classical thought; it leads, however, in the same direction as the present-day theory of the double articulation of language.

As a partisan of the unmotivated relation between sounds and meaning, Aristotle is well aware of the cases of polysemy and synonymy that illustrate this relation. He speaks of them at several points; for example, in *On Sophistical Refutations*, 165a, and in the *Rhetoric*, III, 1405b. These discussions bring clearly to light the noncoincidence of meaning and referent. "The sophist Bryson [claimed] that there is no such thing as foul language, because in whatever words you put a given thing your meaning is the same. This is untrue. One term may describe a thing more truly than another, may be more like it, and set it more intimately before our eyes" (1405b; cf. another example in the *Physics*, 263b). In a more general but also a more complex way, in certain

27

texts the *logos* designates what the word signifies, as opposed to the thing itself; for example, in the *Metaphysics*, 1012a: "The form of words of which the word is a sign will be its definition."

(3) Although they are taken up immediately as the privileged example of a symbol, words are not the only case (it is precisely in this respect that Aristotle's text goes beyond the framework of a strictly linguistic semantics): the second example cited is that of letters. I shall not dwell here on the secondary role attributed to letters with respect to sounds; that has become a well-known theme through the work of Jacques Derrida. Let us note instead that it is hard to imagine how the tripartite division of the symbol (sounds/states of mind/things) would apply to these particular symbols (letters). Here we are speaking only of two elements, written words and spoken words.

(4) One further remark on the central concept of this description, the states of mind. First, we are concerned here with a psychic entity, with something that is not in the word but in the mind of the language user. Second, although it is a psychic phenomenon, this state of mind is in no way individual: it is identical for all. This entity thus stems from a "social" or even a universal psychology rather than from an individual one.

One problem remains that we shall do no more than formulate here: the problem of the relationship between "states of mind" and significance, or signifying capacity, such as the latter appears, for example, in the text of the *Poetics* (1457a), where the noun is defined as "a composite significant sound." It would seem (but I shall refrain from making any categorical affirmations) that it may be possible to speak of two language states: potential, as envisaged in the *Poetics*, where all psychological perspective is lacking; and actualized, as in *On Interpretation*, where meaning becomes an experienced meaning. Whatever the case, the existence of significance limits the psychic nature of meaning in general.

Such are the results of the earliest thinking on the subject to which we have access. We can scarcely speak, here, of a concept of semiotics: the symbol is defined as being broader than the word, but Aristotle does not seem seriously to have raised the question of nonlinguistic symbols, nor to have sought to describe the variety of linguistic symbols.

A second moment of reflection on the sign occurs in Stoic thought. This body of thought is, of course, very little known, for only fragmentary texts have been preserved (and these texts are found, moreover, in authors generally hostile to the Stoics). We must therefore make do with a few succinct remarks. The most important fragment is found in Sextus Empiricus, *Against the Logicians*, ɪɪ, 11-12:

> [The Stoics say] that "three things are linked together, the thing signified and the thing signifying and the thing existing"; and of these the thing signifying is the sound ("Dion," for instance);and the thing signified is the actual thing indicated thereby, and which we apprehend as existing in dependence on our intellect, whereas the barbarians although hearing the sound do not understand it; and the thing existing is the external real object such as Dion himself. And of these, two are bodies—that is, the sound and the existing thing—and one is incorporeal, namely the thing signified and expressible [the *lekton*], and this too is true or false.

Again, let us look at some important points.

(1) The terms "signifier" and "signified" (in a sense that Saussure, by the way, will not maintain) make their appearance here while the term "sign" is not used. This absence, as we shall see shortly, is not accidental. The example given is a word, more precisely a proper noun, and nothing in the passage suggests that other sorts of symbols might exist.

(2) Here, as in Aristotle, three categories are posited simultaneously; in both texts, the object, although exterior to language, is necessary to the definition. And in both of these presentations, no notable difference separates the first and third elements, sound and object.

(3) If there is any difference, it is in the *lekton*; the "expressible" or signified. Modern literature offers numerous discussions concerning the nature of that entity; the inconclusiveness of the debates leads us to keep the Greek term. We must recall first that the *lekton's* status as "incorporeal" is exceptional in the resolutely materialist philosophy of the Stoics. This means that it is impossible to conceive of the *lekton* as an impression in the mind, even a conventional one: such impressions (or "states of mind") are, for the Stoics, corporeal. "Objects," on the other hand, need not necessarily belong to the world that can be observed by the senses: they may be physical or psychic. The *lekton* is not located in speakers' minds but in language itself. The reference to barbarians is revealing. The latter hear the sound and see the man, but they are unacquainted with the *lekton*, that is, with the fact that this sound evokes

that object. The *lekton* is the capacity of the first element to designate the third; in this sense, the fact of having a proper name as an example is highly significant, since the proper name, unlike other words, has no meaning, but, like other words, has a capacity for designation. The *lekton* depends on thought but must not be confused with thought; it is not a concept, and still less—as some would have it—a Platonic idea. It is rather upon the *lekton* that thought operates. By the same token, the internal articulation of these three terms is not what it was for Aristotle: there are no longer two radically distinct relations (of meaning and image); the *lekton* is what allows sounds to be related to objects.

(4) Sextus's last words, according to which the *lekton* may be true or false, suggest that it may be equivalent to a proposition; the example cited, however, which is an isolated word, leads in a different direction. Here, other fragments, reported either by Sextus or by Diogenes Laertius, give us a clearer view of the question.

On the one hand, the *lekton* may be complete (a proposition) or incomplete (a word). Here is Diogenes' text: Speaking of *lekta*, "the Stoics say that some are complete in themselves and others defective. Those are defective the enunciation of which is unfinished, as *e.g.* 'writes,' for we inquire 'Who?' Whereas in those that are complete in themselves the enunciation is finished as, 'Socrates writes'" (*Life*, VII, 63). This distinction was already present in Aristotle, and it leads to the grammatical theory of parts of speech; we shall not be concerned with it here.

On the other hand, propositions are not necessarily true or false. Only assertions can be so evaluated, while imperatives, interrogatives, oaths, curses, hypotheses, vocatives, and so on are not subject to this criterion (ibid., 65). Here again is an argument that was commonplace in its day.

We cannot speak of an explicit semantic theory here, any more than we could in Aristotle's case. For the time being, only the linguistic sign is in question.

Logic

It is somewhat arbitrary to set up independent categories such as "semantics" and "logic" where the classical authors themselves made no such distinctions. By doing so, however, we can see more clearly the autonomous character of texts that, from the modern point of view, deal with related problems.

I shall review the same authors considered before.

Aristotle's logical theory of the sign is presented in the *Prior Analytics* and in the *Rhetoric*. Here, to begin with, is the definition: "Anything such that when it is another thing is, or when it has come into being the other has come into being before or after, is a sign of the other's being or having come into being" (*Pr. an.*, 70a). Aristotle illustrates the concept with the following example (one destined to serve many times over): the fact that a woman has milk is a sign that she has given birth.

The concept of the sign has to be situated first in its own context. For Aristotle, the sign is a truncated syllogism, one that lacks a conclusion. One of its premises (the other may be lacking, too, as we shall see later on) serves as a sign; the referent is the (absent) conclusion. Here a first correction must be offered: for Aristotle, the syllogism illustrated by the preceding example is indistinguishable from conventional syllogisms of the type "If all men are mortal . . . ." We now know that the two must be distinguished: the traditional syllogism describes the relation of predicates within a given proposition (or in adjacent propositions), while the example cited derives from the logic of propositions, not that of predicates. The relations among predicates are not pertinent here; only the interpropositional relations count. In classical logic, this distinction is masked by the term used to describe such cases as we are considering here: "hypothetical syllogism."

The fact that we are moving from one proposition to another (from "this woman has milk" to "this woman has given birth") and not from one predicate to another (from "mortals" to "men") is crucial, for we are passing by the same token from substance to event, and this passage makes it much easier to take nonlinguistic symbolism into consideration. Moreover, we have seen that Aristotle's definition dealt with things and not with propositions (in other texts, the reverse is true). As a result, we are not surprised to note that Aristotle is now explicitly referring to nonlinguistic and, more specifically, to visual signs (70b). The example offered is the following: large extremities may be the sign of courage in lions. Aristotle's perspective here is more epistemological than semiotic: he is speculating about the possibility of acquiring knowledge on the basis of such signs. From this viewpoint, he moves on to distinguish the necessary sign (*tekmêrion*) from the sign that is merely probable. We shall not explore this aspect of Aristotle's thought any further.

31

Another system of classification deals with the content of the predicates in each proposition: "Of signs, one kind bears the same relation to the statement it supports as the particular bears to the universal, the other the same as the universal bears to the particular" (*Rhet.* I, 1357b). The example of the woman who has given birth illustrates the latter case; an example of the former type would be: "A sign that the learned are just is that Socrates was learned and just." Once again, we see the damage done by the confusion between the logic of predicates and the logic of propositions. If Socrates is, in fact, the individual with respect to the universal (learned, just), on the other hand the fact that the woman in question has milk and the fact that she has given birth are two "particulars" with respect to the general law according to which "if a woman has milk it is because she has given birth."

On the linguistic level, signs are implied propositions; but Aristotle cautions that not every implied proposition is evoked by a "sign." In fact, there exist implicit propositions that derive either from collective memory or from the logic of the lexicon ("*e.g.* the man who said 'X is a man' has also said that it is an animal and that it is animate and a biped and capable of acquiring reason and knowledge": *Topics*, 112a); in other words, there are synthetic propositions and analytic propositions. In order for a sign to exist, something more than the implicit meaning must be present; but Aristotle does not say what this additional element is.

Nowhere is the theory of the logical sign articulated with that of the linguistic symbol (nor, as we shall see later on, with that of the rhetorical trope). Even the technical terms are different: here, sign; there, symbol.

The same situation prevails with the Stoics. Here is a transcription from Sextus Empiricus:

> The Stoics. . ., in attempting to establish the conception of the sign, state that "A sign is an antecedent judgement in a valid hypothetical syllogism, which serves to reveal the consequent." . . . "Antecedent," they say, is "the precedent clause in a hypothetical syllogism which begins in truth and ends in truth." And it "serves to reveal the consequent," since in the syllogism "If this woman has milk, she has conceived," the clause "If this woman has milk" seems to be evidential of the clause "she has conceived." [*Outlines of Pyrrhonism*, II, xi, 104, 106]

THE BIRTH OF WESTERN SEMIOTICS

Here we encounter several elements of the Aristotelian analysis, including the key example. Sign theory is linked to the theory of demonstration, and once again what interests its authors is the nature of the knowledge to be derived from it. The only difference—but it is an important one—is that the Stoics, who practice propositional rather than categorical logic, are conscious of the logical properties of this type of reasoning. This preferential attention to propositions has surprising consequences: it is because of such interest in propositions, as we have already noted in the case of Aristotle, that sustained attention begins to be paid to what we would call nonlinguistic signs. Aristotle's logic of classes "is suited to a philosophy of substance and of essence" (Blanché, p.9); propositional logic, for its part, grasps facts in their becoming, facts as events. Now it is precisely events (and not substances) that come to be treated as signs. This change in the object of knowledge (from classes to propositions) thus entails an extension of the material under consideration (the nonlinguistic is added to the linguistic).

The lack of articulation between this theory and the preceding one (that of language) is all the more blatant here because of the close proximity of the terms used in each case. We have observed that, in their semantic theory, the Stoics did not speak of signs, but only of signifiers and signifieds; the relationship is nonetheless striking, and the Skeptic Sextus did not fail to pick it up. His critique, which formally states the necessity of bringing together the various theories of the sign, represents another major step toward the constitution of a semiotics. Purporting to believe that one and the same "sign" is at work in the two cases, Sextus compares the signifier-signified pair with the antecedent-consequent pair and observes several differences. This leads him to formulate the following objections:

(1) The signifier and the signified are simultaneous, whereas the antecedent and the consequent are successive: how can the same name serve for these two relations? "The sign cannot serve to reveal the consequent, if the thing signified is relative to the sign and is, therefore, apprehended along with it.... And if the sign is not apprehended before the thing signified, neither can it really serve to reveal the actual thing which is apprehended along with itself and not after itself" (*Outlines of Pyrrhonism*, II, xi, 117-118).

(2) The signifier is "corporeal," whereas the antecedent, being a proposition, is "incorporeal." "Some things signify, others are signified. Vocal sounds signify, but expressions are signified, and they include also propositions. And as

propositions are signified, but not signifying, the sign will not be a proposition" (*Against the Logicians*, ii, 264).

(3) The passage from antecedent to consequent is a logical operation. Now anyone at all, even animals, can interpret observed facts:

> If the sign is a judgement and an antecedent in a valid major premiss, those who have no conception at all of a judgement, and have made no study of logical technicalities, ought to have been wholly incapable of interpreting by signs. But this is not the case; for often illiterate pilots, and [often] farmers unskilled in logical theorems, interpret by signs excellently—the former on the sea prognosticating squalls and calms, stormy weather and fair, and the latter on the farm foretelling good crops and bad crops, droughts and rainfalls. Yet why do we talk of men, when some of the Stoics have endowed even irrational animals with understanding of the sign? For, in fact, the dog, when he tracks a beast by its footprints, is interpreting by signs; but he does not therefore derive an impression of the judgement "if this is a footprint, a beast is here." The horse, too, at the prod of a goad or the crack of a whip leaps forward and starts to run, but he does not frame a judgement logically in a premiss, such as this—"if a whip has cracked, I must run." Therefore the sign is not a judgement, which is the antecedent in a valid major premiss. [*Against the Logicians*, ii, 269-271]

We have to admit that, although Sextus's criticisms are often purely formal quibbles, here they are not without substance. The assimilation of the two types of signs does pose problems. Let us imagine that Sextus was looking not for inconsistencies in the Stoic doctrine but for the point of articulation between the two theories. His objections then become constructive criticisms that may be reformulated as follows:

(1)Simultaneity and succession are the consequences of a more fundamental difference: in the case of the linguistic sign (word or proposition), the signifier evokes its signified directly; in the case of the logical sign, the antecedent, inasmuch as it is a linguistic segment, has its own meaning, which will be maintained; only secondarily does it evoke something else as well, that is, the consequent. We are dealing then with the difference between direct and indirect signs or in a terminology opposed to Aristotle's, with the difference between signs and symbols.

(2) Direct signs are composed of heterogeneous elements: sounds, incorporeal *lekton*, object; indirect symbols are made up of entities that are like in nature: one *lekton*, for example, evokes another.

(3) These indirect symbols may be either linguistic or nonlinguistic. In the first case, they take the form of two propositions; in the second, of two events. In this latter form, they are accessible not only to logicians but also to the uneducated and even to animals. The substance of the symbol does not dictate its structure. Moreover, no one will confuse the capacity to make inferences with the possibility of talking (as logicians do) about this capacity.

If we consider the classification of *lekta* into two groups, complete and incomplete, we note that it is possible to draw up a chart with a blank space.

	WORD	PROPOSITION
direct	incomplete *lekton*	complete *lekton*
indirect	?	sign

This gap is all the more puzzling (perhaps it may be attributed simply to the fragmentary state of the Stoic writings that have been preserved) in that the Stoics are the founders of a hermeneutic tradition based on the indirect meaning of *words*—on *allegory*. But this line of reasoning draws us into the framework of another discipline.

Before abandoning the logical theory of the Stoics, we must mention one more problem. Sextus reports that the Stoics divide signs into two classes: commemorative and revelatory. This subdivision results from an a priori classification of things according to whether they are clear or obscure, and, in the second case, whether they are always, occasionally, or naturally obscure. In the first two classes that result from this categorization, things that are clear and things that are always obscure, the sign has no role. It is in the latter two classes that the sign comes into play; these classes become the basis for two categories of signs:

> Such objects as are occasionally or naturally non-evident are
> apprehended by means of signs—not of course by the same signs,

but by "suggestive" signs in the case of the occasionally non-evident and by "indicative" signs in the case of the naturally non-evident. Of the signs, then, according to them, some are suggestive, some indicative. [The Stoics] term a sign "suggestive' when, being mentally associated with the thing signified, it by its clearness at the time of its perception, though the thing associated with it remains non-evident, suggests to us the thing associated with it, which is not clearly perceived at the moment—as for instance in the case of smoke and fire. An "indicative" sign, they say, is that which is not clearly associated with the thing signified, but signifies that whereof it is a sign by its own particular nature and constitution, just as, for instance, the bodily motions are signs of the soul. [*Outlines of Pyrrhonism*, II, x, 99-101]

Among the commemorative signs, another example would be a scar for an injury, a stab-wound in the heart for death; among the revelatory signs, perspiration for the pores of the skin.

This distinction does not seem to bring into play the properly semiotic structure of signs, and the problem it poses is simply epistemological. In his critique of the distinction, however, Sextus brings the debate back to a terrain closer to our area of interest. For he does not believe in the existence of revelatory signs. Thus he modifies, first, the relation of these classes, by elevating the one—the class of commemorative signs—to the rank of genus, and relegating the other—the class of revelatory signs—to the rank of species, in whose existence, moreover, he does not believe (*Against the Logicians*, 143). From here on, his discussion brings into play two other oppositions: polysemic and monosemic signs, and natural and conventional signs. The debate may be summarized as follows. Sextus contests the existence of revelatory signs by affirming that they do not allow us to derive any certain knowledge, since one thing may symbolize, potentially, an infinite number of other things; such a thing is therefore not a sign. To which the Stoics retort: yes, but commemorative signs may be polysemic as well, and may evoke several things at once. Sextus admits that this is so, but shows that his argument has another basis: commemorative signs can only be polysemic through the power of a convention. Now revelatory signs are, by definition, natural (they exist as things before being interpreted). Commemorative signs are either natural (for example, smoke for fire)—in which case they are monosemic—or else conventional—in which case they may be either monosemic (for example, words) or polysemic (for example, the lighted torch that announces on one occasion the arrival of friends, on another that of enemies). Here is Sextus's text:

> In reply to those who draw inferences from the commemorative sign and quote the case of the torch, and also of the sound of the bell [which may announce the opening of the meat-market or the need to wet down the streets], we must declare that it is not paradoxical for such signs to be capable of announcing more things than one. For they are determined, as they say, by the lawgivers and lie in our power, whether we wish them to indicate one thing or to be capable of announcing several things. But as the indicative sign is supposed to be essentially suggestive of the thing signified, it must necessarily be indicative of one thing. [*Against the Logicians*, II, 200-201]

Sextus's critique, attesting to the idea that the perfect sign has only one meaning and also to Sextus's preference for conventional signs, is interesting for other reasons as well. We have seen that the natural/conventional opposition has been applied, up to this point, to the origin of words, and that it has been necessary to opt for one solution or the other (or for a compromise between the two). Sextus applies this opposition to signs in general (of which words are only a special case), and he conceives furthermore of the simultaneous existence of *both* types of signs, natural and conventional. In this he shares in a properly semiotic perspective. Is it an accident that this perspective needed a certain eclecticism (that of Sextus) in order to flourish?

Rhetoric

Although Aristotle dealt with the "sign," in his sense of the word, within the framework of rhetoric, he analyzed it in purely logical terms. Here we shall examine under the heading of rhetoric not the "sign" but indirect meanings, or *tropes*.

Once again we must begin with Aristotle, for the proper/transposed opposition—which is of primary interest—originated with him. However, the opposition is not, at the beginning, what it will later become. Not only is all semiotic perspective absent from its description, in Aristotle, but the opposition does not yet have the preponderant role that we are used to seeing it play. Transposition, or metaphor (for Aristotle, the term designates all tropes) is not a symbolic structure that possesses a linguistic manifestation among others. It is rather a type of word: one in which the signified is something other than the conventional signified. This type of word appears within a list of lexical classes that includes, at least at first glance, eight terms; it is a complementary type of neologism, or innovation, in the signifier. To be sure, the existing definitions are a little more ambiguous. We read in the *Poetics*: "Metaphor consists in giving the thing a name that belongs to something else" (1457b). A parallel passage from the *Topics*—but in which the term "metaphor" (transposition) does not appear—states that "those who make false statements and say that an attribute belongs to a thing which does not belong to it, commit error; and those who call objects by the names of other objects (*e.g.* calling a plane-tree a 'man') transgress the established terminology" (109a). The *Rhetoric* speaks, with regard to the tropic operation, of "using metaphors to give names to nameless things" (III, 1405a). It is clear that Aristotle is hesitating between two definitions of metaphor, or else is defining metaphor by this doubleness itself: it is either the improper meaning of a word (transfer, transgression of conventional usage) or the improper expression used to evoke a meaning (a displaced noun, a naming that avoids proper naming). Be that as it may, metaphor remains a purely linguistic category; in fact, it is a subclass of words. The choice of a metaphor rather than a nonmetaphorical term stems from the same tendency that makes us choose one synonym rather than another: we are always seeking what is fitting and appropriate. Here is a passage that says something to this effect:

> If you wish to pay a compliment, you must take your metaphor from something better in the same line; if to disparage, from something worse. To illustrate my meaning: since opposites are in the same class, you do what I have suggested if you say that a man who begs "prays," and a man who prays "begs"; for praying and begging are both variants of asking. [*Rhet.* III, 1405a]

Transposition is but one stylistic device among others (even if it is the one Aristotle preferred), and not a mode of existence of meaning that would have to be articulated with direct signification. Proper meaning, in turn, is not direct meaning, but appropriate meaning. It is understandable that, under these conditions, the theory of transposition as yet shows no opening toward a typology of signs.

This situation does not remain static. As early as the period of Aristotle's disciples, such as Theophrastes, rhetorical figures begin to play a more and more important role; that movement ends only with the death of rhetoric, which comes about when rhetoric is transformed into a "figuratic." The very proliferation of terms is significant. Alongside "transposition," still used in the generic sense, the terms "trope" and "allegory," "irony" and "figure" appear. Their definitions do not diverge much from those Aristotle gives. For example, in the spurious Heraclitus we read: "The stylistic figure that says one thing but means another has its own name, allegory": and in Tryphon: "The trope is a way of speaking that deviates from proper meaning." Here the trope and its synonyms are defined as the appearance of a second meaning, not as the substitution of one signifier for another. But the position and the global role of tropes are gradually modified: tropes tend increasingly to become one of the two possible poles of signification (the other being direct expression); the opposition is much stronger in Cicero, for example, than in Aristotle.

In the work of Quintilian, synthesizer of the tradition, we can rapidly examine the last link of the rhetorical chain in the classical world. We do not find in him, any more than we did in Aristotle, a semiotic analysis of tropes. Owing to the breadth of his treatise, Quintilian ends up incorporating into his discourse several suggestions leading in this direction, but his lack of rigor prevents him from formulating the problem explicitly. Whereas Aristotle classified indirect expression among numerous other lexical devices, Quintilian tends to present it as one of the two possible modes of language: We "regard allusion as better than directness of speech" (*Institutio Oratoria* [The Education of an Orator], VIII, Pr., 24). But his attempt to elaborate a theory that would account for the opposition between "to say" and "to imply," an opposition that functions through the categories of the proper and the transposed, does not bear fruit; in the last analysis, tropes are equally "proper": "Propriety is also made to include the appropriate use of words in metaphor" (VIII, 2, 11).

The presence of onomatopoeia among the tropes constitutes a curious phenomenon. It is difficult to understand this categorization if we limit ourselves to the definition of trope as change of meaning (or as choice of an improper signifier—for both notions are found in Quintilian). The only possible explanation lies precisely in a semiotic conception of the trope, namely, that it is; a motivated sign: this is the only feature common to the metaphor and to onomatopoeia. But this idea is not formulated by Quintilian; it must wait for Lessing to give it expression, in the eighteenth century.

Quintilian devotes lengthy discussions to allegory, but his quantitative emphasis has no theoretical counterpart. He defines allegory, just as Cicero did, as a series of metaphors, as an extended metaphor. This conception sometimes poses problems, which are rediscovered in the definition of the example; for an example, unlike metaphor, maintains the meaning of the initial assertion that contains it; and yet Quintilian links the example to allegory. The problem (of the subdivisions within the category of indirect signs) goes unnoticed, just as the frontier between tropes and figures of speech remains imprecise.

The domain of rhetoric itself contains no semiotic theories. Nonetheless, it prepares the way for the theories to come, by virtue of the attention it focuses on the phenomenon of indirect meaning. Thanks to rhetoric, the proper/transposed opposition is to become familiar to the classical world (even though there is some uncertainty as to its content).

Hermeneutics

The hermeneutic tradition is so extensive and diversified that it is particularly difficult to grasp. Its object seems to have been recognized very early, at least in the form of an opposition between two orders of language, direct and indirect, clear and obscure, *logos* and *muthos*, and, consequently, between two modes of reception, comprehension in the one case and interpretation in the other. As testimony to this we have the famous fragment in which Heraclitus describes the speech of the Delphian oracle: "The master whose oracle is at Delphi says nothing and hides nothing, but he signifies." The teaching of Pythagoras is evoked in similar terms: "When he spoke with his companions, he exhorted them either by pursuing his thought or by employing symbols" (Porphyry). This opposition is maintained in later writings, although it continues to appear without any attempt at justification. The following example is from Dionysius of Halicarnassus: "Some dare to claim that the figurative form is not permitted in discourse. According to them, one should either say a thing or refrain from saying it, but in every case simply, and should henceforth give up speaking by means of innuendo" (*Ars rhetorica*, IX).

Within this extremely general conceptual framework are located a very large number of exegetic practices. We shall be content to divide them into two widely separated groups: textual *commentary* (especially commentary on Homer and on the Bible) and *divination* in its various forms (mantics).

It may be surprising to find divination among hermeneutic practices. Yet here, too, we encounter an effort to discover meaning in objects that had had none, or to find secondary meanings where there had been but one before. As a first step toward a semiotic conception, let us consider the sheer variety of substances that could become the starting point for interpretation: from water to fire, from the flight of birds to animal entrails, everything seems capable of becoming a sign and thus of giving rise to interpretation. We can assert, furthermore, that this type of interpretation is related to the one imposed by the indirect modes of language, that is, to allegory. Two authors can attest here to an extremely heterogeneous tradition.

First, Plutarch, who, when he seeks to characterize the language of the oracles, relates it inevitably to indirect expression:

> The introduction of clearness was attended also by a revolution in belief, which underwent a change along with everything else. And this was the result: in days of old what was not familiar or common, but was expressed altogether indirectly and through circumlocution, the mass of people imputed to an assumed manifestation of divine power, and held it in awe and reverence; but in later times, being well satisfied to apprehend all these various things clearly and easily without the attendant grandiloquence and artificiality, they blamed the poetic language with which the oracles were clothed, not only for obstructing the understanding of these in their true meaning and for combining vagueness and obscurity with the communication, but already they were coming to look with suspicion upon metaphors, riddles, and ambiguous statements, feeling that these were secluded nooks of refuge devised for furtive

> withdrawal and retreat for him that should err in his prophecy.
> [*Moralia*, v: *The Oracles at Delphi*, 407]

Oracular language is assimilated here to the transposed and obscure language of the poets.

Our second witness is Artemidorus of Ephesus, author of the famous *Interpretation of Dreams*, which summarizes and systematizes an already rich tradition. At first, the interpretation of dreams is continually related to that of words; sometimes through resemblance: "School teachers, once they have taught their students the values of the letters, then show them how they are to use the letters together. So too will I add a few small, easy-to-follow guidelines to what has already been said, so that the books will be readily understood by everyone" [III, 66]—sometimes through contiguity: "One must also show some degree of independent skill in judging dreams which are mutilated and which do not, as it were, give one anything to hold on to, especially [in the case of very difficult ones] in which certain letters which do not contain a thought that is whole and entire in itself or a meaningless name are seen, sometimes by transposing, sometimes by changing, sometimes by adding letters and syllables to them" (I, 11).

Moreover, Artemidorus opens his book with a distinction between two types of dreams, and the distinction makes its own origin clear: "Some dreams, moreover, are *theorematic* (direct), while others are *allegorical*. Theorematic dreams are those which correspond exactly to their own dream-vision . . . . Allegorical dreams, on the other hand, are those which signify one thing by means of another" (I, 2; emphasis added). This opposition is probably modeled on that of two rhetorical categories, the proper and the transposed, but here it is applied to a nonlinguistic matter. Furthermore, we find a connection—perhaps an unintentional one—between dream images and rhetorical tropes in Aristotle himself; he affirms, on the one hand, that "a good metaphor implies an intuitive perception of the similarity in dissimilars" (*Poetics*, 1459a), and, on the other hand, that "the most skilful interpreter of dreams is he who has the faculty of observing resemblances" (*Parva Naturalia: On Prophesying by Dreams*, II, 464b). Artemidorus, too, wrote that "the interpretation of dreams is nothing other than the juxtaposition of similarities" (*Interpretation of Dreams*, II, 25).

Let us now return to the principal hermeneutic activity, that of textual exegesis. This is, in the beginning, a practice that implies no particular sign theory but rather what might be called a strategy of interpretation, one that varies from school to school. Not until Clement of Alexandria do we find, within the hermeneutic tradition itself, any effort in the direction of semiotics. First of all, Clement explicitly articulates the unity of the symbolic field; he underlines this unity, moreover, by his systematic use of the word "symbol"; he also speaks of "what is expressed in veiled terms" (*The Miscellanies*, v, ix). He enumerates the varieties of the symbolic, as for example in the following text:

> The observances practised by the Romans in the case of wills have a place here; those balances and small coins to denote justice, and freeing of slaves, and rubbing of the ears. For these observances are, that things may be transacted with justice; and those for the dispensing of honour; and the last, that he who happens to be near, as if a burden were imposed on him, should stand and hear and take the post of mediator. [v, viii]

All of these devices are symbolic, as is, also, indirect language: "'Atœeas king of the Scythians to the people of Byzantium: Do not impair my revenues in case my mares drink your water; for the Barbarian indicated symbolically that he would make war on them" (v, v).

If Clement fails to distinguish here between linguistic and nonlinguistic symbolism, he maintains a clear distinction, in contrast, between symbolic and nonsymbolic (indirect and direct) language. Holy Scripture includes passages written in each style, but different specialists enable us to read both: Didascalus on the one hand, the Pedagogue on the other. This difference derives not only from the fact that *direct* language is opposed to *indirect* language (see for example v, viii), but also from the fact that the one is univocal whereas the other lends itself to multiple interpretations: "Things unconcealed are perceived in one way, [but] we may draw several meanings . . . from what is expressed in veiled form" (v, ix).

Clement is also the author of some reflections on Egyptian writing that profoundly influenced the interpretation of this corpus for centuries to come. These reflections provide a revealing example of his tendency to treat different substances in the same terms, and, more particularly, to apply rhetorical terminology to other types of symbolism (in this case, visual). Clement affirms the existence of several types of writings among the Egyptians, one of which is the hieroglyphic method. Its description follows:

> Now those instructed among the Egyptians learned first of all that style of the Egyptian letters which is called Epistolographic; and second, the Hieratic, which the sacred scribes practise; and finally, and last of all, the Hieroglyphic, of which one kind which is by the first elements is literal (Kyriologic), and the other Symbolic. Of the Symbolic, one kind speaks literally by imitation, and another writes as it were figuratively; and another is quite allegorical, using certain enigmas.
>
> Wishing to express Sun in writing, they make a circle; and Moon, a figure like the Moon, like its proper shape. But in using the figurative style, by transposing and transferring, by changing and by transforming in many ways as suits them, they draw characters. In relating the praises of the kings in theological myths, they write in anaglyphs. Let the following stand as a specimen of the third species—the Enigmatic. For the rest of the stars, on account of their oblique course, they have figures like the bodies of serpents; but the sun like that of a beetle, because it makes a round figure of ox-dung, and rolls it before its face. [v, iv]

In this well-known text several points stand out. First, the possibility of encountering the same structures through different substances: language (metaphors and enigmas), writing (hieroglyphics), painting (imitation). This type of unification constitutes one step toward the elaboration of a semiotic theory. Furthermore, Clement proposes a typology of the whole area of signs: the brevity of his proposition obliges us to make certain hypothetical reconstructions. We can summarize his classification as shown in the diagram.

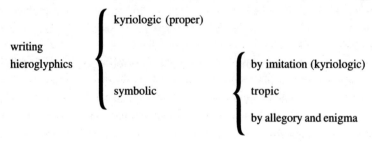

This distribution is obviously problematic in two respects: the fact that the kyriologic (proper) method appears in two different places in the chart, and the fact that allegory, considered a trope in rhetorical terms, here constitutes a separate class. In an attempt to preserve the coherence of the text, one might propose the following explanation, based on the examples quoted. First, the kyriologic genus and the kyriologic symbolic species have some common and some divergent features. They both denote a relation that is *direct*: a letter designates a sound as a circle designates the sun, in an immediate way; the letter and the circle possess no other, prior signification. However, the genus and the species differ as well: the relation between a letter and a sound is *unmotivated*, whereas that of the sun and a circle is *motivated*; this difference may in turn arise from other causes not mentioned here. Thus the opposition between the kyriologic genus and the symbolic genus is the opposition between the unmotivated and the motivated, whereas the opposition within the symbolic genus between the kyriologic species and the other species is the opposition between the direct and the indirect (the transposed).

Furthermore, two steps are required to decipher tropic writing: the pictogram designates one object (by direct imitation); this object in turn evokes another, through resemblance, or participation, or opposition, and so on. What Clement calls enigma, or allegory, on the other hand, implies three relations: between the pictogram and the beetle, that of direct imitation; between the beetle and the piece of dung, a relation of contiguity (metonymic); finally, between the piece of dung and the sun, a relation of resemblance (metaphoric). The difference between trope and allegory lies thus in the length of the chain: in the first case there is a single link, in the second there are two. Allegory has already been defined, in rhetoric, as an extended metaphor; but for Clement, this prolongation does not follow the surface of the text—it occurs instead, as it were, on the spot, in depth.

If we accept the idea that the difference between tropic writing and allegorical writing is the difference between two relations and three, we find that the position of kyriologic symbolic writing is clarified: it takes first place, for it requires the constitution of a single relation, the one between the circle and the sun, between the image and its meaning; it does not depend on any other link. Such an interpretation would explain the classification Clement proposes, and would make manifest, at the same time, the sign theory underlying this system; this theory is plausible to the extent that the category of linkage is indeed present in Clement.

Even apart from this essential (but hypothetical) theoretical contribution, Clement remains a very important figure, for he prepares the way for Augustine on two critical points, by affirming (1) that the material variety of symbolism, which may be communicated by means of all the senses, and which may be linguistic or not, does not diminish its structural unity, and (2) that the symbol is articulated with the sign as transposed meaning is articulated with proper meaning, thus that rhetorical concepts can be applied to nonverbal signs. Finally, it is Clement who first spells out clearly the equivalence between the symbolic and the indirect.

THE AUGUSTINIAN SYNTHESIS

Definition and Description of the Sign

Augustine does not aspire to be a semiotician. His work is organized around a completely different objective, a religious one. It is only in passing, and in terms of this other objective, that he articulates a theory of signs. His interest in the problematics of semiotics, however, seems to be greater than he himself admits or even suspects; in fact, throughout his life he keeps coming back to the same semiotic questions. His thinking in this area does not remain constant; we shall need to examine the course of its evolution. The most important texts, from our point of view, are the following: a treatise of his youth, sometimes considered inauthentic, called *On Dialectics*, written in 387; *On Christian Doctrine*, a central text from every standpoint, of which at least the part that concerns us was written in 397; and *On the Trinity*, dating from 415. But many other texts also contain valuable information.

In *On Dialectics*, Augustine gives the following definition: "A sign is something which is itself sensed and which indicates to the mind something beyond the sign itself. To speak is to give a sign by means of an articulate utterance" (v). Several aspects of this definition merit our attention. First, one property of the sign that will play a major role later on makes its appearance here: a certain nonidentity of the sign with itself, a feature arising from the fact that the sign is originally double, is at once perceptible and intelligible (we found nothing of the sort in Aristotle's description of the symbol). Moreover, Augustine here affirms more strongly than earlier writers have done that words are merely one type of sign; this affirmation, which stands out with increasing sharpness in his later writings, is the cornerstone of the semiotic perspective.

The second important sentence is the one that opens the fifth chapter of *On Dialectics*: "A word is a sign of any sort of thing. It is spoken by a speaker and can be understood by a hearer" (v). This too is a definition, but a double one, for it brings to light two separate relations: first, the relation between sign and thing (this is the framework of designation and signification), second, the relation between speaker and hearer (this is the framework of communication). Augustine links the two in a couple of brief sentences, as if their coexistence posed no problem whatever. His insistence on the communicative dimension is new: that dimension is lacking in the work of the Stoics, who had a pure theory of signification, and it is much less strongly affirmed by Aristotle: he indeed refers to "states of mind," and thus to speakers, but he sheds no light at all on the communicative context. This passage from Augustine provides an early clue to the two major tendencies of his semiotics, its eclecticism and its psychologism.

The very ambiguity produced here by the juxtaposition of several perspectives appears again when the sign is broken down into its constituent elements (in a particularly obscure section of the treatise). "These four are to be kept distinct: the *verbum* [word], the *dicibile* [expressible], the *dictio* [expression], and the *res* [thing]" (v). In the explanation that follows (which is complicated by the fact that Augustine takes *words* as his example of *things*), two excerpts in particular help to clarify the difference between *dicibile* and *dictio*:

> Now that which the mind not the ears perceives from the word and which is held within the mind itself is called a *dicibile* [expressible]. When a word is spoken not for its own sake but for the sake of signifying something else, it is called a *dictio* [expression]. [v]

And:

> Let us take as an example a grammarian questioning a boy in this manner: "What part of speech is '*arma*'?" "*Arma*" is said for its own sake, the word for the sake of the word itself. The other words

that he speaks, "what part of speech," whether or not they are
understood by the mind or uttered by the voice, are not an end in
themselves but concern the word "arma." Now when we consider
words as perceived in the mind, prior to utterance they are *dicibilia*,
but when they are uttered, as I have said, they become *dictiones*.
As for "arma," in the context we supposed, it is a *verbum*, but
when it was uttered by Vergil it was a *dictio*, for it was not said for
its own sake but in order to signify either the wars which Aeneas
waged, or his shield, or the other arms which Vulcan made for the
hero. [v]

On the lexical level, this four-term series clearly has its origin in an amalgam.
As Jean Pépin has shown, *dictio* translates *lexis*; *dicibile* is the exact equivalent
of *lekton*, and *res* may replace *tughanon*; this would give a Latin version of the
tripartite Stoic distribution among signifier, signified, and thing. From another
standpoint, the opposition between *res* and *verba* is commonplace, as we shall
see, in the rhetoric of Cicero and Quintilian. The merging of these two
terminologies creates a problem, for it leaves us with two terms designating the
signifier: *dictio* and *verbum*.

Augustine seems to resolve this terminological muddle by linking it with
another ambiguity that we have encountered before: that of meaning as it
belongs at one and the same time to the process of communication and to the
process of designation. Thus on the one hand we have one term too many, and
on the other hand a double concept: by the same token, *dicibile* is reserved for
the experienced meaning (the Stoics used this term in another sense), and
dictio is associated with referential meaning. *Dicibile* is experienced either by
the person who speaks ("perceived in the mind, prior to utterance") or by the
one who hears ("that which the mind . . . perceives"). *Dictio*, on the contrary, is
a meaning that comes into play not between the interlocutors but (like the
lekton) between sound and thing; it is what the word signifies independently
of any user. By this token, *dicibile* takes its place in a sequence: first the
speaker conceives a meaning, then utters sounds; next the hearer perceives
the sounds, then perceives the meaning. *Dictio* functions in simultaneity: the
referential meaning is realized at the same time the sounds are uttered: a word
only becomes *dictio* if (and when) it is "uttered by the voice." Finally, *dicibile*
is a property of propositions considered in the abstract, whereas *dictio* belongs

48

to each particular utterance of a proposition (in the terminology of modern logic, reference occurs in propositions that are *tokens*, not *types*).

At the same time, *dictio* does not pertain simply to meaning: it is the word uttered, the signifier, endowed with its denotative capacity; it is "the word that comes out of the mouth," that which is "uttered by the voice." Conversely, *verbum* is not simple sonority, as we might be tempted to imagine, but it is the designation of the word as word, the metalinguistic use of language; it is the word that "is uttered for its own sake, that is, so that something is being asked or argued about the word itself. . . . 'Verbum' both is a word and signifies a word" (v).

In *Divine Providence and the Problem of Evil* (*De Ordine*), written a few years later, the compromise is formulated differently. Designation becomes an instrument of communication:

> Now, that which is rational in us, that which uses reason and either produces or seeks after the things that are reasonable—saw that names, or meaningful sounds, had to be assigned to things, so that men might use the sense almost as an interpreter to link them together, inasmuch as they could not perceive one another's minds . . . . Men could not be most firmly associated unless they conversed and thus poured, so to speak, their minds and thoughts back and forth to one another. [II, xii, 35]

In the seventh chapter of *On Dialectics*, Augustine provides another example of his tendency to synthesize. Here he introduces a discussion of what he calls the forcefulness (*vis*) of a word. Forcefulness is what is responsible for the quality of an expression as such, and what determines its perception by the person to whom it is addressed: A word "has efficacy to the extent to which it is able to affect a hearer." Sometimes force and meaning are conceived as two types of signification: "Our reflections give rise to two ways of looking at the subject: partly through presenting truth, partly through observing propriety." We seem to be dealing here with an integration of the rhetorical opposition between clarity and beauty into a theory of signification (the integration is a problematic one, moreover, for the *significance* of a word is not the same thing as its figural nature, or perceptibility). The varieties of this "forcefulness" also bring to mind the rhetorical context: "forcefulness" is manifested by sound, by meaning, or by harmony between the two.

The same theme is developed in *Concerning the Teacher*, written in 389. Here the two types of signification seem to become properties either of the signifier or of the signified: the function of the first is to act on the senses, that of the second is to assure interpretation. "Everything which is expressed by the articulate voice with some signification both strikes the ear so that it can be sensed and is committed to memory so that it can be known" (v, 12). This relation is made explicit by means of a pseudo-etymological argument. "What if words be called such because of one fact and names be called names because of another, that is, words [*verba*] from the striking [*a verberando*] and nouns from the knowing [*a noscendo*]. As the first is called such with regard to the ears, should not the second be called such in reference to the soul?" (*ibid.*) In this dual process, perception is subject to intellection, for, as soon as we understand it, the signifier becomes transparent for us: "that law . . . by nature is very strong, namely, that when signs are heard the attention is turned toward the things signified" (vIII, 24). This second formulation, from the treatise *Concerning the Teacher*, seems a step backward from the one in *On Dialectics*, since here Augustine no longer imagines that the signified may have a perceptible form (a "forcefulness") that attracts attention.

Let us now move on to the central treatise, *On Christian Doctrine*. Given its importance in our context, we can justify a rapid glance at its overall plan. This is a work devoted to the theory of the interpretation—and, to a lesser degree, of the expression—of Christian texts. Its exposition is articulated around several oppositions: signs/things, interpretation/expression, difficulties arising from ambiguity or obscurity. Its outline can be presented in schematic form, with numbers designating the four parts of the treatise (the end of the third and the fourth were written in 427, thirty years after the first three.

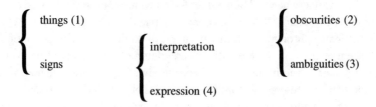

We shall not linger here to consider the tenor of Augustine's ideas about the way discourse is understood and uttered (H. I. Marrou has demonstrated their originality); the attempt at synthesis, apparent even in the outline, is what particularly concerns us. Augustine's project is hermeneutic at the outset; but he adds a section on production (the fourth part) which is to become the first Christian rhetoric. What is more, he inserts the whole into a general sign theory in which a properly semiotic undertaking encompasses what we distinguished earlier under the headings "logic" and "semantics." This text has a better claim than any other to be considered the first semiotic work.

Returning to the sign theory formulated in *On Christian Doctrine*: if we compare it to the one in *On Dialectics*, we observe that only the experienced meaning is preserved; thus the inconsistency of the schema is diminished. Even more surprising is the disappearance of the "thing," or referent. In fact, Augustine does speak of things and of signs in this treatise (and in this he is faithful to the rhetorical tradition handed down from Cicero's time), but he does not take the former to be referents of the latter. The world is divided into signs and things according to whether the perceived object has transitive value or not. Things participate in signs as signifiers, not as referents. Let us note before going any further that this sweeping affirmation is moderated by another assertion, one which, however, remains more an abstract principle than a characteristic of the sign: "Things are learned by signs" (I, ii, 2).

The articulation between signs and things is further developed through the articulation between two basic processes, use and enjoyment. This second distinction is located in fact within the category of things; but things used are transitive, like signs, and things enjoyed are intransitive (here we have a category that allows us to oppose things to signs). "To enjoy something is to cling to it with love for its own sake. To use something, however, is to employ it in obtaining that which you love, provided that it is worthy of love" (I, iv, 4).

This distinction has an important theological extension. In the last analysis, nothing other than God deserves to be enjoyed, to be cherished for itself alone. Augustine develops this idea when he speaks of the love that man can bear to man:

> It is to be asked whether man is to be loved by man for his own
> sake or for the sake of something else. If for his own sake, we enjoy
> him; if for the sake of something else, we use him. But I think that
> man is to be loved for the sake of something else. In that which is

> to be loved for its own sake the blessed life resides; and if we do not
> have it for the present, the hope for it now consoles us. But "cursed
> be the man that trusteth in man" [Jer. 17:5]. But no one ought to
> enjoy himself either, if you observe the matter closely, because he
> should not love himself on account of himself but on account of
> Him who is to be enjoyed. [ɪ, xxii, 20-21]

It follows that the only thing that is absolutely not a sign (because it is the object of enjoyment *par excellence*) is God. This fact, in our culture, imparts a reciprocal coloration of divinity to every ultimate signified (that is, to everything that is signified without signifying anything in turn).

The relation between signs and things having been articulated in this fashion, we now come to the definition of a sign: "A sign is a thing which causes us to think of something beyond the impression the thing itself makes upon the senses" (ɪɪ, i, 1). We are not far from the definition given in *On Dialectics*; "thought" has simply replaced "mind." Another formula is more explicit: "Nor is there any other reason for signifying, or for giving signs, except for bringing forth and transferring to another mind the action of the mind in the person who makes the sign" (ɪɪ, ii, 3). It is no longer a question of defining the sign, but of describing the reasons for the activity of signification. It is no less revealing to note that the relation of designation plays no part here; we are dealing only with the relation of communication. What signs bring to mind is the experienced meaning, the one the speaker has in mind. To signify is to externalize.

The schema of communication is spelled out and developed in certain later texts, for example, in *The First Catechetical Instructions* (405), in which Augustine mentions the problem of the temporal divergence between language and thought. Noting his own frequent dissatisfaction with the way a thought is expressed, he explains it as follows:

> This is so chiefly because intuition floods the mind, as it were,
> with a sudden flash of light, while the expression of it in speech is
> a slow, drawn-out, and far different process, and while speech is
> being formed, intellectual apprehension has already hidden itself in
> its secret recesses; nevertheless, because it has stamped in a
> wonderful way certain imprints upon the memory, these endure

for the length of time it takes to pronounce the words; and from
these imprints we construct those audible symbols which are called
language, whether it be Latin, or Greek, or Hebrew, or any other
tongue, whether these symbols exist in the mind or are actually
uttered by the voice, though these marks are neither Latin nor
Greek, nor Hebrew, nor peculiar to any other race. [II, 3]

Thus Augustine imagines a state of meaning in which meaning does not
yet belong to any language (it is not entirely clear whether or not there exists a
Latin signified, a Greek signified, and so on, apart from the universal meaning;
this would seem unlikely, since language is described exclusively in its phonetic
dimension). The situation is not very different from the one Aristotle described;
there, as here, states of mind are universal and languages are particular. But
Aristotle accounts for this identity of psychic states by the identity with itself
of the referent-object, while Augustine's text does not deal with objects at all.
We must also note the instantaneous nature of the "intuition," and the inevitable
duration of (linear) discourse; in more general terms, this passage points to the
necessity of thinking of linguistic activity as endowed with a temporal dimension
(a dimension undermined by the role of the imprints). All of these features are,
once again, characteristic of the process of communication (the entire passage,
moreover, reflects a highly nuanced psychological analysis).

The sign theory presented in *On the Trinity* is yet another extension of the
one in *The First Catechetical Instructions* (as is the one appearing in the
eleventh book of the *Confessions*). The schema here remains entirely within
the realm of communication. "When we speak to others, we apply to the word,
remaining within us, the ministry of the voice or of some bodily sign, that by
some kind of sensible remembrance some similar thing may be wrought also in
the mind of him that hears—similar, I say, to that which does not depart from
the mind of him who speaks" (IX, ii, 12).

This description remains very close to that of the act of signification that
we found in *On Christian Doctrine*. However, Augustine distinguishes still
more clearly here between what he calls the *word* that precedes the division
into languages, and the linguistic *signs* that make the word known to us.

For those are called words in one way, which occupy spaces of
time by their syllables, whether they are pronounced or only thought;

and in another way, all that is known is called a word imprinted on the mind. [ix, x,15]

This [word] belongs to no tongue, to wit, of those which are called the tongues of nations, of which our Latin tongue is one. . . . The thought that is formed by the thing which we know, is the word which we speak in the heart: which word is neither Greek nor Latin, nor of any other tongue. But when it is needful to convey this to the knowledge of those to whom we speak, then some sign is assumed whereby to signify it. [xv, x, 19]

Words do not designate things directly; they merely express. What they express, however, is not the speaker's individuality, but an internal, prelinguistic word. This latter is determined in turn by other factors—two of them, it would seem. These are, on the one hand, the imprints left in the soul by the objects of knowledge, and, on the other hand, immanent knowledge whose source can only be God.

We must go on, then, to that word of man . . . which is neither utterable in sound nor capable of being thought under the likeness of sound, such as must needs be with the word of any tongue; but which precedes all the signs by which it is signified, and is begotten from the knowledge that continues in the mind, when that same knowledge is spoken inwardly according as it really is. [xv, xi, 20]

This human process of expression and signification, taken as a whole, constitutes an analogue to the Word of God, whose outward sign is not the word but the world; the two sources of knowledge are in the last analysis but one, to the extent that the world is the divine language.

That which is uttered with the mouth of the flesh is the articulate sound of a word; and is itself also called a word, on account of that to make which outwardly apparent it is itself assumed. For our word is so made in some way into an articulate sound of the body, by assuming that articulate sound by which it may be manifested to men's senses, as the Word of God was made flesh, by assuming that flesh in which itself also might be manifested to men's senses. [xv, xi, 20].

The doctrine of universal symbolism, which is to dominate medieval tradition, can be observed in the process of formulation here.

In summary, we may establish a circuit (which is the same, in symmetrically inverse form, for speaker and hearer) as shown in the diagram.

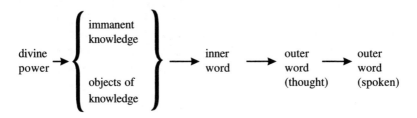

This schema makes it clear to what extent the word-thing relation in particular is the bearer of successive mediations.

It remains the case, so far as semiotic theory is concerned, that the materialist doctrine of the Stoics, which depends upon the analysis of designation, is progressively but decisively displaced in the work of Augustine by a doctrine of communication.

Classification of Signs

It is especially in *On Christian Doctrine* that Augustine concentrates on classifying the signs and thus on nuancing the very notion of sign; his other writings help to clarify certain details. In considering the Augustinian classifications, one is struck at once by their considerable number (even after attempting to group them together, we are left with at least five oppositions), as well as by the absence of real coordination among them: in this area, as elsewhere, Augustine displays a theoretical ecumenicalism by juxtaposing what might be articulated. Thus we shall examine his classifications, and the underlying oppositions, one at a time.

(1) *According to the mode of transmission.* This classification, destined to become canonical, in itself exemplifies Augustine's synthetic bent: since the signifier must be perceptible, all signifiers may be classified according to the sense by means of which they are perceived. Thus Aristotle's psychological

55

theory converges with semiotic description. Two details warrant our attention here. First, the limited role of the signs that are transmitted by senses other than sight and hearing: Augustine conceives of their existence for obvious theoretical reasons, but he immediately limits their importance. "Among the signs by means of which men express their meanings to one another, some pertain to the sense of sight, more to the sense of hearing, and very few to the other senses" (ii, iii, 4). A single example will suffice to illustrate the other channels of transmission: "Our Lord gave a sign with the odor of the ointment with which his feet were anointed [John 12:3-8]; and the taste of the sacrament of His body and blood signified what He wished [Luke 22:19-20]; and when the woman was healed by touching the hem of His garment, something was signified" [Matt. 9:20-22]. These examples emphasize the exceptional character of the signs that are based on smell, taste, or touch.

In *On the Trinity*, there remain only two modes of transmission of signs, sight and hearing. Augustine likes to stress their resemblance: "And generally a sound, sometimes a nod, is exhibited, the former to the ears, the latter to the eyes, that the word which we bear in our mind may become known also by bodily signs to the bodily senses. For what is to nod or beckon, except to speak in some way to the sight?" (xv, x, 19).

The opposition of sight and hearing allows us, in a first approximation, to situate words among the signs (and this is the second point that concerns us here). Indeed, for Augustine, language is phonic by nature (we shall return to his description of writing). Thus the immense majority of signs are phonic—for the immense majority are words. "A multitude of innumerable signs by means of which men express their thoughts is made up of words" (ii, iii, 4). The advantage words enjoy is, apparently, only quantitative.

(2) *According to origin and use.* A new distinction produces two pairs of sign types, but it is possible to bring them together, as Augustine himself shows, in a single category. The way is paved for this distinction in the first book of *On Christian Doctrine*. This part of the work begins with a division between signs and things. No sooner is the distinction made than it is abolished, for signs, far from being opposed to things, are things themselves—"things" being understood in the broadest sense of everything that is. "Every sign is also a thing, for that which is not a thing is nothing at all" (i, ii, 2). The opposition

can be reconstituted only at another level—at the level of function, not of substance. A sign indeed may be considered from two points of view: as thing or as sign (Augustine's discussion follows this order): "Just as I began, when I was writing about things, by warning that no one should consider them except as they are, without reference to what they signify beyond themselves, now when I am discussing signs I wish it understood that no one should consider them for what they are but rather for their value as signs which signify something else" (II, i, 1).

The opposition does not lie between things and signs, but between pure things and sign-things. Nevertheless, there are things that owe their existence entirely to the fact that they are used as signs; these are obviously the closest things to pure signs that can be found (since it is impossible to reach the limiting case). It is this capacity of signs to bracket, as it were, their nature as things, that opens the door to Augustine's new categorization.

Augustine in fact opposes natural signs to intentional signs (*data*). This opposition has often been misunderstood. It has been confused with another opposition, more common in the classical period, between natural and conventional; a study by J. Engels has shed useful light on this point. Augustine writes: "Among signs, some are natural and others are conventional. Those are natural which, without any desire or intention of signifying, make us aware of something beyond themselves" (II, i, 2). As examples of natural signs, he proposes smoke for fire, animal tracks, the human face. "Conventional signs are those which living creatures show to one another for the purpose of conveying, in so far as they are able, the motion of their spirits or something which they have sensed or understood" (II, ii, 3). His examples of intentional signs are chiefly human (words), but he also mentions animal cries, which can indicate the presence of food or simply the presence of the sign-maker.

It is clear how the opposition between natural signs and intentional signs is related to the opposition between things and signs. Intentional signs are things that have been produced for the purpose of serving as signs (origin) and that serve only to this end (usage); in other words, they are things whose function as things is reduced to a minimum. These signs thus come as close as possible to being pure signs (given that pure signs do not exist). Intentional signs are not necessarily human, and there is no obligatory correlation between their natural or intentional character and their mode of transmission (the classification of these modes comes up with regard to the intentional signs, but it is hard to see why). Let us note also that words are intentional signs: this constitutes their second characteristic (phoneticism being the first).

We can discern, in this opposition, echos of another we have already found in Aristotle (*On Interpretation*, 16a). However, the example of animal cries, appearing in both texts but in opposing categories, allows us to clarify Aristotle's position. For Aristotle, the fact that these cries do not depend upon any convention suffices for them to be considered "natural." For Augustine, on the other hand, the intention to signify, once attested, justifies including animal cries among the intentional signs: Augustine does not equate intentional with conventional. We may suppose that this distinction is Augustine's own: based on the notion of intention, it squares well with his general project which, as we have seen, is psychological and oriented toward communication. It allows him to overcome the objection that Sextus addressed to the Stoics, namely, that the existence of signs does not necessarily imply a logical structure generating this existence: certain signs are given in nature. We may also note that here the two types of signs—which remained completely separate for Augustine's predecessors—are integrated: what was sign for Aristotle and the Stoics becomes "natural sign," Aristotle's symbol and the Stoics' combination of signifier and signified become "intentional signs" (moreover, the same examples are always used). The term "natural" is somewhat misleading: it would be clearer to oppose signs that *already exist* as things to those that are *deliberately created* for the purpose of signification.

(3) *According to social function*. Such a terminological precaution would be all the more desirable since, elsewhere in his text, Augustine introduces a subdivision—a much more familiar one, as we have seen—between natural (and universal) signs and institutional (or conventional) signs. The former are comprehensible in a spontaneous and immediate fashion; the latter have to be learned. In fact, in *On Christian Doctrine*, Augustine considers only the case of the institutional sign, and he does so by means of an example leading apparently in the opposite direction.

> If those signs which the actors make in their dances had a natural
> meaning and not a meaning dependent on the institution and consent
> of men, the public crier in early times would not have had to

> explain to the Carthaginian populace what the dancer wished to
> convey during the pantomime. Many old men still remember the
> custom, as we have heard them say. And they are to be believed,
> for even now if anyone unacquainted with such trifles goes to the
> theater and no one else explains to him what these motions signify,
> he watches the performance in vain. [II, xxv, 38]

Even pantomime, at first glance a natural sign, requires a convention, and thus needs to be learned. So Augustine reincorporates within his own topology the opposition customarily applied to the origin of language (as Sextus had done before him).

This opposition is no more explicitly connected to the others than its predecessors. We may suppose that if Augustine fails in this instance to provide any example of a natural sign (in the sense given above), it is because his treatise is explicitly concerned with the intentional signs. Now natural signs may be found only among already existing signs; the intentionally created sign implies learning and thus convention. But is every already existing sign natural, that is, capable of being grasped apart from any convention? Augustine does not make such an assertion, and counterexamples come readily to mind. Still, in *The First Catechetical Instructions* he describes as natural a sign that appears in *On Christian Doctrine* among the nonintentional signs.

> [These imprints] are produced in the mind as is the expression of
> the face in the body. For instance, anger is designated by one word
> in Latin, by another in Greek, and by others again in the various
> other tongues; but the expression on the face of an angry man is
> neither Latin nor Greek. Thus it is that not all nations understand
> when a man says: *Iratus sum*, but Latins only; but if the feeling
> present in his mind as it kindles to white heat comes out upon his
> features and gives him a certain look, all who see him understand
> that he is angry. [II, 3]

The same affirmation appears in the *Confessions*:

> The movements of their bodies [are] a kind of universal language,
> expressed by the face, the direction of the eye, gestures of the
> limbs and tones of the voice, all indicating the state of feeling in the

mind as it seeks, enjoys, rejects or avoids various objects. [I, viii, 13]

Natural signs (although the example chosen seems questionable to us) here share the universality of the imprints of the soul whose properties we have already seen. Augustine, who is fairly close to Aristotle on this issue, sees the relation between words and things as arbitrary (conventional) and the relation between thoughts and things as universal, and thus natural.

This insistence on the necessarily conventional nature of language suggests how little stock Augustine places in motivation: in his view, motivation cannot be substituted for knowledge of the convention: "It is true that everyone seeks a certain verisimilitude in making signs so that these signs, in so far as is possible, may resemble the things that they signify. But since one thing may resemble another in a great variety of ways, signs are not valid among men except by common consent" (*On Christian Doctrine*, II, xxv, 38).

Motivation does not permit us to dispense with convention. The argument summarized here in one sentence is developed at length in *Concerning the Teacher*, in which Augustine shows that one can never be certain of the meaning of a gesture without the help of a linguistic commentary, that is, without the help of the institution that is language. By the same token, he refuses to concede any decisive importance to the natural/conventional (or natural/arbitrary) opposition; the eighteenth-century attempts, renewed by Hegel and Saussure, to found on that cornerstone the opposition between (arbitrary) signs and (natural) symbols, had already been outdistanced.

This "arbitrariness of the sign" leads naturally to polysemy.

> But since things are similar to other things in a great many ways, we must not think it to be prescribed that what a thing signifies by similitude in one place must always be signified by that thing. For the Lord used "leaven" in vituperation when He said, "Beware of the leaven of the Pharisees" [Matt 16:11], and in praise when He said, "The kingdom of God. . . is like to leaven, which a woman took and hid in three measures of meal, till the whole was leavened" [Luke 13:20-21]. [*On Christian Doctrine*, III, xxv, 35)

(4) *According to the nature of the symbolic relation.* After classifying signs as intentional or nonintentional, and as conventional or natural,

Augustine considers the same facts a third time and arrives at yet another articulation: that of *proper* signs and *transposed* signs (*translata*). The rhetorical origin of this opposition is obvious, but Augustine—like Clement before him, although more clearly—generalizes with regard to signs what rhetoric had to say about words.

The opposition is introduced in the following manner:

> Signs are either literal or figurative. They are called literal when they are used to designate those things on account of which they were instituted: thus we say *bos* [ox] when we mean an animal of a herd because all men using the Latin language call it by that name just as we do. Figurative signs occur when that thing which we designate by a literal sign is used to signify something else; thus we say "ox" and by that syllable understand the animal which is ordinarily designated by that word, but again by that animal we understand an evangelist, as is signified in the Scripture, according to the interpretation of the Apostle, when it says, "Thou shalt not muzzle the ox that treadeth out the corn" [1 Cor. 9:9]. [*On Christian Doctrine*, II, x, 15)

The proper signs are defined in the same way as the intentional signs; they have been created in view of their use as signs. But the definition of the transposed sign is not precisely parallel: these are not "natural" signs; that is, they are not among those whose existence precedes their use as signs. They are defined, more generally, by their secondary status: a sign is transposed when its signified becomes, in turn, a signifier; in other words, the proper sign is based on a single relation, the transposed sign on two successive operations (we have already seen this idea taking shape in the work of Clement).

In fact, we find ourselves from the outset within the category of intentional signs (since Augustine is exclusively preoccupied with these), and it is within this category that the operation that distinguished them from other signs is repeated: the proper signs are at once created expressly for the purpose of signification and used in accordance with this initial intention. The transposed signs are also intentional signs (words are the only examples given), but, instead of being used for their original purpose, they are redirected toward a second function, just as things were when they became signs.

This structural analogy—which is not identity—accounts for the affinity between transposed signs (which are linguistic nonetheless) and nonintentional signs ("natural" and nonlinguistic). It is not by chance that the two sets of examples overlap: the ox does not owe its existence to a semiotic intentionality, but it *can* signify; it is thus both a natural sign and a (possible ingredient of) a transposed sign. This third approach to the same phenomenon is, from the formal point of view, the most satisfying; we no longer depend upon empirical contingency to distinguish among signs (whether already existing or deliberately created, comprehensible directly or by means of a convention), but upon a difference in structure: the single or double symbolic relation. By this same token, language no longer forms a separate class among signs: one group of linguistic signs (indirect expressions) is found on the same side as the nonlinguistic signs. The formulation of this opposition, based upon an analysis of form and not of substance, represents in my view the most important theoretical acquisition of Augustinian semiotics; I can only regret the preference of the later tradition for the motivated/unmotivated, or natural/conventional, opposition (to the detriment of the opposition between indirect and direct). Let us note at the same time that this articulation itself contributes to the partial eradication of the difference between the two phenomena, which were much farther apart for Aristotle (symbol vs. sign), for the Stoics (signifier-signified vs. sign), and for Clement (direct language vs. indirect or symbolic language).

The proper/transposed opposition has its origin in rhetoric. However, Augustine's departure from rhetorical tradition is not limited to his extension of it beyond the word to the sign. With Augustine the very definition of "transposed" is new: the term no longer refers to a word that changes meaning, but to a word that designates an object which in turn carries meaning. This description applies to the example cited, in fact (the evangelist, just like the ox . . .), an example which does not resemble a rhetorical trope. On the following page, however, Augustine gives another example of a transposed sign which conforms perfectly to the rhetorical definition. Rather than confusing two types of indirect meaning, Augustine is probably attempting here to broaden the category of transposed meaning so that it can include Christian allegory. Speaking of the difficulties that arise in the course of interpretation, he considers two sorts which correspond closely to the two forms of indirect meaning. The opposition is better formulated in *On the Trinity*, where Augustine conceives of two types of allegory (that is, of transposed signs), the one based on words, the other on things. This distinction may be derived from one of Clement's texts; Clement, however, believed that he was dealing with two alternative definitions of one and the same notion.

Another attempt at subdividing the category of transposed meaning leads, later on, to the well-known doctrine of the four meanings of Scripture. Whether this doctrine originated with Augustine remains subject to controversy; in our consideration of it we can draw upon several series of texts. In the first, represented by *On the Advantage of Believing*, 3, 5, and by a closely parallel but shorter passage from the *Unfinished Book on the Literal Meaning of Genesis*, 2, four terms are clearly distinguished: history, etiology, analogy, and allegory. But it is not certain that these are meanings, properly speaking; the terms may refer instead to the various operations carried out on the text that is being interpreted. Analogy in particular is a device that consists in drawing upon one text in order to explain another. Etiology has a problematic status: it consists in seeking the cause of the event evoked by the text. It constitutes an explanation, and thus a meaning, but this meaning does not seem to belong, in a strict sense, to the text under analysis: it is rather a supplement provided by the commentator. There remain, then, only two meanings: historical (literal) meaning and allegorical meaning. The examples Augustine gives of the latter indicate that he does not distinguish between the various types of allegory in the way that a later tradition would. These examples include the following: Jonah in the whale representing Christ in the tomb (typology, in the later tradition); the Jews' sufferings during the Exodus as an incitation not to sin (tropology); the two women, symbol of the two Churches (analogy). I must add here that Augustine does not distinguish, either, between spiritual meaning and transposed meaning (he attributes the same definition to both). If his approach is compared to the later tradition as codified by Thomas Aquinas, we observe the redistribution as shown in the chart.

	PROPER MEANING	TRANSPOSED MEANING	SPIRITUAL MEANING
Augustine	proper meaning	transposed meaning	
Thomas	literal meaning		spiritual meaning

To summarize: only the proper/transposed dichotomy is essential to Augustine; the others are of little importance.

But one other text must be examined here. It is found in *On the Literal Meaning of Genesis*, II, 1, where Augustine speaks of the contents of the various books of the Bible. There are some, he says, that evoke eternity, others that recount facts, others that announce the future, still others that indicate rules of behavior. He does not assert, here, that a single passage may have a quadruple meaning; the theory is nonetheless present in embryonic form.

In his attempt to clarify the status of transposed signs, Augustine associates them with two related semantic phenomena: ambiguity and lies. Ambiguity is a long-term preoccupation, one encountered in as early a work as *On Dialectics*, where difficulties in communication are classified according to whether they can be attributed to obscurities or to ambiguities (Aristotle had already introduced this subdivision). Among its own subdivisions, the category of ambiguity includes those arising from transposed meaning. The same hierarchical articulation reappears in *On Christian Doctrine*: "The ambiguity of Scripture arises either from words used literally or figuratively" (III, 1, 1). An ambiguity due to proper (literal) meaning is an ambiguity in which semantics plays no role: phonic, graphic, or syntactic ambiguity. Semantic ambiguities simply coincide with those that can be attributed to the presence of a transposed meaning. Augustine does not entertain the possibility of semantic ambiguities based on lexical polysemy.

Transposed signs, a species within the genus "ambiguity," must be sharply distinguished from lies, on the other hand—although neither transposed signs nor lies reveal the truth if taken literally.

> If we call "Jacob's deception of his father" a lie, then all parables and figures for signifying anything which are not to be taken literally, but in which one thing must be understood for another, will be called lies. A deplorable consequence! He who thinks this can bring this charge against all figurative expressions, be they ever so many. In this way even what is named a metaphor, that is, the so-called transfer of some word from its own object to an object not its own, could be called a lie. Thus, it will be considered a lie when we say that grain fields wave and the eyes sparkle or when we speak of the flower of youth and the autumn of life, because, undoubtedly, we

do not find waves or sparks or flower or autumn in those objects to which we have transferred the words from another source. [*Against Lying*, x, 24)

This difference is explained soon afterward: it resides precisely in the existence of a transposed meaning, one absent in lies, which allows truth to be restored to the tropes. Such words or actions "should be judged as prophetic expressions and actions put for the understanding of those things which are true" (ibid.). Or again: "What is said or done figuratively is not a lie. Every pronouncement must be referred to that which it expresses. Everything said or done figuratively expresses what is signified to those to whom it was related" (*Lying*, v, 7). Lies are not true in the literal sense, nor do they have a transposed meaning.

(5) *According to the nature of the designatum, sign or thing.* Transposed signs are characterized by the fact that their "signifier" is already a full-fledged sign; we may now consider the complementary case, in which not the signifier but the signified is in its turn a complete sign. We shall in fact combine under this heading two cases that remain separate for Augustine: that of letters, signs of sounds, and that of the metalinguistic uses of language. In each of these cases, the sign is designated, but in the first instance we are concerned with its signifier, and in the second with its signified.

LETTERS. As far as letters are concerned, Augustine does not go beyond the Aristotelian adage according to which letters are the signs of sounds. Thus, in *On Dialectics*, he states: "Every word is a sound, for when it is written it is not a word but the sign of a word. When we read, the letters we see suggest to the mind the sounds of the utterance. For written letters indicate to the eyes something other than themselves and indicate to the mind utterances beyond themselves" (v). Similarly, in *Concerning the Teacher*: "What do we find about written words? Are they not better understood as signs of words than as words?" (IV, 8). Or in *On Christian Doctrine*: "Words are shown to the eyes, not in themselves but through certain signs which stand for them" (II, iv, 5). And in *On the Trinity*: "Letters . . . are signs of words, as words themselves are signs in our conversation of those things which we think" (xv, x, 19).

We discover, however, that Augustine has identified several additional characteristics of letters. The first one, noted in *On Dialectics*, constitutes a paradox: letters are signs of sounds, but not of just any sounds—they signify articulate sounds alone. Now articulate sounds are those that can be designated by a letter. "By an articulate sound I mean one which can be expressed in letters" (v). One might argue that letters are based on an implicit phonological analysis, since they represent only invariable elements. In a broader sense, "writing" appears equally indispensable to language: thus it is with the "imprints" that are mentioned in *The First Catechetical Instructions* and of which words are only the translation.

In *On Christian Doctrine*, Augustine insists on the durative nature of letters, as opposed to the punctual character of sounds: "Because vibrations in the air soon pass away and remain no longer than they sound, signs of words have been constructed by means of letters" (ii, iv, 5). Thus letters permit an escape from the constraining "now" that weighs upon the spoken word. In *On the Trinity*, Augustine goes even further: writing makes it possible to envisage not only "once upon a time" but also "elsewhere." "Whereas we exhibit . . . bodily signs either to ears or eyes of persons present to whom we speak, letters have been invented that we might be able to converse also with the absent" (xv, x, 19). Writing is defined by its complicity with absence.

METALINGUISTIC USAGE. At no point does Augustine take into account the singular capacity of letters to designate other signs (sounds). This situation is nevertheless familiar to him, for he shows continuing interest in the problem of the metalinguistic use of words. In *On Dialectics*, he notes that words may be used either as signs of things or as names of words; the distinction persists throughout *Concerning the Teacher*, in which Augustine warns against the confusions that may result from these two quite separate uses of language.

Again, in *On Dialectics*, Augustine notes in passing: "We are unable to speak of words except by words" (v). This observation is generalized in *On Christian Doctrine*: "I could express the meaning of all signs of the type here touched upon in words, but I would not be able at all to make the meanings of words clear by these signs" (ii, iii, 4). Thus words are not only available for metalinguistic use, but they are also uniquely capable of metasemiotic use. Unfortunately, Augustine does not pursue this argument and subject it to theoretical development; nowhere does he try to articulate it with the other classifications he is outlining. One might wonder, for instance, whether all verbal signs (proper and transposed) possess this capacity to the same degree; or again, what property of words it is that fits them for assuming this role. Here again, Augustine is content to observe and to juxtapose, without advancing to a theoretical conclusion.

SOME CONCLUSIONS

Let me attempt to draw some conclusions concerning the dual object of this first chapter, Augustine and semiotics.

We have seen, first of all, how Augustine's own position is constituted. Throughout his semiotic work, he is guided by a tendency to inscribe the semiotic problem within the framework of a psychological theory of communication. This impetus is all the more striking in that it contrasts with his own point of departure, namely, Stoic sign theory. For all this, Augustine's approach is not entirely original: a psychological perspective was present in Aristotle's work. Still, Augustine developed this tendency further than any of his predecessors; we can account for this by the theological and exegetic use to which he sought to put sign theory.

Yet if Augustine's originality is limited in its detail, his synthetic "originality"—or rather his ecumenical capacity—is tremendous, and leads to the first construction in the history of Western thought that deserves to be called semiotic. Let us review the principal articulations of this ecumenicalism. A rhetorician by training, Augustine first applied his knowledge to the interpretation of particular texts (the Bible): thus hermeneutics absorbed rhetoric. Moreover, he also annexed to hermeneutics the logical theory of signs—at the price, to be sure, of a slide from structure to substance, since in the place of Aristotle's "symbol" and "sign" we discover intentional and natural signs. These two conglomerates converge in *On Christian Doctrine* to give rise to a general theory of signs, or semiotics, in which the "signs" that emerged from the rhetorical tradition (which has meanwhile become hermeneutics), that is, the "transposed signs," take their place. In modern terminology, signs (in the restricted sense) are opposed to symbols as the proper is opposed to the transposed, or, better yet, as the direct is to the indirect.

Augustine's extraordinary gift for synthesis (which is not diminished by the fact that he does have precursors on the path of eclecticism) is entirely consistent with his place in history: his work is a locus through which classical tradition will be transmitted to the Middle Ages. Augustine's synthesizing capacity is apparent in many other areas, which bear occasionally upon the one that concerns us: thus, for instance, in several passages of the treatise *On Dialectics* (in the section on etymology), we find that historical changes of meaning are described in terms of rhetorical tropes, and history appears as no more than a projection of the typology in time. An even more important instance: for the first time, the Aristotelian classification of associations, found in the second chapter of the treatise on memory (association by resemblance, by proximity, by opposition), is used to describe the variety of these synchronic and diachronic relations of meaning.

It is precisely at this point that we have to set aside the question of Augustine's personal destiny to consider at what cost to knowledge semiotics was born. Since language exists, the question that has empirical if not ontological priority for any semiotics must be: What is the place of linguistic signs among signs in general? So long as our consideration is limited to verbal language alone, we remain inside a science (or philosophy) of language; only the shattering of the linguistic framework justifies the establishment of a semiotics. And this is precisely the inaugural move that Augustine makes: what has been said of words, in the context of rhetoric or semantics, he transfers to the level of signs, where words occupy merely one place among others. But which place?

We may well ask, while seeking the answer to that last question, whether the price paid for the birth of semiotics is not too high. At the level of general utterances, Augustine locates words (linguistic signs) within only two classifications. Words belong on the one hand to the auditory realm, on the other to the intentional realm: the intersection of these two categories yields linguistic signs. In so stating, Augustine fails to observe that he is leaving himself no way to distinguish linguistic signs from other "intentional auditory signs," except for their frequency of use. His text is quite revealing on this point: "Most signs, as I have said, pertain to the ears, and most of these consist of words. But the trumpet, the flute, and the harp make sounds which are not only pleasing but also significant, although as compared with the number of verbal signs the number of signs of this kind are few" (*On Christian Doctrine*, II, iii, 4). Between the trumpet announcing an attack (to take an example where intentionality is unmistakable) and words, the difference would lie only in the frequency of the latter? This is all that Augustine's semiotics offers us explicitly. We can see to what extent the phonetic prejudice, among others, is responsible for his blindness to the problem of the nature of language:

the need to connect words with "meaning" conceals their specificity (a purely "visual" conception of language that identifies language with writing would invite the same reproach). Augustine's gift for synthesis works against him here: it is perhaps not by accident that the Stoics were no more prepared than Aristotle to give a single name to "natural" signs (associated, for them, with inference) and to words. Synthesis is fruitful only if it does not obliterate difference.

In fact, as we have also seen, Augustine identifies certain properties of language that cannot be explained by its intentional-auditory character: above all, its metasemiotic capacity. Yet he does not ask what property of language endows it with this capacity. Now, only a response to this fundamental question would make it possible to resolve another problem, one that grows out of the first: the problem of the "price" of instituting semiotics, the question whether it is useful to unify within a single notion—that of the sign—both what possesses this metasemiotic property and what lacks it (note that this new question contains, in circular fashion, the word "semiotics" itself). Such usefulness cannot be measured until we know what is at stake in the opposition between the linguistic and the nonlinguistic sign. It is thus in a context of ignorance—not to say repression—of the difference between words and other signs that Augustine's semiotics is born—just like Saussure's, fifteen centuries later. Which makes the very existence of semiotics problematic.

Still, Augustine had glimpsed a possible way out of this impasse (although he probably remained as unconscious of the possibility as of the impasse itself). The way out lay in his extension of the proper/transposed category from rhetoric to the domain of signs. For this category, transcending the substantive opposition between linguistic and nonlinguistic signs (since this opposition is found in both areas) as well as the pragmatic and contingent oppositions between intentional and natural signs or conventional and universal signs, allows for the articulation of two major modes of designation for which today one would be tempted to use two distinct terms: signification and symbolization. With this, as our point of departure, we can inquire into the difference that underlies these two modes—the difference that explains, indirectly, the presence or absence of a metasemiotic capacity. In other words, semiotics deserves to exist only if, in the very move that inaugurates it, the semantic/symbolic articulation is present. That is what allows us to appreciate Augustine's groundbreaking work—sometimes in spite of itself.

2

LOGIC AS SEMIOTIC: THE THEORY OF SIGNS

Charles S. Peirce

1. WHAT IS A SIGN? THREE DIVISIONS OF LOGIC

Logic, in its general sense, is, as I believe I have shown, only another name for semiotic (σημειτικη), the quasi-necessary, or formal, doctrine of signs. By describing the doctrine as "quasi-necessary," or formal, I mean that we observe the characters of such signs as we know, and from such an observation, by a process which I will not object to naming Abstraction, we are led to statements, eminently fallible, and therefore in one sense by no means necessary, as to what *must be* the characters of all signs used by a "scientific" intelligence, that is to say, by an intelligence capable of learning by experience. As to that process of abstraction, it is itself a sort of observation. The faculty which I call abstractive observation is one which ordinary people perfectly recognize, but for which the theories of philosophers sometimes hardly leave room. It is a familiar experience to every human being to wish for something quite beyond his present means, and to follow that wish by the question, "Should I wish for

Peirce, Charles S. "Logic as Semiotic: The Theory of Signs." In Charles Hartshorne and Paul Weiss (eds.), *The Collected Papers of Charles Sanders Peirce*, volumes I and II. Cambridge, Mass.: The Belknal Press of Harvard University Press. Reprinted with permission from Harvard University Press.

that thing just the same, if I had ample means to gratify it?" To answer that question, he searches his heart, and in doing so makes what I term an abstractive observation. He makes in his imagination a sort of skeleton diagram, or outline sketch, of himself, considers what modifications the hypothetical state of things would require to be made in that picture, and then examines it, that is, *observes* what he has imagined, to see whether the same ardent desire is there to be discerned. By such a process, which is at bottom very much like mathematical reasoning, we can reach conclusions as to what *would be* true of signs in all cases, so long as the intelligence using them was scientific. The modes of thought of a God, who should possess an intuitive omniscience superseding reason, are put out of the question. Now the whole process of development among the community of students of those formulations by abstractive observation and reasoning of the truths which *must* hold good of all signs used by a scientific intelligence is an observational science, like any other positive science, notwithstanding its strong contrast to all the special sciences which arises from its aiming to find out what *must be* and not merely what *is* in the actual world.

A sign, or *representamen*, is something which stands to somebody for something in some respect or capacity. It addresses somebody, that is, creates in the mind of that person an equivalent sign, or perhaps a more developed sign. That sign which it creates I call the *interpretant* of the first sign. The sign stands for something, its *object*. It stands for that object, not in all respects, but in reference to a sort of idea, which I have sometimes called the *ground* of the representamen. "Idea" is here to be understood in a sort of Platonic sense, very familiar in everyday talk; I mean in that sense in which we say that one man catches another man's idea, in which we say that when a man recalls what he was thinking of at some previous time, he recalls the same idea, and in which when a man continues to think anything, say for a tenth of a second, in so far as the thought continues to agree with itself during that time, that is to have a *like* content, it is the same idea, and is not at each instant of the interval a new idea.

In consequence of every representamen being thus connected with three things, the ground, the object, and the interpretant, the science of semiotic has three branches. The first is called by Duns Scotus *grammatica speculativa*. We may term it *pure grammar*. It has for its task to ascertain what must be true of the representamen used by every scientific intelligence in order that they may embody any *meaning*. The second is logic proper. It is the science of what is quasi-necessarily true of the representamina of any scientific intelligence in order that they may hold good of any *object*, that is, may be true. Or say, logic proper is the formal science of the conditions of the truth of representations. The third, in imitation of Kant's fashion of preserving old associations of words in finding nomenclature for new conceptions, I call pure *rhetoric*. Its task is to ascertain the laws by which in every scientific intelligence one sign gives birth to another, and especially one thought brings forth another.

A *Sign*, or *Representamen*, is a First which stands in such a genuine triadic relation to a Second, called its *Object*, as to be capable of determining a Third, called its *Interpretant*, to assume the same triadic relation to its Object in which it stands itself to the same Object. The triadic relation is *genuine*, that is its three members are bound together by it in a way that does not consist in any complexus of dyadic relations. That is the reason the Interpretant, or Third, cannot stand in a mere dyadic relation to the Object, but must stand in such a relation to it as the Representamen itself does. Nor can the triadic relation in which the Third stands be merely similar to that in which the First stands, for this would make the relation of the Third to the First a degenerate Secondness merely. The Third must indeed stand in such a relation, and thus must be capable of determining a Third of its own; but besides that, it must have a second triadic relation in which the Representamen, or rather the relation thereof to its Object, shall be its own (the Third's) Object, and must be capable of determining a Third to this relation. All this must equally be true of the Third's Thirds and so on endlessly; and this, and more, is involved in the familiar idea of a Sign; and as the term Representamen is here used, nothing more is implied. A *Sign* is a Representamen with a mental Interpretant. Possibly there may be Representamens that are not Signs. Thus, if a sunflower, in turning toward the sun, becomes by that very act fully capable, without further condition, of reproducing a sunflower which turns in precisely corresponding ways toward the sun, and of doing so with the same reproductive power, the sunflower would become a Representamen of the sun. But *thought* is the chief, if not the only, mode of representation.

The Sign can only represent the Object and tell about it. It cannot furnish acquaintance with or recognition of that Object; for that is what is meant in this volume by the Object of a Sign; namely, that with which it presupposes an acquaintance in order to convey some further information concerning it. No doubt there will be readers who will say they cannot comprehend this. They think a Sign need not relate to anything otherwise known, and can make neither head nor tail of the statement that every sign must relate to such an Object. But if there be anything that conveys information and yet has absolutely no relation nor reference to anything with which the person to whom it conveys the information has, when he comprehends that information, the slightest acquaintance, direct or indirect—and a very strange sort of information that would be—the vehicle of that sort of information is not, in this volume, called a Sign.

Two men are standing on the seashore looking out to sea. One of them says to the other, "That vessel there carries no freight at all, but only passengers." Now, if the other, himself, sees no vessel, the first information he derives from the remark has for its Object the part of the sea that he does see, and informs him that a person with sharper eyes than his, or more trained in looking for such things, can see a vessel there; and then, that vessel having been thus introduced to his acquaintance, he is prepared to receive the information about it that it carries passengers exclusively. But the sentence as a whole has, for the person supposed, no other Object than that with which it finds him already acquainted. The Objects—for a Sign may have any number of them—may each be a single known existing thing or thing believed formerly to have existed or expected to exist, or a collection of such things, or a known quality or relation or fact, which single Object may be a collection, or whole of parts, or it may have some other mode of being, such as some act permitted whose being does not prevent its negation from being equally permitted, or something of a general nature desired, required, or invariably found under certain general circumstances.

2. THREE TRICHOTOMIES OF SIGNS

Signs are divisible by three trichotomies; first, according as the sign in itself is a mere quality, is an actual existent, or is a general law; secondly, according as the relation of the sign to its object consists in the sign's having some character in itself, or in some existential relation to that object, or in its relation to an interpretant; thirdly, according as its Interpretant represents it as a sign of possibility or as a sign of fact or a sign of reason.

I

According to the first division, a Sign may be termed a *Qualisign*, a *Sinsign*, or a *Legisign*.

A *Qualisign* is a quality which is a Sign. It cannot actually act as a sign until it is embodied; but the embodiment has nothing to do with its character as a sign.

A *Sinsign* (where the syllable *sin* is taken as meaning "being only once," as in *single, simple,* Latin *semel,* etc.) is an actual existent thing or event which is a sign. It can only be so through its qualities; so that it involves a qualisign, or rather, several qualisigns. But these qualisigns are of a peculiar kind and only form a sign through being actually embodied.

A *Legisign* is a law that is a Sign. This law is usually established by men. Every conventional sign is a legisign [but not conversely]. It is not a single object, but a general type which, it has been agreed, shall be significant. Every legisign signifies through an instance of its application, which may be termed a *Replica* of it. Thus, the word "the" will usually occur from fifteen to twenty-five times on a page. It is in all these occurrences one and the same word, the same legisign. Each single instance of it is a Replica. The Replica is a Sinsign. Thus, every Legisign requires Sinsigns. But these are not ordinary Sinsigns, such as are peculiar occurrences that are regarded as significant. Nor would the Replica be significant if it were not for the law which renders it so.

II

According to the second trichotomy, a Sign may be termed an *Icon*, an *Index*, or a *Symbol*.

An *Icon* is a sign which refers to the Object that it denotes merely by virtue of characters of its own, and which it possesses, just the same, whether any such Object actually exists or not. It is true that unless there really is such an Object, the Icon does not act as a sign; but this has nothing to do with its character as a sign. Anything whatever, be it quality, existent individual, or law, is an Icon of anything, in so far as it is like that thing and used as a sign of it.

An *Index* is a sign which refers to the Object that it denotes by virtue of being really affected by that Object. It cannot, therefore, be a Qualisign, because qualities are whatever they are independently of anything else. In so far as the

Index is affected by the Object, it necessarily has some Quality in common with the Object, and it is in respect to these that it refers to the Object. It does, therefore, involve a sort of Icon, although an Icon of a peculiar kind; and it is not the mere resemblance of its Object, even in these respects which makes it a sign, but it is the actual modification of it by the Object.

A *Symbol* is a sign which refers to the Object that it denotes by virtue of a law, usually an association of general ideas, which operates to cause the Symbol to be interpreted as referring to that Object. It is thus itself a general type or law, that is, a Legisign. As such it acts through a Replica. Not only is it general itself, but the Object to which it refers is of a general nature. Now that which is general has its being in the instances which it will determine. There must, therefore, be existent instances of what the Symbol denotes, although we must here understand by "existent," existent in the possibly imaginary universe to which the Symbol refers. The Symbol will indirectly, through the association or other law, be affected by those instances; and thus the Symbol will involve a sort of Index, although an Index of a peculiar kind. It will not, however, be by any means true that the slight effect upon the Symbol of those instances accounts for the significant character of the Symbol.

III

According to the third trichotomy, a Sign may be termed a *Rheme*, a *Dicisign* or *Dicent Sign* (that is, a proposition or quasiproposition), or an *Argument*.

A *Rheme* is a Sign which, for its interpretant, is a Sign of qualitative Possibility, that is, is understood as representing such and such a kind of possible Object. Any Rheme, perhaps, will afford some information; but it is not interpreted as doing so.

A *Dicent Sign* is a Sign, which, for its interpretant, is a Sign of actual existence. It cannot, therefore, be an Icon, which affords no ground for an interpretation of it as referring to actual existence. A Dicisign necessarily involves, as a part of it, a Rheme, to describe the fact which it is interpreted as indicating. But this is a peculiar kind of Rheme; and while it is essential to the Dicisign, it by no means constitutes it.

An *Argument* is a Sign which, for its Interpretant, is a Sign of law. Or we may say that a Rheme is a sign which is understood to represent its object in its characters merely; that a Dicisign is a sign which is understood to represent its object in respect to actual existence; and that an Argument is a Sign which is understood to represent its Object in its character as Sign. Since these definitions touch upon points at this time much in dispute, a word may be added in defence of them. A question often put is: What is the essence of a judgment? A judgment is the mental act by which the judger seeks to impress upon himself the truth of a proposition. It is much the same as an act of asserting the proposition, or going before a notary and assuming formal responsibility for its truth, except that those acts are intended to affect others, while the judgment is only intended to affect oneself. However, the logician, as such, cares not what the psychological nature of the act of judging may be. The question for him is: What is the nature of the sort of sign of which a principal variety is called a proposition, which is the matter upon which the act of judging is exercised? The proposition need not be asserted or judged. It may be contemplated as a sign capable of being asserted or denied. This sign itself retains its full meaning whether it be actually asserted or not. The peculiarity of it, therefore, lies in its mode of meaning; and to say this is to say that its peculiarity lies in its relation to its interpretant. The proposition professes to be really affected by the actual existent or real law to which it refers. The argument makes the same pretension, but that is not the principal pretension of the argument. The rheme makes no such pretension.

3.   Icon, Index, and Symbol

A. Synopsis

A sign is either an *icon*, an *index*, or a *symbol*. An *icon* is a sign which would possess the character which renders it significant, even though its object had no existence; such as a lead-pencil streak as representing a geometrical line. An *index* is a sign which would, at once, lose the character which makes it a sign if its object were removed, but would not lose that character if there were no interpretant. Such, for instance, is a piece of mould with a bullet-hole in it as sign of a shot; for without the shot there would have been no hole; but there is a hole there, whether anybody has the sense to attribute it to a shot or not. A *symbol* is a sign which would lose the character

77

which renders it a sign if there were no interpretant. Such is any utterance of speech which signifies what it does only by virtue of its being understood to have that signification.

B. Icon

. . . While no Representamen actually functions as such until it actually determines an Interpretant, yet it becomes a Representamen as soon as it is fully capable of doing this; and its Representative Quality is not necessarily dependent upon its ever actually determining an Interpretant, nor even upon its actually having an Object.

An *Icon* is a Representamen whose Representative Quality is a Firstness of it as a First. That is, a quality that it has *qua* thing renders it fit to be a representamen. Thus, anything is fit to be a *Substitute* for anything that it is like. (The conception of "substitute" involves that of a purpose, and thus of genuine thirdness.) Whether there are other kinds of substitutes or not we shall see. A Representamen by Firstness alone can only have a similar Object. Thus, a Sign by Contrast denotes its object only by virtue of a contrast, or Secondness, between two qualities. A sign by Firstness is an image of its object and, more strictly speaking, can only be an *idea*. For it must produce an Interpretant idea; and an external object excites an idea by a reaction upon the brain. But most strictly speaking, even an idea, except in the sense of a possibility, or Firstness, cannot be an Icon. A possibility alone is an Icon purely by virtue of its quality; and its object can only be a Firstness. But a sign may be *iconic*, that is, may represent its object mainly by its similarity, no matter what its mode of being. If a substantive be wanted, an iconic representamen may be termed a *hypoicon*. Any material image, as a painting, is largely conventional in its mode of representation; but in itself, without legend or label it may be called a *hypoicon*.

Hypoicons may be roughly divided according to the mode of Firstness of which they partake. Those which partake of simple qualities, or First Firstnesses, are *images*; those which represent the relations, mainly dyadic, or so regarded, of the parts of one thing by analogous relations in their own parts, are *diagrams*; those which represent the representative character of a representamen by representing a parallelism in something else, are *metaphors*.

The only way of directly communicating an idea is by means of an icon; and every indirect method of communicating an idea must depend for its establishment upon the use of an icon. Hence, every assertion must contain an icon or set of icons, or else must contain signs whose meaning is only explicable by icons. The idea which the set of icons (or the equivalent of a set of icons) contained in an assertion signifies may be termed the *predicate* of the assertion.

Turning now to the rhetorical evidence, it is a familiar fact that there are such representations as icons. Every picture (however conventional its method) is essentially a representation of that kind. So is every diagram, even although there be no sensuous resemblance between it and its object, but only an analogy between the relations of the parts of each. Particularly deserving of notice are icons in which the likeness is aided by conventional rules. Thus, an algebraic formula is an icon, rendered such by the rules of commutation, association, and distribution of the symbols. It may seem at first glance that it is an arbitrary classification to call an algebraic expression an icon; that it might as well, or better, be regarded as a compound conventional sign. But it is not so. For a great distinguishing property of the icon is that by the direct observation of it other truths concerning its object can be discovered than those which suffice to determine its construction. Thus, by means of two photographs a map can be drawn, etc. Given a conventional or other general sign of an object, to deduce any other truth than that which it explicitly signifies, it is necessary, in all cases, to replace that sign by an icon. This capacity of revealing unexpected truth is precisely that wherein the utility of algebraical formulae consists, so that the iconic character is the prevailing one.

That icons of the algebraic kind, though usually very simple ones, exist in all ordinary grammatical propositions is one of the philosophic truths that the Boolean logic brings to light. In all primitive writing, such as the Egyptian hieroglyphics, there are icons of a non-logical kind, the ideographs. In the earliest form of speech, there probably was a large element of mimicry. But in all languages known, such representations have been replaced by conventional auditory signs. These, however, are such that they can only be explained by icons. But in the syntax of every language there are logical icons of the kind that are aided by conventional rules . . . .

Photographs, especially instantaneous photographs, are very instructive, because we know that they are in certain respects exactly like the objects they represent. But this resemblance is due to the photographs having been produced under such circumstances that they were physically forced to correspond point by point to nature. In that aspect, then, they belong to the second class of signs, those by physical connection. The case is different if I surmise that zebras are likely to be obstinate, or otherwise disagreeable animals, because they seem to have a general resemblance to donkeys, and donkeys are self-willed. Here the donkey serves precisely as a probable likeness of the zebra. It is true we suppose that resemblance has a physical cause in heredity; but then, this hereditary affinity is itself only an inference from the likeness between the two animals, and we have not (as in the case of the photograph) any independent knowledge of the circumstances of the production of the two species. Another example of the use of a likeness is the design an artist draws of a statue, pictorial composition, architectural elevation, or piece of decoration, by the contemplation of which he can ascertain whether what he proposes will be beautiful and satisfactory. The question asked is thus answered almost with certainty because it relates to how the artist will himself be affected. The reasoning of mathematicians will be found to turn chiefly upon the use of likenesses, which are the very hinges of the gates of their science. The utility of likenesses to mathematicians consists in their suggesting in a very precise way, new aspects of supposed states of things . . . .

Many diagrams resemble their objects not at all in looks; it is only in respect to the relations of their parts that their likeness consists. Thus, we may show the relation between the different kinds of signs by a brace, thus:

$$
\text{Signs:} \quad
\left\{
\begin{array}{l}
\text{Icons,} \\
\text{Indices,} \\
\text{Symbols.}
\end{array}
\right.
$$

This is an icon. But the only respect in which it resembles its object is that the brace shows the classes of *icons*, *indices*, and *symbols* to be related to one another and to the general class of signs, as they really are, in a general way. When, in algebra, we write equations under one another in a regular array, especially when we put resembling letters for corresponding coefficients, the array is an icon. Here is an example:

$$
a_1 x + b_1 y = n_1,
$$
$$
a_2 x + b_2 y = n_2.
$$

This is an icon, in that it makes quantities look alike which are in analogous relations to the problem. In fact, every algebraical equation is an icon, in so far as it *exhibits*, by means of the algebraical signs (which are not themselves icons), the relations of the quantities concerned.

It may be questioned whether all icons are likenesses or not. For example, if a drunken man is exhibited in order to show, by contrast, the excellence of temperance, this is certainly an icon, but whether it is a likeness or not may be doubted. The question seems somewhat trivial.

C. Index

[An index is] a sign, or representation, which refers to its object not so much because of any similarity or analogy with it, nor because it is associated with general characters which that object happens to possess, as because it is in dynamical (including spatial) connection both with the individual object, on the one hand, and with the senses of memory of the person for whom it serves as a sign, on the other hand . . . . While demonstrative and personal pronouns are, as ordinarily used, "genuine indices," relative pronouns are "degenerate indices"; for though they may, accidentally and indirectly, refer to existing things, they directly refer, and need only refer, to the images in the mind which previous words have created.

Indices may be distinguished from other signs, or representations, by three characteristic marks: first, that they have no significant resemblance to their objects; second, that they refer to individuals, single units, single collections of units, or single continua; third, that they direct the attention to their objects by blind compulsion. But it would be difficult, if not impossible, to instance an absolutely pure index, or to find any sign absolutely devoid of the indexical quality. Psychologically, the action of indices depends upon association by contiguity, and not upon association by resemblance or upon intellectual operations.

An *Index* or *Seme* (σημα) is a Representamen whose Representative character consists in its being an individual second. If the Secondness is an existential relation, the Index is *genuine*. If the Secondness is a reference, the Index is *degenerate*. A genuine Index and its Object must be existent individuals (whether things or facts), and its immediate Interpretant must be of the same character. But since every individual must have characters, it follows that a genuine Index may contain a Firstness, and so an Icon is a constituent part of it. Any individual is a degenerate Index of its own characters.

Subindices or *Hyposemes* are signs which are rendered such principally by an actual connection with their objects. Thus a proper name, personal demonstrative, or relative pronoun or the letter attached to a diagram, denotes what it does owing to a real connection with its object, but none of these is an Index, since it is not an individual.

Let us examine some examples of indices. I see a man with a rolling gait. This is a probable indication that he is a sailor. I see a bowlegged man in corduroys, gaiters, and a jacket. These are probable indications that he is a jockey or something of the sort. A sundial or a clock *indicates* the time of day. Geometricians mark letters against the different parts of their diagrams and then use these letters to indicate those parts. Letters are similarly used by lawyers and others. Thus, we may say: If A and B are married to one another and C is their child while D is brother of A, then D is uncle of C. Here A, B, C, and D fulfill the office of relative pronouns, but are more convenient since they require no special collocation of words. A rap on the door is an index. Anything which focusses the attention is an index. Anything which startles us is an index, in so far as it marks the junction between two portions of experience. Thus a tremendous thunderbolt indicates that *something* considerable happened, though we may not know precisely what the event was. But it may be expected to connect itself with some other experience.

. . . A low barometer with moist air is an index of rain; that is we suppose that the forces of nature establish a probable connection between the low barometer with moist air and coming rain. A weathercock is an index of the direction of the wind; because in the first place it really takes the self-same direction as the wind, so that there is a real connection between them, and in the second place we are so constituted that when we see a weathercock pointing in a certain direction it draws our attention to that direction, and when we see the weathercock veering with the wind, we are forced by the law of mind to think that direction is connected with the wind. The pole star is an index, or pointing finger, to show us which way is north. A spirit-level, or a plumb bob, is an index of the vertical direction. A yard-stick might seem, at first sight, to be an icon of a yard; and so it would be, if it were merely intended to show a yard as near as it can be seen and estimated to be a yard. But the very purpose of a yard-stick is to show a yard nearer than it can be estimated by its appearance. This it does in consequence of an accurate mechanical comparison made with the bar in London called the yard. Thus it is a real connection which gives the yardstick its value as a representamen; and thus it is an *index*, not a mere *icon*.

When a driver to attract the attention of a foot passenger and cause him to save himself, calls out "Hi!" so far as this is a significant word, it is, as will be seen below, something more than an index; but so far as it is simply intended to act upon the hearer's nervous system and to rouse him to get out of the way, it is an index, because it is meant to put him in real connection with the object, which is his situation relative to the approaching horse. Suppose two men meet upon a country road and one of them says to the other, "The chimney of that house is on fire." The other looks about him and descries a house with green blinds and a verandah having a smoking chimney. He walks on a few miles and meets a second traveller. Like a Simple Simon he says, "The chimney of that house is on fire." "What house?" asks the other. "Oh, a house with green blinds and a verandah," replies the simpleton. "Where is the house?" asks the stranger. He desires some *index* which shall connect his apprehension with the house meant. Words alone cannot do this. The demonstrative pronouns, "this" and "that," are indices. For they call upon the hearer to use his powers of observation, and so establish a real connection between his mind and the object; and if the demonstrative pronoun does that—without which its meaning is not understood—it goes to establish such a connection; and so is an index. The relative pronouns, *who* and *which*, demand observational activity in much the same way, only with them the observation has to be directed to the words that have gone before. Lawyers use A, B, C, practically as very effective relative pronouns. To show how effective they are, we may note that Messrs. Allen and Greenough, in their admirable (though in the edition of 1877 [?], too small) Latin Grammar, declare that no conceivable syntax could wholly remove the ambiguity of the following sentence, "A replied to B that he thought C (his brother) more unjust to himself than to his own friend." Now, any lawyer would state that with perfect clearness, by using A, B, C, as relatives, thus:

$$A \text{ replied to B that he } \left\{ \begin{array}{c} A \\ B \end{array} \right\}, \text{ thought C (his } \left\{ \begin{array}{c} A's \\ B's \end{array} \right\}, \text{ brother) more unjust}$$

$$\text{to himself, } \left\{ \begin{array}{c} A \\ B \\ C \end{array} \right\} \text{ than to his } \left\{ \begin{array}{c} A's \\ B's \\ C's \end{array} \right\} \text{ own friend.}$$

The terminations which in any inflected language are attached to words "governed" by other words, and which serve to show which the governing word is, by repeating what is elsewhere expressed in the same form, are likewise *indices* of the same relative pronoun character. Any bit of Latin poetry illustrates this, such as the twelve-line sentence beginning, "*Jam satis terris.*" Both in these terminations and in the A, B, C, a likeness is relied upon to carry the attention to the right object. But this does not make them icons, in any important way; for it is of no consequence how the letters A, B, C, are shaped or what the terminations are. It is not merely that one occurrence of an A is like a previous occurrence that is the important circumstance, but that *there is an understanding that like letters shall stand for the same thing*, and this acts as a force carrying the attention from one occurrence of A to the previous one. A possessive pronoun is two ways an index: first it indicates the possessor, and, second, it has a modification which syntactically carries the attention to the word denoting the thing possessed.

Some indices are more or less detailed directions for what the hearer is to do in order to place himself in direct experiential or other connection with the thing meant. Thus, the Coast Survey issues "Notices to Mariners," giving the latitude and longitude, four or five bearings of prominent objects, etc., and saying *there* is a rock, or shoal, or buoy, or lightship. Although there will be other elements in such directions, yet in the main they are indices.

Along with such indexical directions of what to do to find the object meant, ought to be classed those pronouns which should be entitled *selective* pronouns [or quantifiers] because they inform the hearer how he is to pick out one of the objects intended, but which grammarians call by the very indefinite designation of *indefinite* pronouns. Two varieties of these are particularly important in logic, the *universal selectives*, such as *quivis, quilibet, quisquam, ullus, nullus, nemo, quisque, uterque,* and in English, *any, every, all, no, none, whatever, whoever, everybody, anybody, nobody.* These mean that the hearer is at liberty to select any instance he likes within limits expressed or understood, and the assertion is intended to apply to that one. The other logically important variety consists of the *particular selectives, quis, quispiam, nescio quis, aliquis, quidam,* and in English, *some, something, somebody, a, a certain, some or other, a suitable, one.*

Allied to the above pronouns are such expressions as *all but one, one or two, a few, nearly all, every other one,* etc. Along with pronouns are to be classed adverbs of place and time, etc.

Not very unlike these are, *the first, the last, the seventh, two-thirds of, thousands of,* etc.

Other indexical words are prepositions, and prepositional phrases, such as, "on the right (or left) of." Right and left cannot be distinguished by any general description. Other prepositions signify relations which may, perhaps, be described; but when they refer, as they do oftener than would be supposed, to a situation relative to the observed, or assumed to be experientially known, place and attitude of the speaker relatively to that of the hearer, then the indexical element is the dominant element.

Icons and indices assert nothing. If an icon could be interpreted by a sentence, that sentence must be in a "potential mood," that is, it would merely say, "Suppose a figure has three sides," etc. Were an index so interpreted, the mood must be imperative, or exclamatory, as "See there!" or "Look out!" But the kind of signs which we are now coming to consider are, by nature, in the "indicative," or, as it should be called, the *declarative* mood. Of course, they can go to the expression of any other mood, since we may declare assertions to be doubtful, or lucre interrogations, or imperatively requisite.

D. Symbol

A Symbol is a Representamen whose Representative character consists precisely in its being a rule that will determine its interpretant. All words, sentences, books, and other conventional signs are Symbols. We speak of writing or pronouncing the word "man"; but it is only a *replica*, or embodiment of the word, that is pronounced or written. The word itself has no existence although it has a real being, *consisting* in the fact that existents *will* conform to it. It is a general mode of succession of three sounds or representamens of sounds, which becomes a sign only in the fact that a habit, or acquired law, will cause replicas of it to be interpreted as meaning a man or men. The word and its meaning are both general rules; but of the two, the word alone prescribes the qualities of its replicas in themselves. Otherwise the "word" and its "meaning" do not differ, unless some special sense be attached to "meaning."

A Symbol is a law, or regularity of the indefinite future. Its Interpretant must be of the same description; and so must be also the complete immediate Object, or meaning. But a law necessarily governs, or "is embodied in" individuals, and prescribes some of their qualities. Consequently, a constituent of a Symbol may be an Index, and a constituent may be an Icon. A man walking with a child points his arm up into the air and says, "There is a balloon." The pointing arm is an essential part of the symbol without which the latter would convey no information. But if the child asks, "What is a balloon?" and the man replies, "It is something like a great big soap bubble," he makes the image a part of the symbol. Thus, while the complete object of a symbol, that is to say, its meaning, is of the nature of a law, it must *denote* an individual, and must *signify* a character. A *genuine* symbol is a symbol that has a general meaning. There are two kinds of degenerate symbols, the *Singular Symbol* whose Object is an existent individual and which signifies only such characters as that individual may realize; and the *Abstract Symbol*, whose only Object is a character.

Although the immediate interpretant of an Index must be an Index, yet since its Object may be the Object of an Individual [Singular] Symbol, the Index may have such a Symbol for its indirect interpretant. Even a genuine Symbol may be an imperfect interpretant of it. So an icon may have a degenerate Index, or an Abstract Symbol, for an indirect Interpretant, and a genuine Index or Symbol for an imperfect Interpretant.

A *Symbol* is a sign naturally fit to declare that the set of objects which is denoted by whatever set of indices may be in certain ways attached to it is represented by an icon associated with it. To show what this complicated definition means, let us take as an example of a symbol the word "loveth." Associated with this word is an idea, which is the mental icon of one person loving another. Now we are to understand that "loveth" occurs in a sentence; for what it may mean by itself, if it means anything, is not the question. Let the sentence, then, be "Ezekiel loveth Huldah." Ezekiel and Huldah must, then, be or contain indices; for without indices it is impossible to designate what one is talking about. Any mere description would leave it uncertain whether they were not mere characters in a ballad; but whether they be so or not, indices can designate them. Now the effect of the word "loveth" is that the pair of objects denoted by, the pair of indices Ezekiel and Huldah is represented by the icon, or the image we have in our minds of a lover and his beloved.

The same thing is equally true of every verb in the declarative mood; and indeed of every verb, for the other moods are merely declarations of a fact somewhat different from that expressed by the declarative mood. As for a noun, considering the meaning which it has in the sentence, and not as standing by itself, it is most conveniently regarded as a portion of a symbol. Thus the sentence, "every man loves a woman" is equivalent to "whatever is a man loves something that is a woman." Here "whatever" is a universal selective index, "is a man" is a symbol, "loves" is a symbol, "something that" is a particular selective index, and "is a woman" is a symbol . . . .

The word *Symbol* has so many meanings that it would be an injury to the language to add a new one. I do not think that the signification I attach to it, that of a conventional sign, or one depending upon habit (acquired or inborn), is so much a new meaning as a return to the original meaning. Etymologically, it should mean a thing thrown together, just as εμβολου (embolum) is a thing thrown into something, a bolt, is παραβολου (parabolum) and a thing thrown besides, collateral security, and υποβολου (hypobolum) is a thing thrown underneath, an antenuptial gift. It is usually said that in the word *symbol* the throwing together is to be understood in the sense of "to conjecture"; but were that the case, we ought to find that sometimes at least it meant a conjecture, a meaning for which literature may be searched in vain. But the Greeks used "throw together" (συμβαλλειν) very frequently to signify the making of a contract or convention. Now, we do find symbol (συμβολου) early and often used to mean a convention or contract. Aristotle calls a noun a "symbol," that is, a conventional sign. In Greek, watchfire is a "symbol," that is, a signal agreed upon; a standard or ensign is a "symbol," a watchword is a "symbol," a badge is a "symbol"; a church creed is called a "symbol," because it serves as a badge or shibboleth; a theatre ticket is called a "symbol"; any ticket or check entitling one to receive anything is a "symbol." Moreover, any expression of sentiment was called a "symbol." Such were the principal meanings of the word in the original language. The reader will judge whether they suffice to establish my claim that I am not seriously wrenching the word in employing it as I propose to do.

Any ordinary word, as "give," "bird," "marriage," is an example of a symbol. It is *applicable to whatever may be found to realize the idea connected with the word*; it does not, in itself, identify those things. It does not show us a bird, nor enact before our eyes a giving or a marriage, but supposes that we are able to imagine those things, and have associated the word with them.

A regular progression of one, two, three may be remarked in the three orders of signs, Icon, Index, Symbol. The Icon has no dynamical connection with the object it represents; it simply happens that its qualities resemble those of that object, and excite analogous sensations in the mind for which it is a likeness. But it really stands unconnected with them. The index is physically connected with its object; they make an organic pair, but the interpreting mind has nothing to do with this connection, except remarking it, after it is established. The symbol is connected with its object by virtue of the idea of the symbol-using mind, without which no such connection would exist.

Every physical force reacts between a pair of particles, either of which may serve as an index of the other. On the other hand, we shall find that every intellectual operation involves a triad of symbols.

A symbol, as we have seen, cannot indicate any particular thing; it denotes a kind of thing. Not only that, but it is itself a kind and not a single thing. You can write down the word "star," but that does not make you the creator of the word, nor if you erase it have you destroyed the word. The word lives in the minds of those who use it. Even if they are all asleep, it exists in their memory. So we may admit, if there be reason to do so, that generals are mere words without at all saying, as Ockham supposed, that they are really individuals.

Symbols grow. They come into being by development out of other signs, particularly from icons, or from mixed signs partaking of the nature of icons and symbols. We think only in signs. These mental signs are of mixed nature; the symbol-parts of them are called concepts. If a man makes a new symbol, it is by thoughts involving concepts. So it is only out of symbols that a new symbol can grow. *Omne symbolum de symbolo*. A symbol, once in being, spreads among the peoples. In use and in experience, its meaning grows. Such words as force, law, wealth, marriage, bear for us very different meanings from those they bore to our barbarous ancestors. The symbol may, with Emerson's sphynx, say to man,

Of thine eye I am eyebeam.

4. Ten Classes of Signs

The three trichotomies of Signs result together in dividing Signs into TEN CLASSES OF SIGNS, of which numerous subdivisions have to be considered. The ten classes are as follows:

First: A Qualisign [*e.g.*, a feeling of "red"] is any quality in so far as it is a sign. Since a quality is whatever it is positively in itself, a quality call only

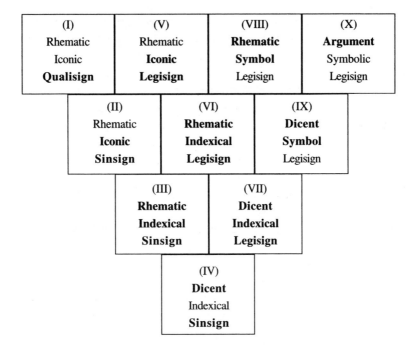

denote an object by virtue of some common ingredient or similarity; so that a Qualisign is necessarily an Icon. Further, since a quality is a mere logical possibility, it can only be interpreted as a sign of essence, that is, as a Rheme.

Second: An Iconic Sinsign [*e.g.*, an individual diagram] is any object of experience in so far as some quality of it makes it determine the idea of an object. Being an Icon, and thus a sign by likeness purely, of whatever it may be like, it can only be interpreted as a sign of essence, or Rheme. It will embody a Qualisign.

Third: A Rhematic Indexical Sinsign [*e.g.*, a spontaneous cry] is any object of direct experience so far as it directs attention to an Object by which its presence is caused. It necessarily involves an Iconic Sinsign of a peculiar kind, yet is quite different since it brings the attention of the interpreter to the very Object denoted.

Fourth: A Dicent Sinsign [*e.g.*, a weathercock] is any object of direct experience, in so far as it is a sign, and, as such, affords information concerning its Object. This it can only do by being really affected by its Object; so that it is necessarily an Index. The only information it can afford is of actual fact. Such a Sign must involve an Iconic Sinsign to embody the information and a Rhematic Indexical Sinsign to indicate the Object to which the information refers. But the mode of combination, or *Syntax*, of these two must also be significant.

Fifth: An Iconic Legisign [*e.g.*, a diagram, apart from its factual individuality] is any general law or type, in so far as it requires each instance of it to embody a definite quality which renders it fit to call up in the mind the idea of a like object. Being an Icon, it must be a Rheme. Being a Legisign, its mode of being is that of governing single Replicas, each of which will be an Iconic Sinsign of a peculiar kind.

Sixth: A Rhematic Indexical Legisign [*e.g.*, a demonstrative pronoun] is any general type or law, however established, which requires each instance of it to be really affected by its Object in such a manner as merely to draw attention to that Object. Each Replica of it will be a Rhematic Indexical Sinsign of a peculiar kind. The Interpretant of a Rhematic Indexical Legisign represents it as an Iconic Legisign; and so it is, in a measure—but in a very small measure.

Seventh: A Dicent Indexical Legisign [*e.g.*, a street cry] is any general type or law, however established, which requires each instance of it to be really affected by its Object in such a manner as to furnish definite information concerning that Object. It must involve an Iconic Legisign to signify the information and a Rhematic Indexical Legisign to denote the subject of that information. Each Replica of it will be a Dicent Sinsign of a peculiar kind.

Eighth: A Rhematic Symbol or Symbolic Rheme [*e.g.*, a common noun] is a sign connected with its Object by an association of general ideas in such a way that its Replica calls up an image in the mind, which image, owing to certain habits or dispositions of that mind, tends to produce a general concept, and the Replica is interpreted as a Sign of an Object that is an instance of that concept. Thus, the Rhematic Symbol either is, or is very like, what the logicians call a General Term. The Rhematic Symbol, like any Symbol, is necessarily itself of the nature of a general type, and is thus a Legisign. Its Replica, however, is a Rhematic Indexical Sinsign of a peculiar kind, in that the image it suggests to the mind acts upon a Symbol already in that mind to give rise to a General Concept. In this it differs from other Rhematic Indexical Sinsigns, including those which are Replicas of Rhematic Indexical Legisigns. Thus, the demonstrative pronoun "that" is a Legisign, being a general type; but it is not a Symbol, since it does not signify a general concept. Its Replica draws attention to a single Object, and is a Rhematic Indexical Sinsign. A Replica of the word "camel" is likewise a Rhematic Indexical Sinsign, being really affected, through the knowledge of camels, common to the speaker and auditor, by the real camel it denotes, even if this one is not individually known to the auditor; and it is through such real connection that the word "camel" calls up the idea of a camel. The same thing is true of the word "phoenix." For although no phoenix really exists, real descriptions of the phoenix are well known to the speaker and his auditor; and thus the word is really affected by the Object denoted. But not only are the Replicas of Rhematic Symbols very different from ordinary Rhematic Indexical Sinsigns, but so likewise are Replicas of Rhematic Indexical Legisigns. For the thing denoted by "that" has not affected the replica of the word in any such direct and simple manner as that in which, for example, the ring of a telephone-bell is affected by the person at the other end who wants to make a communication. The Interpretant of the Rhematic Symbol often represents it as a Rhematic Indexical Legisign; at other times as an Iconic Legisign; and it does in a small measure partake of the nature of both.

Ninth: A Dicent Symbol, or ordinary Proposition, is a sign connected with its object by an association of general ideas, and acting like a Rhematic Symbol, except that its intended interpretant represents the Dicent Symbol as being, in respect to what it signifies, really affected by its Object, so that the existence or law which it calls to mind must be actually connected with the indicated Object. Thus, the intended Interpretant looks upon the Dicent Symbol as a Dicent Indexical Legisign; and if it be true, it does partake of this nature, although this does not represent its whole nature. Like the Rhematic Symbol, it is necessarily a Legisign. Like the Dicent Sinsign it is composite inasmuch as it necessarily involves a Rhematic Symbol (and thus is for its interpretant an Iconic Legisign) to express its information and a Rhematic Indexical Legisign to indicate the subject of that information. But its Syntax of these is significant. The Replica of the Dicent Symbol is a Dicent Sinsign of a peculiar kind. This is easily seen to be trite when the information the Dicent Symbol conveys is of actual fact. When that information is of a real law, it is not true in the same fullness. For a Dicent Sinsign cannot convey information of law. It is, therefore, true of the Replica of such a Dicent Symbol only in so far as the law has its being in instances.

Tenth: An Argument is a sign whose interpretant represents its object as being an ulterior sign through a law, namely, the law that the passage from all such premises to such conclusions tends to the truth. Manifestly, then, its object must be general; that is, the Argument must be a Symbol. As a Symbol it must, further, be a Legisign. Its Replica is a Dicent Sinsign.

The affinities of the ten classes are exhibited by arranging their designations in the triangular table here shown, which has heavy boundaries between adjacent squares that are appropriated to classes alike in only one respect. All other adjacent squares pertain to classes alike in two respects. Squares not adjacent pertain to classes alike in one respect only, except that each of the three squares of the vertices of the triangle pertains to a class differing in all three respects from the classes to which the squares along the opposite side of the triangle are appropriated. The lightly printed designations are superfluous.

In the course of the above descriptions of the classes, certain subdivisions of some of them have been directly or indirectly referred to. Namely, beside the normal varieties of Sinsigns, Indices, and Dicisigns, there are others which are Replicas of Legisigns, Symbols, and Arguments, respectively. Beside the normal varieties of Qualisigns, Icons, and Rhemes, there are two series of others; to wit, those which are directly involved in Sinsigns, Indices, and Dicisigns, respectively, and also those which are indirectly involved in Legisigns, Symbols, and Arguments, respectively. Thus, the ordinary Dicent Sinsign is exemplified by a weathercock and its veering and by a photograph. The fact that the latter is known to be the effect of the radiations from the object renders it an index and highly informative. A second variety is a Replica of a Dicent Indexical Legisign. Thus, any given street cry, since its tone and theme identifies the individual, is not a symbol, but an Indexical Legisign; and any individual instance of it is a Replica of it which is a Dicent Sinsign. A third variety is a Replica of a Proposition. A fourth variety is a Replica of an Argument. Beside the normal variety of the Dicent Indexical Legisign, of which a street cry is an example, there is a second variety, which is that sort of proposition which has the name of a well-known individual as its predicate; as if one is asked, "Whose statue is this?" the answer may be, "It is Farragut." The meaning of this answer is a Dicent Indexical Legisign. A third variety may be a premise of an argument. A Dicent Symbol, or ordinary proposition, insofar as it is a premise of an Argument, takes on a new force, and becomes a second variety of the Dicent Symbol. It would not be worthwhile to go through all the varieties; but it may be well to consider the varieties of one class more. We may take the Rhematic Indexical Legisign. *The* shout of "Hullo!" is an example of the ordinary variety— meaning, not an individual shout, but this shout "Hullo!" in general—this type of shout. A second variety is a constituent of a Dicent Indexical Legisign; as the word "that" in the reply, "that is Farragut." A third variety is a particular application of a Rhematic Symbol; as the exclamation "Hark!" A fourth and fifth variety are in the peculiar force a general word may have in a proposition or argument. It is not impossible that some varieties are here overlooked. It is a nice problem to say to what class a given sign belongs; since all the circumstances of the case have to be considered. But it is seldom requisite to be very accurate; for if one does not locate the sign precisely, one will easily come near enough to its character for any ordinary purpose of logic.

3

THE LINGUISTIC SIGN

Ferdinand de Saussure

1. THE OBJECT OF LINGUISTICS

Definition of Language

What is both the integral and concrete object of linguistics? The question is especially difficult; later we shall see why; here I wish merely to point up the difficulty.

Other sciences work with objects that are given in advance and that can then be considered from different viewpoints; but not linguistics. Someone pronounces the French word *nu* 'bare': a superficial observer would be tempted to call the word a concrete linguistic object; but a more careful examination would reveal successively three or four quite different things, depending on whether the word is considered as a sound, as the expression of an idea, as the equivalent of Latin *nudum*, etc. Far from it being the object that antedates the viewpoint, it would seem that it is the viewpoint that creates the object; besides,

De Saussure, Ferdinand. "The Linguistic Sign." In Charles Bally and Albert Sechehaye (eds.), in collaboration with Albert Riedinger, translated from the French by Wade Baskin, *Course in General Linguistics*. London: Peter Owen. Reprinted with permission from Peter Owen.

nothing tells us in advance that one way of considering the fact in question takes precedence over the others or is in any way superior to them.

Moreover, regardless of the viewpoint that we adopt, the linguistic phenomenon always has two related sides, each deriving its values from the other. For example:

1)   Articulated syllables are acoustical impressions perceived by the ear, but the sounds would not exist without the vocal organs; an *n*, for example, exists only by virtue of the relationship between the two sides. We simply cannot reduce language to sound or detach sound from oral articulation; reciprocally, we cannot define the movements of the vocal organs without taking into account the acoustical impression.

2)   But suppose that sound were a simple thing: would it constitute speech? No, it is only the instrument of thought; by itself, it has no existence. At this point a new and redoubtable relationship arises: a sound, a complex acoustical-vocal unit, combines in turn with an idea to form a complex physiological-psychological unit. But that is still not the complete picture.

3)   Speech has both an individual and a social side, and we cannot conceive of one without the other. Besides:

4)   Speech always implies both an established system and an evolution; at every moment it is an existing institution and a product of the past. To distinguish between the system and its history, between what it is and what it was, seems very simple at first glance; actually the two things are so closely related that we can scarcely keep them apart. Would we simplify the question by studying the linguistic phenomenon in its earliest stages—if we began, for example, by studying the speech of children? No, for in dealing with speech, it is completely misleading to assume that the problem of early characteristics differs from the problem of permanent characteristics. We are left inside the vicious circle.

From whatever direction we approach the question, nowhere do we find the integral object of linguistics. Everywhere we are confronted with a dilemma: if we fix our attention on only one side of each problem, we run the risk of failing to perceive the dualities pointed out above; on the other hand, if we study speech from several viewpoints simultaneously, the object of linguistics appears to us as a confused mass of heterogeneous and unrelated things. Either procedure opens the door to several sciences—psychology, anthropology, normative grammar, philology, etc.—which are distinct from linguistics, but which might claim speech, in view of the faulty method of linguistics, as one of their objects.

As I see it there is only one solution to all the foregoing difficulties: *from the very outset we must put both feet on the ground of language and use language as the norm of all other manifestations of speech.* Actually, among so many dualities, language alone seems to lend itself to independent definition and provide a fulcrum that satisfies the mind.

But what is language [*langue*]? It is not to be confused with human speech [*langage*], of which it is only a definite part, though certainly an essential one. It is both a social product of the faculty of speech and a collection of necessary conventions that have been adopted by a social body to permit individuals to exercise that faculty. Taken as a whole, speech is many-sided and heterogeneous; straddling several areas simultaneously—physical, physiological, and psychological—it belongs both to the individual and to society; we cannot put it into any category of human facts, for we cannot discover its unity.

Language, on the contrary, is a self-contained whole and a principle of classification. As soon as we give language first place among the facts of speech, we introduce a natural order into a mass that lends itself to no other classification.

One might object to that principle of classification on the ground that since the use of speech is based on a natural faculty whereas language is something acquired and conventional, language should not take first place but should be subordinated to the natural instinct.

That objection is easily refuted.

First, no one has proved that speech, as it manifests itself when we speak, is entirely natural, i.e. that our vocal apparatus was designed for speaking just as our legs were designed for walking. Linguists are far from agreement on this point. For instance Whitney, to whom language is one of several social institutions, thinks that we use the vocal apparatus as the instrument of language purely through luck, for the sake of convenience: men might just as well have chosen gestures and used visual symbols instead of acoustical symbols. Doubtless his thesis is too dogmatic; language is not similar in all respects to other social institutions; moreover, Whitney goes too far in saying that our choice happened to fall on the vocal organs; the choice was more or less imposed by nature. But on the essential point the American linguist is right: language is a convention, and the nature of the sign that is agreed upon does not matter. The question of the vocal apparatus obviously takes a secondary place in the problem of speech.

One definition of *articulated speech* might confirm that conclusion. In Latin, *articulus* means a member, part, or subdivision of a sequence; applied to speech, articulation designates either the subdivision of a spoken chain into syllables or the subdivision of the chain of meanings into significant units; *gegliederte Sprache* is used in the second sense in German. Using the second definition, we can say that what is natural to mankind is not oral speech but the faculty of constructing a language, i.e. a system of distinct signs corresponding to distinct ideas.

Broca discovered that the faculty of speech is localized in the third left frontal convolution; his discovery has been used to substantiate the attribution of a natural quality to speech. But we know that the same part of the brain is the center of *everything* that has to do with speech, including writing. The preceding statements, together with observations that have been made in different cases of aphasia resulting from lesion of the centers of localization, seem to indicate: (1) that the various disorders of oral speech are bound up in a hundred ways with those of written speech; and (2) that what is lost in all cases of aphasia or agraphia is less the faculty of producing a given sound or writing a given sign than the ability to evoke by means of an instrument, regardless of what it is, the signs of a regular system of speech. The obvious implication is that beyond the functioning of the various organs there exists a more general faculty which governs signs and which would be the linguistic faculty proper. And this brings us to the same conclusion as above.

To give language first place in the study of speech, we can advance a final argument: the faculty of articulating words—whether it is natural or not—is exercised only with the help of the instrument created by a collectivity and provided for its use; therefore, to say that language gives unity to speech is not fanciful.

Place of Language in the Facts of Speech

In order to separate from the whole of speech the part that belongs to language, we must examine the individual act from which the speaking-circuit can be reconstructed. The act requires the presence of at least two persons; that is the minimum number necessary to complete the circuit. Suppose that two people, A and B, are conversing with each other:

A   B

Suppose that the opening of the circuit is in A's brain, where mental facts (concepts) are associated with representations of the linguistic sounds (sound-images) that are used for their expression. A given concept unlocks a corresponding sound-image in the brain; this purely *psychological* phenomenon is followed in turn by a *physiological* process: the brain transmits an impulse corresponding to the image to the organs used in producing sounds. Then the sound waves travel from the mouth of A to the ear of B: a purely *physical* process. Next, the circuit continues in B, but the order is reversed: from the ear to the brain, the physiological transmission of the sound-image; in the brain, the psychological association of the image with the corresponding concept. If B then speaks, the new act will follow—from his brain to A's— exactly the same course as the first act and pass through the same successive phases, which I shall diagram as follows:

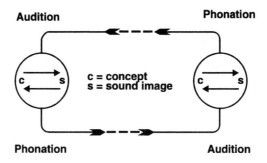

99

The preceding analysis does not purport to be complete. We might also single out the pure acoustical sensation, the identification of that sensation with the latent sound-image, the muscular image of phonation, etc. I have included only the elements thought to be essential, but the drawing brings out at a glance the distinction between the physical (sound waves), physiological (phonation and audition), and psychological parts (word-images and concepts). Indeed, we should not fail to note that the word-image stands apart from the sound itself and that it is just as psychological as the concept which is associated with it.

The circuit that I have outlined can be further divided into:

(a) an outer part that includes the vibrations of the sounds which travel from the mouth to the ear, and an inner part that includes everything else;

(b) a psychological and a nonpsychological part, the second including the physiological productions of the vocal organs as well as the physical facts that are outside the individual;

(c) an active and a passive part: everything that goes from the associative center of the speaker to the ear of the listener is active, and everything that goes from the ear of the listener to his associative center is passive;

(d) finally, everything that is active in the psychological part of the circuit is executive (c→s), and everything that is passive is receptive (s→c).

We should also add the associative and co-ordinating faculty that we find as soon as we leave isolated signs; this faculty plays the dominant role in the organization of language as a system.

But to understand clearly the role of the associative and co-ordinating faculty, we must leave the individual act, which is only the embryo of speech, and approach the social fact.

Among all the individuals that are linked together by speech, some sort of average will be set up: all will reproduce—not exactly of course, but approximately—the same signs united with the same concepts.

How does the social crystallisation of language come about? Which parts of the circuit are involved? For all parts probably do not participate equally in it.

The nonpsychological part can be rejected from the outset. When we hear people speaking a language that we do not know, we perceive the sounds but remain outside the social fact because we do not understand them.

Neither is the psychological part of the circuit wholly responsible: the executive side is missing, for execution is never carried out by the collectivity. Execution is always individual, and the individual is always its master: I shall call the executive side *speaking* [*parole*].

Through the functioning of the receptive and co-ordinating faculties, impressions that are perceptibly the same for all are made on the minds of speakers. How can that social product be pictured in such a way that language will stand apart from everything else? If we could embrace the sum of word-images stored in the minds of all individuals, we could identify the social bond that constitutes language. It is a storehouse filled by the members of a given community through their active use of speaking, a grammatical system that has a potential existence in each brain, or, more specifically, in the brains of a group of individuals. For language is not complete in any speaker; it exists perfectly only within a collectivity.

In separating language from speaking we are at the same time separating: (1) what is social from what is individual; and (2) what is essential from what is accessory and more or less accidental.

Language is not a function of the speaker; it is a product that is passively assimilated by the individual. It never requires premeditation, and reflection enters in only for the purpose of classification, which we shall take up later.

Speaking, on the contrary, is an individual act. It is wilful and intellectual. Within the act, we should distinguish between: (1) the combinations by which the speaker uses the language code for expressing his own thought; and (2) the psychophysical mechanism that allows him to exteriorize those combinations.

Note that I have defined things rather than words; these definitions are not endangered by certain ambiguous words that do not have identical meanings in different languages. For instance, German *Sprache* means both "language" and "speech"; *Rede* almost corresponds to "speaking" but adds the special connotation of "discourse." Latin *sermo* designates both "speech" and "speaking," while *lingua* means "language," etc. No word corresponds exactly to any of the notions specified above; that is why all definitions of words are made in vain; starting from words in defining things is a bad procedure.

To summarize, these are the characteristics of language:

(1) Language is a well-defined object in the heterogeneous mass of speech facts. It can be localized in the limited segment of the speaking-circuit where an auditory image becomes associated with a concept. It is the social side of speech, outside the individual who can never create nor modify it by himself; it exists only by virtue of a sort of contract signed by the members of a community. Moreover, the individual must always serve an apprenticeship in order to learn the functioning of language; a child assimilates it only gradually. It is such a distinct thing that a man deprived of the use of speaking retains it provided that he understands the vocal signs that he hears.

(2) Language, unlike speaking, is something that we can study separately. Although dead languages are no longer spoken, we can easily assimilate their linguistic organisms. We can dispense with the other elements of speech; indeed, the science of language is possible only if the other elements are excluded.

(3) Whereas speech is heterogeneous, language, as defined, is homogeneous. It is a system of signs in which the only essential thing is the union of meanings and sound-images, and in which both parts of the sign are psychological.

(4) Language is concrete, no less so than speaking; and this is a help in our study of it. Linguistic signs, though basically psychological, are not abstractions; associations which bear the stamp of collective approval—and which added together constitute language—are realities that have their seat in the brain. Besides, linguistic signs are tangible; it is possible to reduce them to conventional written symbols, whereas it would be impossible to provide detailed photographs of acts of speaking [*actes de parole*]; the pronunciation of even the smallest

word represents an infinite number of muscular movements that could be identified and put into graphic form only with great difficulty. In language, on the contrary, there is only the sound-image, and the latter can be translated into a fixed visual image. For if we disregard the vast number of movements necessary for the realization of sound-images in speaking, we see that each sound-image is nothing more than the sum of a limited number of elements or phonemes that can in turn be called up by a corresponding number of written symbols. The very possibility of putting the things that relate to language into graphic form allows dictionaries and grammars to represent it accurately, for language is a storehouse of sound-images, and writing is the tangible form of those images.

Place of Language in Human Facts: Semiology

The foregoing characteristics of language reveal an even more important characteristic. Language, once its boundaries have been marked off within the speech data, can be classified among human phenomena, whereas speech cannot.

We have just seen that language is a social institution; but several features set it apart from other political, legal, etc. institutions. We must call in a new type of facts in order to illuminate the special nature of language.

Language is a system of signs that express ideas, and is therefore comparable to a system of writing, the alphabet of deaf-mutes, symbolic rites, polite formulas, military signals, etc. But it is the most important of all these systems.

A science that studies the life of signs within society is conceivable; it would be a part of social psychology and consequently of general psychology; I shall call it *semiology* (from Greek *sēmeîon* 'sign'). Semiology would show what constitutes signs, what laws govern them. Since the science does not yet exist, no one can say what it would be; but it has a right to existence, a place staked out in advance. Linguistics is only a part of the general science of semiology; the laws discovered by semiology will be applicable to linguistics, and the latter will circumscribe a well-defined area within the mass of anthropological facts.

103

To determine the exact place of semiology is the task of the psychologist. The task of the linguist is to find out what makes language a special system within the mass of semiological data. This issue will be taken up again later; here I wish merely to call attention to one thing: if I have succeeded in assigning linguistics a place among the sciences, it is because I have related it to semiology.

Why has semiology not yet been recognized as an independent science with its own object like all the other sciences? Linguists have been going around in circles: language, better than anything else, offers a basis for understanding the semiological problem; but language must, to put it correctly, be studied in itself; heretofore language has almost always been studied in connection with something else, from other viewpoints.

There is first of all the superficial notion of the general public: people see nothing more than a name-giving system in language, thereby prohibiting any research into its true nature.

Then there is the viewpoint of the psychologist, who studies the sign-mechanism in the individual; this is the easiest method, but it does not lead beyond individual execution and does not reach the sign, which is social.

Or even when signs are studied from a social viewpoint, only the traits that attach language to the other social institutions—those that are more or less voluntary—are emphasized; as a result, the goal is by-passed and the specific characteristics of semiological systems in general and of language in particular are completely ignored. For the distinguishing characteristic of the sign—but the one that is least apparent at first sight—is that in some way it always eludes the individual or social will.

In short, the characteristic that distinguishes semiological systems from all other institutions shows up clearly only in language where it manifests itself in the things which are studied least, and the necessity or specific value of a semiological science is therefore not clearly recognized. But to me the language problem is mainly semiological, and all developments derive their significance from that important fact. If we are to discover the true nature of language we must learn what it has in common with all other semiological systems; linguistic forces that seem very important at first glance (e.g., the role of the vocal apparatus) will receive only secondary consideration if they serve only to set language apart from the other systems. This procedure will do more than to clarify the linguistic problem. By studying rites, customs, etc. as signs, I believe that we shall throw new light on the facts and point up the need for including them in a science of semiology and explaining them by its laws.

2.   NATURE OF THE LINGUISTIC SIGN

Sign, Signified, Signifier

Some people regard language, when reduced to its elements, as a naming-process only—a list of words, each corresponding to the thing that it names. For example:

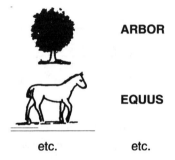

ARBOR

EQUUS

etc.   etc.

This conception is open to criticism at several points. It assumes that ready-made ideas exist before words; it does not tell us whether a name is vocal or psychological in nature (*arbor*, for instance, can be considered from either viewpoint); finally, it lets us assume that the linking of a name and a thing is a very simple operation—an assumption that is anything but true. But this rather naive approach can bring us near the truth by showing us that the linguistic unit is a double entity, one formed by the associating of two terms.

We have seen in considering the speaking-circuit that both terms involved in the linguistic sign are psychological and are united in the brain by an associative bond. This point must be emphasized.

The linguistic sign unites, not a thing and a name, but a concept and a sound-image. The latter is not the material sound, a purely physical thing, but the psychological imprint of the sound, the impression that it makes on our senses. The sound-image is sensory, and if I happen to call it "material," it is only in that sense, and by way of opposing it to the other term of the association, the concept, which is generally more abstract.

The psychological character of our sound-images becomes apparent when we observe our own speech. Without moving our lips or tongue, we can talk to ourselves or recite mentally a selection of verse. Because we regard the words of our language as sound-images, we must avoid speaking of the "phonemes" that make up the words. This term, which suggests vocal activity, is applicable to the spoken word only, to the realization of the inner image in discourse. We can avoid that misunderstanding by speaking of the *sounds* and *syllables* of a word provided we remember that the names refer to the sound-image.

The linguistic sign is then a two-sided psychological entity that can be represented by the drawing:

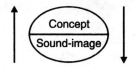

The two elements are intimately united, and each recalls the other. Whether we try to find the meaning of the Latin word *arbor* or the word that Latin uses to designate the concept "tree," it is clear that only the associations sanctioned by that language appear to us to conform to reality, and we disregard whatever others might be imagined.

Our definition of the linguistic sign poses an important question of terminology. I call the combination of a concept and a sound-image a *sign*, but in current usage the term generally designates only a sound-image, a word, for example (*arbor*, etc.). One tends to forget that *arbor* is called a sign only because it carries the concept "tree," with the result that the idea of the sensory part implies the idea of the whole.

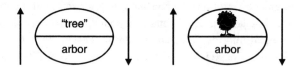

106

Ambiguity would disappear if the three notions involved here were designated by three names, each suggesting and opposing the others. I propose to retain the word *sign* [*signe*] to designate the whole and to replace *concept* and *sound-image* respectively by *signified* [*signifié*] and *signifier* [*signifiant*]; the last two terms have the advantage of indicating the opposition that separates them from each other and from the whole of which they are parts. As regards *sign*, if I am satisfied with it, this is simply because I do not know of any word to replace it, the ordinary language suggesting no other.

The linguistic sign, as defined, has two primordial characteristics. In enunciating them I am also positing the basic principles of any study of this type.

Principle I: The Arbitrary Nature of the Sign

The bond between the signifier and the signified is arbitrary. Since I mean by sign the whole that results from the association of the signifier with the signified, I can simply say: *the linguistic sign is arbitrary.*

The idea of "sister" is not linked by any inner relationship to the succession of sounds *s-ö-r* which serves as its signifier in French; that it could be represented equally by just any other sequence is proved by differences among languages and by the very existence of different languages: the signified "ox" has as its signifier *b-ö-f* on one side of the border and *o-k-s* (*Ochs*) on the other.

No one disputes the principle of the arbitrary nature of the sign, but it is often easier to discover a truth than to assign to it its proper place. Principle I dominates all the linguistics of language; its consequences are numberless. It is true that not all of them are equally obvious at first glance; only after many detours does one discover them, and with them the primordial importance of the principle.

One remark in passing: when semiology becomes organized as a science, the question will arise whether or not it properly includes modes of expression based on completely natural signs, such as pantomime. Supposing that the new science welcomes them, its main concern will still be the whole group of systems grounded on the arbitrariness of the sign. In fact, every means of expression used in society is based, in principle, on collective behavior or—what amounts to the same thing—on convention. Polite formulas, for instance, though often imbued with a certain natural expressiveness (as in the case of a

Chinese who greets his emperor by bowing down to the ground nine times), are nonetheless fixed by rule; it is this rule and not the intrinsic value of the gestures that obliges one to use them. Signs that are wholly arbitrary realize better than the others the ideal of the semiological process; that is why language, the most complex and universal of all systems of expression, is also the most characteristic; in this sense linguistics can become the master-pattern for all branches of semiology although language is only one particular semiological system.

The word *symbol* has been used to designate the linguistic sign, or more specifically, what is here called the signifier. Principle I in particular weighs against the use of this term. One characteristic of the symbol is that it is never wholly arbitrary; it is not empty, for there is the rudiment of a natural bond between the signifier and the signified. The symbol of justice, a pair of scales, could not be replaced by just any other symbol, such as a chariot.

The word *arbitrary* also calls for comment. The term should not imply that the choice of the signifier is left entirely to the speaker (we shall see below that the individual does not have the power to change a sign in any way once it has become established in the linguistic community); I mean that it is unmotivated, i.e. arbitrary in that it actually has no natural connection with the signified.

In concluding let us consider two objections that might be raised to the establishment of Principle I:

1) *Onomatopoeia* might be used to prove that the choice of the signifier is not always arbitrary. But onomatopoeic formations are never organic elements of a linguistic system. Besides, their number is much smaller than is generally supposed. Words like French *fouet* 'whip' or *glas* 'knell' may strike certain ears with suggestive sonority, but to see that they have not always had this property we need only examine their Latin forms (*fouet* is derived from *fāgus* 'beech-tree,' *glas* from *classicum* 'sound of a trumpet'). The quality of their present sounds, or rather the quality that is attributed to them, is a fortuitous result of phonetic evolution.

As for authentic onomatopoeic words (e.g. *glug-glug, tick-tock*, etc.), not only are they limited in number, but also they are chosen somewhat arbitrarily, for they are only approximate and more or less conventional imitations of certain sounds (cf. English *bow-wow* and French *ouaoua*). In addition, once these words have been introduced into the language, they are to a certain extent subjected to the same evolution—phonetic, morphological, etc.—that other words undergo (cf. *pigeon*, ultimately from Vulgar Latin *pīpiō*, derived in turn from an onomatopoeic formation): obvious proof that they lose something of their original character in order to assume that of the linguistic sign in general, which is unmotivated.

2) *Interjections*, closely related to onomatopoeia, can be attacked on the same grounds and come no closer to refuting our thesis. One is tempted to see in them spontaneous expressions of reality dictated, so to speak, by natural forces. But for most interjections we can show that there is no fixed bond between their signified and their signifier. We need only compare two languages on this point to see how much such expressions differ from one language to the next (e.g. the English equivalent of French *aïe!* is *ouch!*). We know, moreover, that many interjections were once words with specific meanings (cf. French *diable!* 'darn!' *mordieu!* 'golly!' from *mort Dieu* 'God's death,' etc.).

Onomatopoeic formations and interjections are of secondary importance, and their symbolic origin is in part open to dispute.

Principal II: The Linear Nature of the Signifier

The signifier, being auditory, is unfolded solely in time from which it gets the following characteristics: (a) it represents a span, and (b) the span is measurable in a single dimension; it is a line.

While Principle II is obvious, apparently linguists have always neglected to state it, doubtless because they found it too simple; nevertheless, it is fundamental, and its consequences are incalculable. Its importance equals that of Principle I; the whole mechanism of language depends upon it. In contrast to visual signifiers (nautical signals, etc.) which can offer simultaneous groupings in several dimensions, auditory signifiers have at their command only the dimension of time. Their elements are presented in succession; they form a chain. This feature becomes readily apparent when they are represented in writing and the spatial line of graphic marks is substituted for succession in time.

Sometimes the linear nature of the signifier is not obvious. When I accent a syllable, for instance, it seems that I am concentrating more than one significant element on the same point. But this is an illusion; the syllable and its accent constitute only one phonational act. There is no duality within the act but only different oppositions to what precedes and what follows.

3. IMMUTABILITY AND MUTABILITY OF THE SIGN

Immutability

The signifier, though to all appearances freely chosen with respect to the idea that it represents, is fixed, not free, with respect to the linguistic community that uses it. The masses have no voice in the matter, and the signifier chosen by language could be replaced by no other. This fact, which seems to embody a contradiction, might be called colloquially "the stacked deck." We say to language: "Choose!" but we add: "It must be this sign and no other." No individual, even if he willed it, could modify in any way at all the choice that has been made; and what is more, the community itself cannot control so much as a single word; it is bound to the existing language.

No longer can language be identified with a contract pure and simple, and it is precisely from this viewpoint that the linguistic sign is a particularly interesting object of study; for language furnishes the best proof that a law accepted by a community is a thing that is tolerated and not a rule to which all freely consent.

Let us first see why we cannot control the linguistic sign and then draw together the important consequences that issue from the phenomenon.

No matter what period we choose or how far back we go, language always appears as a heritage of the preceding period. We might conceive of an act by which, at a given moment, names were assigned to things and a contract was formed between concepts and sound-images; but such an act has never been recorded. The notion that things might have happened like that was prompted by our acute awareness of the arbitrary nature of the sign.

No society, in fact, knows or has ever known language other than as a product inherited from preceding generations, and one to be accepted as such. That is why the question of the origin of speech is not so important as it is generally assumed to be. The question is not even worth asking; the only real object of linguistics is the normal, regular life of an existing idiom. A particular language-state is always the product of historical forces, and these forces explain why the sign is unchangeable, i.e. why it resists any arbitrary substitution.

Nothing is explained by saying that language is something inherited and leaving it at that. Can not existing and inherited laws be modified from one moment to the next?

To meet that objection, we must put language into its social setting and frame the question just as we would for any other social institution. How are other social institutions transmitted? This more general question includes the question of immutability. We must first determine the greater or lesser amounts of freedom that the other institutions enjoy; in each instance it will be seen that a different proportion exists between fixed tradition and the free action of society. The next step is to discover why in a given category, the forces of the first type carry more weight or less weight than those of the second. Finally, coming back to language, we must ask why the historical factor of transmission dominates it entirely and prohibits any sudden widespread change.

There are many possible answers to the question. For example, one might point to the fact that succeeding generations are not superimposed on one another like the drawers of a piece of furniture, but fuse and interpenetrate, each generation embracing individuals of all ages—with the result that modifications of language are not tied to the succession of generations. One might also recall the sum of the efforts required for learning the mother language and conclude that a general change would be impossible. Again, it might be added that reflection does not enter into the active use of an idiom—speakers are largely unconscious of the laws of language; and if they are unaware of them, how could they modify them? Even if they were aware of these laws, we may be sure that their awareness would seldom lead to criticism, for people are generally satisfied with the language they have received.

The foregoing considerations are important but not topical. The following are more basic and direct, and all the others depend on them.

(1) *The arbitrary nature of the sign.* Above, we had to accept the theoretical possibility of change; further reflection suggests that the arbitrary nature of the sign is really what protects language from any

attempt to modify it. Even if people were more conscious of language than they are, they would still not know how to discuss it. The reason is simply that any subject in order to be discussed must have a reasonable basis. It is possible, for instance, to discuss whether the monogamous form of marriage is more reasonable than the polygamous form and to advance arguments to support either side. One could also argue about a system of symbols, for the symbol has a rational relationship with the thing signified; but language is a system of arbitrary signs and lacks the necessary basis, the solid ground for discussion. There is no reason for preferring *soeur* to *sister*, *Ochs to boeuf*, etc.

(2) *The multiplicity of signs necessary to form any language.* Another important deterrent to linguistic change is the great number of signs that must go into the making of any language. A system of writing comprising twenty to forty letters can in case of need be replaced by another system. The same would be true of language if it contained a limited number of elements; but linguistic signs are numberless.

(3) *The over-complexity of the system.* A language constitutes a system. In this one respect (as we shall see later) language is not completely arbitrary but is ruled to some extent by logic; it is here also, however, that the inability of the masses to transform it becomes apparent. The system is a complex mechanism that can be grasped only through reflection; the very ones who use it daily are ignorant of it. We can conceive of a change only through the intervention of specialists, grammarians, logicians, etc.; but experience shows us that all such meddlings have failed.

(4) *Collective inertia toward innovation.* Language—and this consideration surpasses all the others—is at every moment everybody's concern; spread throughout society and manipulated by it, language is something used daily by all. Here we are unable to set up any comparison between it and other institutions. The prescriptions of codes, religious rites, nautical signals, etc., involve only a certain number of individuals simultaneously and then only during a limited period of time; in language, on the contrary, everyone participates at

all times, and that is why it is constantly being influenced by all. This capital fact suffices to show the impossibility of revolution. Of all social institutions, language is least amenable to initiative. It blends with the life of society, and the latter, inert by nature, is a prime conservative force.

But to say that language is a product of social forces does not suffice to show clearly that it is unfree; remembering that it is always the heritage of the preceding period, we must add that these social forces are linked with time. Language is checked not only by the weight of the collectivity but also by time. These two are inseparable. At every moment solidarity with the past checks freedom of choice. We say *man* and *dog*. This does not prevent the existence in the total phenomenon of a bond between the two antithetical forces—arbitrary convention by virtue of which choice is free and time which causes choice to be fixed. Because the sign is arbitrary, it follows no law other than that of tradition, and because it is based on tradition, it is arbitrary.

Mutability

Time, which insures the continuity of language, wields another influence apparently contradictory to the first: the more or less rapid change of linguistic signs. In a certain sense, therefore, we can speak of both the immutability and the mutability of the sign.

In the last analysis, the two facts are interdependent: the sign is exposed to alteration because it perpetuates itself. What predominates in all change is the persistence of the old substance; disregard for the past is only relative. That is why the principle of change is based on the principle of continuity.

Change in time takes many forms, on any one of which an important chapter in linguistics might be written. Without entering into detail, let us see what things need to be delineated.

First, let there be no mistake about the meaning that we attach to the word change. One might think that it deals especially with phonetic changes undergone by the signifier, or perhaps changes in meaning which affect the signified concept. That view would be inadequate. Regardless of what the forces of change are, whether in isolation or in combination, they always result in *a shift in the relationship between the signified and the signifier*.

113

Here are some examples. Latin *necāre* 'kill' became *noyer* 'drown' in French. Both the sound-image and the concept changed; but it is useless to separate the two parts of the phenomenon; it is sufficient to state with respect to the whole that the bond between the idea and the sign was loosened, and that there was a shift in their relationship. If instead of comparing Classical Latin *necāre* with French *noyer*, we contrast the former term with *necare* of Vulgar Latin of the fourth or fifth century meaning 'drown' the case is a little different; but here again, although there is no appreciable change in the signifier, there is a shift in the relationship between the idea and the sign.

Old German *dritteil* 'one-third' became *Drittel* in Modern German. Here, although the concept remained the same, the relationship was changed in two ways: the signifier was changed not only in its material aspect but also in its grammatical form; the idea of *Teil* 'part' is no longer implied; *Drittel* is a simple word. In one way or another there is always a shift in the relationship.

In Anglo-Saxon the preliterary form *fot* 'foot' remained while its plural **fōti* became *fēt* (Modern English *feet*). Regardless of the other changes that are implied, one thing is certain: there was a shift in their relationship; other correspondences between the phonetic substance and the idea emerged.

Language is radically powerless to defend itself against the forces which from one moment to the next are shifting the relationship between the signified and the signifier. This is one of the consequences of the arbitrary nature of the sign.

Unlike language, other human institutions—customs, laws, etc.—are all based in varying degrees on the natural relations of things; all have of necessity adapted the means employed to the ends pursued. Even fashion in dress is not entirely arbitrary; we can deviate only slightly from the conditions dictated by the human body. Language is limited by nothing in the choice of means, for apparently nothing would prevent the associating of any idea whatsoever with just any sequence of sounds.

To emphasize the fact that language is a genuine institution, Whitney quite justly insisted upon the arbitrary nature of signs; and by so doing, he placed linguistics on its true axis. But he did not follow through and see that the arbitrariness of language radically separates it from all other institutions. This is apparent from the way in which language evolves. Nothing could be more complex. As it is a product of both the social force and time, no one can change anything in it, and on the other hand, the arbitrariness of its signs theoretically entails the freedom of establishing just any relationship between phonetic substance and ideas. The result is that each of the two elements united in the sign maintains its own life to a degree unknown elsewhere, and that language changes, or rather evolves, under the influence of all the forces which can affect either sounds or meanings. The evolution is inevitable; there is no example of a single language that resists it. After a certain period of time, some obvious shifts can always be recorded.

Mutability is so inescapable that it even holds true for artificial languages. Whoever creates a language controls it only so long as it is not in circulation; from the moment when it fulfills it mission and becomes the property of everyone, control is lost. Take Esperanto as an example; if it succeeds, will it escape the inexorable law? Once launched, it is quite likely that Esperanto will enter upon a fully semiological life; it will be transmitted according to laws which have nothing in common with those of its logical creation, and there will be no turning backwards. A man proposing a fixed language that posterity would have to accept for what it is would be like a hen hatching a duck's egg: the language created by him would be borne along, willy-nilly, by the current that engulfs all languages.

Signs are governed by a principle of general semiology: continuity in time is coupled to change in time; this is confirmed by orthographic systems, the speech of deaf-mutes, etc.

But what supports the necessity for change? I might be reproached for not having been as explicit on this point as on the principle of immutability. This is because I failed to distinguish between the different forces of change. We must consider their great variety in order to understand the extent to which they are necessary.

The causes of continuity are *a priori* within the scope of the observer, but the causes of change in time are not. It is better not to attempt giving an exact account at this point, but to restrict discussion to the shifting of relationships in general. Time changes all things; there is no reason why language should escape this universal law.

Let us review the main points of our discussion and relate them to the principles set up in the Introduction.

1) Avoiding sterile word definitions, within the total phenomenon represented by speech we first singled out two parts: language and speaking.

Language is speech less speaking. It is the whole set of linguistic habits which allow an individual to understand and to be understood.

2) But this definition still leaves language outside its social context; it makes language something artificial since it includes only the individual part of reality; for the realization of language, a community of speakers [*masse parlante*] is necessary. Contrary to all appearances, language never exists apart from the social fact, for it is a semiological phenomenon. Its social nature is one of its inner characteristics. Its complete definition confronts us with two inseparable entities, as shown in this drawing:

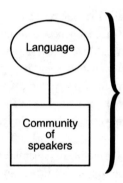

But under the conditions described language is not living—it has only potential life; we have considered only the social, not the historical, fact.

3) The linguistic sign is arbitrary; language, as defined, would therefore seem to be a system which, because it depends solely on a rational principle, is free and can be organized at will. Its social nature, considered independently, does not definitely rule out this viewpoint. Doubtless it is not on a purely logical basis that group psychology operates; one must consider everything that deflects reason in actual contacts between individuals. But the thing which keeps language from being a simple convention that can be modified at the whim of interested parties is not its social nature; it is rather the action of time combined with the social force. If time is left out, the linguistic facts are incomplete and no conclusion is possible.

If we considered language in time, without the community of speakers—imagine an isolated individual living for several centuries—we probably would notice no change; time would not influence language. Conversely, if we considered the community of speakers without considering time, we would not see the effect of the social forces that influence language. To represent the actual facts, we must then add to our first drawing a sign to indicate passage of time:

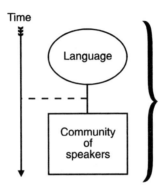

Language is no longer free, for time will allow the social forces at work on it to carry out their effects. This brings us back to the principle of continuity, which cancels freedom. But continuity necessarily implies change, varying degrees of shifts in the relationship between the signified and the signifier.

117

4

THE WHORFIAN
HYPOTHESIS TODAY

Rick Osborn

INTRODUCTION—THE WHORFIAN HYPOTHESIS?

Every student of every subject which has anything to do with the relationship between language and society knows that there was somebody called Whorf who had a hypothesis which has two versions, one of which is strong and the other weak. Abilities to say much more than this vary, but most will be able to state that the 'strong version' suggests that the language spoken by an individual determines the way in which that person thinks, whereas the weak version suggests influence rather than determination. Many will also be able to draw the conclusion that such ideas have implications for the extent to which different cultures and language communities can communicate with each other.

What is also noticeable about such students is that very few of them will ever have read anything which was actually written by Whorf. Virtually all will have read some introductory text (in linguistics, sociology, etc.).

They will have obtained from this some statement of the 'hypothesis'. Many will have read a number of refutations of the 'strong version'. Depending

Rick Osborn. "The Whorfian Hypothesis Today." In Asher Cashdan and Martin Jordin (eds.), *Studies in Communication*. Oxford: Basil Blackwell, 1987. Reprinted with permission from Basil Blackwell.

on their predilections and those of their teachers, they will have read a variety of texts which either refute all 'Whorfianism' or make use of it more or less explicitly or implicitly.

Finally, there is a very small group who are on courses for which the 'Whorfian' hypothesis is a central concept, or who find the theoretical issues inherently interesting or who are possessed of enquiring and critical minds. These students actually read Whorf and discover to their surprise that he never made any explicit statement of the 'Whorfian' hypothesis. This fact is also the cause of much frustration to those who teach in this area and probably accounts for the fact that the most often quoted passage used to express the 'Whorfian' hypothesis was written not by Whorf but by Sapir, though it is quoted by Whorf at the beginning of 'The relation of habitual thought and behaviour to language (1939, p. 134). Thus we find use of the term 'the Sapir-Whorf hypothesis' and occasionally reference in student essays to the work of one Benjamin Lee Sapir-Whorf!

Whorf certainly speaks of a principle of 'linguistic relativity'. It is certainly the case that his writings are peppered with observations and assertions which seem to lead to a deterministic view of language. However, there are also passages which view language as formed by social and historical forces. Thus, later in the same work we find:

> In the Middle Ages the patterns already formed in Latin began to interweave with the increased mechanical invention, industry, trade, and scholastic and scientific thought. The need for measurement in industry and trade, the stores and bulks of 'stuffs' in various containers, the typebodies in which various goods were handled, standardizing of measure and weight units, invention of clocks and measurement of 'time', keeping of records, accounts, chronicles, histories, growth of mathematics and the partnership of mathematics and science, all cooperated to bring our thought and language world into its present form. (Whorf, 1939, p. 157)

What are we to make of this? Did Whorf see the clock as a product for the tense systems of European languages or vice versa. My view is that Whorf would have rejected as meaningless so simplistic a dichotomy and would have rejected also other such equally simplistic dichotomies though couched in more sophisticated and circuitous language. I would also suggest that the notion of a Whorfian hypothesis, though obviously based in statements made by Whorf, is a product of the hermeneutic study of his texts rather than something which is directly contained in them. This is particularly the case when attempting to locate its 'strong' and 'weak' versions.

I do not, in this chapter, intend to pursue this 'case for Whorf' any further. I believe that it emerges fairly obviously from a careful reading of his texts unprejudiced by intervening interpretations of them. My main concern is not with the origins of the 'Whorfian' hypothesis but more with some of its effects upon current issues of academic interest. I am not so much concerned with the hypothesis as the product of any one person, but more with its status as an element within our current academic culture. One of the more cogent presentations of the 'Whorfian' hypothesis contained in an introductory text is to be found in Lyons (1981). He alerts the reader to the fact that the hypothesis contains two fundamental concepts: 'linguistic relativity'—different languages express different views of the universe and there is no absolute scale by which they may be judged; and 'linguistic determinism'—the form of our language determines the way in which we view the world. As a final observation on Whorf's writings, it is worth noting that it is the former concept which is most emphasized within them. Most of his conclusions result from a comparison of non-European languages with English or the mythical 'Standard Average European'. However, most of the current explicit or implicit uses of the hypothesis stress 'linguistic determinism' and are more concerned with differences within rather than between language communities. Given this, together with the problems I have outlined above, I propose to use the term 'concept of linguistic determinism' hereafter in preference to the more problematic 'Whorfian hypothesis'.

Two Examples of 'Linguistic Determinism' in Current Debates

The concept of linguistic determinism does of course antedate Whorf, whose work had the effect of reformulating it and spreading it to a wider audience. It has, of course, been a subject of debate in its own right. What I also find of interest, however, is the way in which it has permeated a wide range of areas of study which because their main focus is elsewhere, have used it rather than debated it. In order to illustrate this breadth of influence, I give a (very brief) discussion below of two manifestations of this concept in very different fields: namely, the concern within software engineering about the suitability of computer programming of languages, and debates around the concept of sexist language.

Linguistic determinism in software engineering

Even people outside the computer world may have detected the distant rumblings of a debate concerning programming languages from, say, headlines in the *Guardian's* micro page like 'Does BASIC rot the mind?'. The contention centres around the notion that certain programming languages, if they are used as a vehicle for training programmers, bring about bad attitudes to programming which are very difficult to reverse. What is meant by 'bad' attitudes is that they result in the production of programs which are difficult to interpret, difficult to modify and sometimes incorrect as a result of errors which are difficult to locate. It is argued by some that people who have become habituated to a 'bad' language find it difficult to learn more appropriate ones and, even if they do, difficult to think in them.

The problem stems from the fact that virtually all existing computing machines can operate with only the most rudimentary units of information. These units are termed 'machine instructions' and involve operations such as moving an item of data from one part of the machine to another or performing some simple arithmetic operation upon a data item. In the early days of computing, programmers had to transform operations which are utterly rudimentary to a human into complex sets of 'sub-instructions' so that a machine could carry them out. Thus a program which multiplied two numbers together might look like the following:

```
(1)      LOD X
         MOV B A
         LOD Y
         MOV H A
         MOV A B
    LOOP ADD B
         DECR H
         JNZ LOOP
         STO Z
```

The basic multiplication process is carried out in lines 6 to 8 of the program through the repeated addition of the first number to itself; the number of repetitions being determined by the value of the second number. All the other instructions involve the movement of data between locations so that the right answer ends up in the right place. Clearly, if a programmer has to go to such lengths to multiply two numbers, then the writing of a program to carry out a complex computation will be tedious in the extreme. Worse, the amount of detail required will almost inevitably lead to errors in the writing. So in the mid to late fifties people began to design and implement what have become known as high level languages (HLL). The basic objective of such projects was to provide programmers with means of expressing computations in a way which was more comprehensible to humans. The core of such a project is to write a program which translates a program written in an HLL into one which has the same effect but is comprehensible to a machine. Such a program is called a compiler. Obviously, a compiler would be very complex and would have to be written in a machine level language. However, once written and demonstrated to be correct it could be the last program which would need to be written in a machine level language (assuming that you can say anything in the HLL that you could in the machine level language). Thus in the HLL called Standard BASIC, everything in (1) can be rendered as:

LET Z= X * Y

Given that the symbol '*' is a standard computer keyboard symbol meaning 'multiplied by', the meaning of this statement becomes fairly obvious. What the inventors of the first HLLs achieved was the benefit of abstraction: in other words, the ability to state a complex concept succinctly so that it can participate in a higher level through the explicit statement of its internal complexity. The problem which arises at this point, however, is which abstractions do you incorporate in your HLL and to what level do you allow the abstraction process to proceed? An analogy with natural language can be drawn. If we take a concept like the economics term 'inflation', we can see that it is an abstraction which can be decomposed into a number of concepts such as 'change over time', 'wage rates', 'price levels' etc. Each of these in turn can be seen as abstractions which can be further decomposed, and so on. Of course, the point at which such decomposition stops in natural language is not as clear-cut as it is in programming languages. Also difficult to define in natural languages is the process whereby some complexes of concepts become selected for abstraction whilst others do not. Thus we have a single word for inflation but 'the right of each person to health and financial security' is expressible only by a phrase.

In programming languages the process of abstraction is unproblematic—the language designer simply makes a decision as to which abstractions to implement. The criteria of decision are, however, hard to define. Thus whilst it is obvious that the language will require abstractions for basic arithmetic operations—multiply, divide, etc.—other less basic operations are less obvious. One could allow the process of abstraction to continue to a point where what in some systems would be a large program is implemented in an HLL as a single statement. At this point, however, one begins to find the HLL becoming confusing because of the plethora of constructs within it. Languages of this type have been called 'baroque' (see, for example, Dijkstra, 1972). Choices have to be made between low level languages which have lexical systems which are so simple that the expression of a simple meaning requires a long sentence, and the possibility of high level languages whose lexical systems are so rich that the user finds learning all their elements and distinguishing between their sometimes close shades of meaning somewhat problematic.

Another issue which has caused considerable debate is that of structuredness. We can illustrate this by examining the device of repetition in a program. Many programs achieve their desired result by repeating a simple operation in a controlled way. The program in (1) achieves the effect of multiplication by repeated addition. Let us consider the simpler example written in BASIC in (2).

(2) 10 PRINT "hello"
    20 PRINT "goodbye"

This program has the effect of simply printing on the screen the words 'hello' and 'goodbye'. Now consider (3).

(3) 10 PRINT "hello"
    20 GOTO 10
    30 PRINT "goodbye"

This program will print an endless sequence of 'hello's. It will never print 'goodbye' and it will never terminate. The reason is that it begins at line 10, prints 'hello' and then at line 20, instead of proceeding to line 30, it is told to go to line 10 where it prints 'hello' and then goes, via line 20, to line 10, and so on. Suppose, however, that we want a program which prints six 'hello's and then a 'goodbye'. (4) will do this.

```
(4) 5 LET A = 6
    10 PRINT "hello"
    20 LET A = A - 1
    30 IF A > 0 then goto 10
    40 PRINT "goodbye"
```

(4) introduces a variable called A which can take any integer number value. Line 5 sets the value of A to 6. At line 20 the value of A is reduced by 1. At line 30 the program is told to repeat the sequence starting at line 10 only if A is greater than 0. After line 20 has been repeated six times, the value of A is 0 and the program does not go back to line 10 but proceeds to line 40. (4) embodies all the necessary constructs to write virtually any program. Using LET, IF . . . THEN and GOTO statements, programs of considerable complexity and sophistication can be written. The use of GOTO however, can cause considerable problems. Consider (5). Its effect is identical to that of (3). Readers who are not familiar with programming languages may care to work out why.

```
(5) 5 LET A = 6
    10 PRINT "hello"
    20 LET A = A - 1
    30 IF A > 0 THEN GOTO 100
    40 PRINT "goodbye"
    100 LET A = 2
    110 GOTO 10
```

If you experience any difficulty in working out what is happening in (5), then consider the problem posed by a program of several hundreds or thousands of lines which is liberally sprinkled with GOTO statements. The use of GOTO statements can destroy the structure of a program. The reason for this is that the fundamental structural principle of this type of language is the sequencing of operations. GOTO disrupts this principle, resulting sometimes in chaos.

However, as we have seen, we need to be able to embody repetition in programs and repetition necessarily entails the disruption of sequencing. How are we to reconcile these apparently contradictory requirements? The answer is to restrict repetition to single definable sub-sequences within the program. We do this using structured repetition constructs of which REPEAT . . . UNTIL is an example. Using this construct we can rewrite (4) as (6).

```
(6) 10 LET A = 6
    20 REPEAT
    30 PRINT "hello"
    40 LET A = A - 1
    50 UNTIL A = 0
    60 PRINT "goodbye"
```

The sequence between lines 20 and 50 is repeated until the value of A has been reduced to 0. Anyone wishing to test the value of this construct should try rewriting (5), using it. For the reasons illustrated above, among others, designers of high level languages have favoured implementing structured rather than unstructured constructs in them.

The reasons for using structured constructs are in most cases obvious. Recently, however, the use or non-use of such concepts has been claimed to have effects not only on programs but upon programmers. Consider the following:

> Language is the vehicle by which we express our thoughts and the relation between our thoughts and our language is a subtle and involuted one. The nature of language actually shapes and models the way we think . . .If by providing appropriate language constructs we can improve the programs written using these structures, then the entire field will benefit. (Wulf, 1977)

Here then is a clear statement of belief in linguistic determinism. Not only does the use of 'structureless' languages produce bad programs but programmers who learned programming by using such languages are likely to approach the programming task in an unstructured way. Wulf goes on:

> A. language design should at least provide facilities which allow
> comprehensible expression of algorithms; at best a language suggests
> better forms of expression. But language is not a panacea. A language
> cannot for example, prevent the creation of obscure programs; the
> ingenious programmer can always find an infinite number of paths
> to obfuscation. (Wulf, 1977)

The implication is that unless programmers are trained initially in structured languages, then even when later presented with them they will fail to avail themselves of their virtues. Wulf's comments are by no means atypical of the current orthodoxy in software engineering. Interestingly, these comments, coming as they do from 'hard' scientists, are rarely substantiated by any evidence that would lend support to their assertion of the doctrine of linguistic determinism. They are frequently made by people who are unaware that such ideas are in the least contentious. Equally interestingly, investigations to test such notions in this area would be considerably easier to set up than in the context of natural language. They might, by operating in a more easily defined microcosm, shed some light on the wider issues of linguistic determinism.

Linguistic determinism in debates around sexist language

> In order to live in the world we must name it. Names are essential
> for the construction of reality, for without a name it is difficult to
> accept the existence of an object, an event, a feeling. Naming is the
> means whereby we attempt to order and structure the chaos and
> flux of existence which would otherwise be an undifferentiated
> mass. (Spender, 1980)

The principle of linguistic determinism could hardly be more forcefully stated. It comes as the preamble to a chapter called 'The politics of naming' in which it is suggested, among other things, that many of the experiences habitually undergone by women are not named in English and, therefore, seen by speakers of English as less real than others for which a name exists. Elsewhere it is suggested that children who are socialized within a community whose language unequally categorizes men and women will learn to think of this inequality as natural. Language determines thought and thence behaviour and therefore the social structures which are realized by habitual patterns of behaviour. If such a contention is accepted then there is ample rationale for attempting to change linguistic structures which lead to inequality. Thus we might argue that the use of 'he' as a non-specified gender pronoun should be replaced by the use of 'he or she'.

In the same way we should not use nouns like 'chairman', 'spokesman' etc. but rather, newer coinages such as 'chairperson', 'spokesperson' which do not make use of the suffix '-man'. Interestingly, the arguments in favour of such changes in the language are advanced in a 'strong' and a 'weak' form. The former is exemplified in the quotation from Spender above and depends for its validity on the correctness of linguistic determinism. Such a view, if taken to its logical conclusion, would imply that, if we could succeed in eradicating such usages from the language, then the inequalities produced by them would also disappear. A view which depends on a 'weaker' view of determinism suggests that whilst the eradication of such usage will not in itself eradicate social inequalities, the use of the more marked, preferred usages—'he or she', 'chairperson' etc.—serves to highlight the inequalities which exist and draw them into the conscious consideration of the language user.

With equal frequency, it seems to me, we encounter the notion that sexist language is a product of a sexist society. In other words, a reverse principle of the social determination of language is proposed. We can also construct a third position which affirms that neither of these contentions is correct. Rather, language and social structure are separate entities each with its own history and internal momentum; apparent convergences are accidental. Such a position has very respectable antecedents, following as it does from the concept of the arbitrary relationship between the form and the meaning of the sign. At first sight, these three possibilities, which we may term linguistic determinism, social determinism and non-determinism, are both exhaustive and mutually exclusive. That is to say, between them they cover all the logical possibilities and only one of them can be correct. Such a view seems to be advanced by Pateman (1981) when contrasting 'functionalism or materialism with 'Whorfianism'.

> the explanatory functionalism has been married to a substantive
> materialism: human interests, desires, beliefs etc. themselves arise
> in and are conditioned by determinate material circumstances . . .

But it cannot be reconciled with . . . Whorfian tendencies . . . For if
Whorfianism is any distinctive theory at all, it must be a theory
about the conditioning of people's . . . 'world view' by the language
they speak. The direction of causation is exactly the reverse of that
proposed by any materialism.

It would seem therefore that we have to choose between these options and
cannot have our logical cake and eat it. Yet the feeling persists for many people,
myself included, that each of these three logically exclusive options lends
coherence to some aspects of our experience and therefore has some truth in it.

SOME SUGGESTIONS TOWARDS A RESOLUTION

Two logical fallacies

I would argue that the sort of arguments that purport to see linguistic
determinism, social determinism and non-determinism as logically mutually
exclusive are based upon a simplistic use of logic which confuses situations in
which certain statements are obviously true, with others where their validity is
at least questionable. It seems to me that there are two areas of fallacy.
The first arises from a misconception of the generality of statements about
causality and can be illustrated using a simple example.

1 This chicken laid this egg.
2 This chicken hatched from this egg.

Assuming only one egg and one chicken to be involved throughout both 1
and 2 then to assert that both statements are true would be patently absurd.
Few people however would have any difficulty in believing and indeed verifying
3 and 4.

3 Chickens lay eggs.
4 Chickens hatch from eggs.

It would seem to me that 5 and 6 are of the same character as 3 and 4, not of 1
and 2.

5 Language influences social behaviour.
6 Social behaviour influences language.

The second fallacy stems from regarding the sort of entity which is denoted by the term 'language' as monolithic. Anyone who has spent time attempting to describe and analyse languages knows that each is a complex of systems and structures, comprised of complex sub-systems and sub-structures, many of which are relatively autonomous. It would, therefore, be quite logical, though hardly plausible, to assert that the phonology of a language is determined by the social structure of its speakers whilst the latter is determined by the syntax of the language. Equally logically and rather more plausibly, we may assert that social relationships can be influenced by habitually used linguistic forms, whilst changes in social attitudes can influence habitual forms of linguistic usage. Allowing ourselves a little slide into the Whorfian heresy, we might consider whether the apparent validity of the 'monolithic fallacy' stems from the fact that 'language' in English and many other languages is an abstract singular noun.

The establishment of the feasibility of our intuition that both linguistic and social deterministic influences coexist within a language community, allows us to proceed on a sounder theoretical basis to an examination of how such influences interact. To do so here is beyond the scope of this essay. However, I shall finish with a small example which illustrates some aspects of such an attempt.

The importance of lexicalized meanings

Most people, I think, would reject what is depicted as 'strong' linguistic determinism. If the existing classification system embodied in a language were an absolute rule, then conceptual change would be impossible. It does seem reasonable to suggest, however, that the existing classification system influences the ways in which we habitually conceptualize our surroundings, including the social environment which we inhabit. A rejection of 'strong' relativity leads us to the conclusion that anything that can be said in any one language can be said in any other. A weaker form of relativity leads us to the realization that a concept which might be expressed in one language using a single word may be expressible in another only by the construction of a phrase, sentence, or longer chunk of language. Anyone who has any experience with translation will be familiar with this phenomenon. The most obvious explanation of this disparity is that concepts which are important for a language community become lexicalized—the community establishes them within a single word. Languages differ in the relative degree of importance which they attach to different concepts. If this is the case then a dictionary is not just a word list, but a record of the concepts which a particular society considers to be important.

We may see here some similarity with the transition from low level, machine-oriented computer languages to high level languages. Just as certain frequently used sequences of low-level code are abstracted to single high-level constructs, meanings in natural language which are habitually articulated in the form of supra-lexical entities are abstracted to single words. Those which are used less frequently remain unlexicalized. But why should lexicalized meanings appear more important than those which are expressible only by syntactic devices? The answer resides in the permanence of their form. The second time a phrasal meaning is uttered it is likely to be rephrased or paraphrased. The form which is adopted for this meaning is variable. This is not the case with a lexicalized meaning which will be 'the same word' whenever it is uttered.

What we see here is an aspect of social determinism. Meanings within a society which are considered important are established and made permanent within that society's coding system. We can see linguistic determinism within another aspect of this situation. Lexicalized meanings are not only privileged by virtue of their wordhood. They are more easily manipulable within the language and can be used to develop the concept which they represent and to participate in the modification of other concepts. This results not only from the more succinct expression which a word brings to a meaning, but also from the fact that a word can participate in the morphological productivity system of the language in a way that larger units cannot.

Thus, if I invent a verb 'repone' to denote a process which has hitherto been expressible only by the use of a phrase, say, 'to elect someone to an office which they once held but were not holding at the time of the election', then the morphological productivity system of English allows me to construct naturally a whole set of other words. 'Tories set to repone Heath', says the headline. The process can be placed in time and given aspectual properties: 'At an election held last night the Tory party reponed Edward Heath to the party leadership'; 'They are reponing Heath.' A noun and adjective emerge: 'The reponation of

Edward Heath . . .'; 'The Tory party is not one which is usually thought of as being reponacious'; 'Edward Heath, the reponed leader . . .'; and so on. The point is that on the formal level, the invention of one word is all that is necessary; the others are virtually automatically invented by the system. On the semantic level, the creation of a word does not create a new meaning since that meaning was always expressible by the phrase. What happens is that the meaning becomes 'normalized': that is to say, easier to express and easier to use in relation to the other normalized meanings within the culture. The meaning, once lexicalized, can be extended through its use in the modification of other meanings. Thus we might find that a once fashionable author who is back in favour with the critics after spending a period in the wilderness might be spoken of as 'having undergone a sort of literary reponation after the publication of her most recent novel'.

The overall effect is that the meaning becomes legal communicative tender rather than a promissory note. Let us take an actual example. Part of this chapter has touched upon sexist language. Fifteen years ago I would probably have had to write 'sexist' language. Twenty-five years ago I would have had to say something like: the use of language which tends to express and reproduce male dominance in our society. What is more likely is that it would not have occurred to me to write about such an obscure area of communication at all. The reasons why this subject has been lifted from obscurity to the status of a live issue are multiple. The most fundamental is without doubt social: the emergence during the mid-sixties of the contemporary women's movement. However, the coining of the word 'sexist' has also been a factor. Its coining did not create a new meaning in the language. That meaning existed in the structure of our society for centuries and was always expressible by syntactic constructs. What it did was to 'normalize' that meaning and make it part of current usage. To say that the coining of 'sexist' produced a new consciousness of the status of women in our culture would be wrong, but it certainly accelerated the development of that consciousness. It has therefore exerted some influence on social change. We can thus see that the relationship between language and society in this area of lexicalization is a dialectical one. Meanings become lexicalized as a result of social change. The fact of their lexicalization can accelerate the rate of change and perhaps produce changes which otherwise might not happen, or would happen with greater difficulty. It is worth noting that the ease with which 'sexism' came into the language was probably a product of the previous coining of 'racism'. The emergence of 'ageism' and more recently 'speciesism' seems to indicate the establishment at a meta-lexical level of a means of articulating oppression.

The study of the interplay of social and linguistic forces is an interesting one. It will not be served by posing theories about them in a spurious either/or logic. It can make a contribution to the study of the shifting balances between ideologies, and in this the concept of 'normalized' meanings may prove fruitful. In any case, the ideas of Whorf can still be seen as a useful catalyst in making sense of areas as diverse as software engineering and the development of social movements.

REFERENCES

Dijkstra, E. W. (1972) 'The humble programmer', *Communications of the Association for Computing Machinery*, 15, 859-66.

Lyons, J. (1981) *Language and Linguistics*, Cambridge University Press.

Pateman, T. (1981) 'Linguistics as a branch of critical theory', *UEA Papers in Linguistics*, 14/15, 1-29.

Spender, D. (1980) *Man Made Language*, Routledge.

Whorf, B. L. (1939) 'The relation of habitual. thought and behaviour to language', in J. B. Carroll (1953), *Language and Thought*, Prentice-Hall.

Wulf, W. A. (1977) 'Language and structural programs', in R. T. Yeh (ed.), *Current Trends in Programming Methodology*, I, Prentice-Hall.

5

CONCEPTS WE LIVE BY

George Lakoff
Mark Johnson

Metaphor is for most people a device of the poetic imagination and the rhetorical flourish—a matter of extraordinary rather than ordinary language. Moreover, metaphor is typically viewed as characteristic of language alone, a matter of words rather than thought or action. For this reason, most people think they can get along perfectly well without metaphor. We have found, on the contrary, that metaphor is pervasive in everyday life, not just in language but in thought and action. Our ordinary conceptual system, in terms of which we both think and act, is fundamentally metaphorical in nature.

The concepts that govern our thought are not just matters of the intellect. They also govern our everyday functioning, down to the most mundane details. Our concepts structure what we perceive, how we get around in the world, and how we relate to other people. Our conceptual system thus plays a central role in defining our everyday realities. If we are right in suggesting that our conceptual system is largely metaphorical, then the way we think, what we experience, and what we do every day is very much a matter of metaphor.

But our conceptual system is not something we are normally aware of. In most of the little things we do every day, we simply think and act more or less

George Lakoff and Mark Johnson. "Concepts We Live By." In *Metaphors We Live By*. Chicago: University of Chicago Press, 1980. Reprinted with permission from the University of Chicago Press.

automatically along certain lines. Just what these lines are is by no means obvious. One way to find out is by looking at language. Since communication is based on the same conceptual system that we use in thinking and acting, language is an important source of evidence for what that system is like.

Primarily on the basis of linguistic evidence, we have found that most of our ordinary conceptual system is metaphorical in nature. And we have found a way to begin to identify in detail just what the metaphors are that structure how we perceive, how we think, and what we do.

To give some idea of what it could mean for a concept to be metaphorical and for such a concept to structure an everyday activity, let us start with the concept ARGUMENT and the conceptual metaphor ARGUMENT IS WAR. this metaphor is reflected in our everyday language by a wide variety of expressions.

ARGUMENT IS WAR

Your claims are *indefensible*.

He *attacked every weak point* in my argument.

His criticisms were *right on target*.

I *demolished* his argument.

I've never *won* an argument with him.

You disagree? Okay, *shoot*!

If you use that *strategy*, he'll *wipe you out*.

He *shot down* all of my arguments.

It is important to see that we don't just *talk* about arguments in terms of war. We can actually win or lose arguments. We see the person we are arguing with as an opponent. We attack his positions and we defend our own. We gain and lose ground. We plan and use strategies. If we find a position indefensible, we can abandon it and take a new line of attack. Many of the things we *do* in arguing are partially structured by the concept of war. Though there is no physical battle, there is a verbal battle, and the structure of an argument—attack, defense, counterattack, etc.—reflects this. It is in this sense that the ARGUMENT IS WAR metaphor is one that we live by in this culture; it structures the actions we perform in arguing.

Try to imagine a culture where arguments are not viewed in terms of war, where no one wins or loses, where there is no sense of attacking or defending, gaining or losing ground. Imagine a culture where an argument is viewed as a dance, the participants are seen as performers, and the goal is to perform in a balanced and aesthetically pleasing way. In such a culture, people would view arguments differently, experience them differently, carry them out differently. But *we* would probably not view them as arguing at all: they would simply be doing something different. It would seem strange even to call what they are doing "arguing." Perhaps the most neutral way of describing this difference between their culture and ours would be to say that we have a discourse form structured in terms of battle and they have one structured in terms of dance.

This is an example of what it means for a metaphorical concept, namely, ARGUMENT IS WAR, to structure (at least in part) what we do and how we understand what we are doing when we argue. *The essence of metaphor is understanding and experiencing one kind of thing in terms of another.* It is not that arguments are a subspecies of war. Arguments and wars are different kinds of things—verbal discourse and armed conflict—and the actions performed are different kinds of actions. But ARGUMENT is partially structured, understood, performed, and talked about in terms of WAR. The concept is metaphorically structured, the activity is metaphorically structured, and, consequently, the language is metaphorically structured.

Moreover, this is the *ordinary* way of having an argument and talking about one. The normal way for us to talk about attacking a position is to use the words "attack a position." Our conventional ways of talking about arguments presuppose a metaphor we are hardly ever conscious of. The metaphor is not merely in the words we use—it is in our very concept of an argument. The language of argument is not poetic, fanciful, or rhetorical; it is literal. We talk about arguments that way because we conceive of them that way—and we act according to the way we conceive of things.

The most important claim we have made so far is that metaphor is not just a matter of language, that is, of mere words. We shall argue that, on the contrary, human *thought processes* are largely metaphorical. This is what we mean when we say that the human conceptual system is metaphorically structured and defined. Metaphors as linguistic expressions are possible precisely because there are metaphors in a person's conceptual system. Therefore, whenever in this book we speak of metaphors, such as ARGUMMENNT IS WAR, it should be understood that *metaphor* means *metaphorical concept*.

6

A.J. Greimas: An Introduction to His Writings

Paul J. Perron

1. Introduction

The intention of this introduction is not to retrace the development of semiotics in Europe, or to situate in every detail all of Algirdas Julien Greimas's works within the intellectual tradition of his times. J.-C. Coquet, in his lengthy and informative introductory chapter in *Sémiotique—l'École de Paris* (1982) and his "Éléments de bio-bibliographie" (1985), provides us with a detailed overview of the fundamental role played by Greimas in the history of semiotics as well as a complete bibliography of his numerous works. In addition, Herman Parret and Hans George Ruprecht in their perceptive introduction to *Recueil d'hommages pour/Essays in honor of Algirdas Julien Greimas* (1985) not only discuss some of the salient features of the theory but also sketch the intellectual horizon in which it was elaborated. The essays in this volume of translations have been selected from three major works: *Du sens* (1970), *Sémiotique et sciences sociales* (1976), and *Du sens II* (1983a), both to provide the English reader with the founding texts of Greimassian semiotics and to highlight the

Paul J. Perron. "A.J. Greimas: An Introduction to His Writings." In Paul J. Perron (ed.) *Theory and Literature*, vol. 38. University of Minnesota Press.

heuristic value of narrativity theory as applied to literary, historical, ethnological, sociological, psychological, and scientific discourses.

2. BEGINNINGS

The essays appearing in *Du sens* (1970), which opens with the cursory remark "It is extremely difficult to speak about meaning and to say something meaningful about it" (p. 7), explore and set into place the first two phases of Greimassian semiotics. In 1956, Greimas published a programmatic article in *Le Français Moderne* entitled "L'actualité du saussurisme," in which he examined works by Maurice Merleau-Ponty and Claude Lévi-Strauss and concluded that the "Saussurian postulate of a structured world apprehensible in its significations" (p. 193) can in fact contribute to the elaboration of a unified methodology for the human sciences. At this time Greimas became aware that although structuralism in its many forms focused mainly on problems of language from a linguistic perspective (e.g., Lévi-Strauss and Georges Dumézil in anthropology, Roland Barthes in literature, and Jacques Lacan in psychoanalysis to name but a few of the dominant figures who revolutionized their respective disciplines), no structural linguists per se were striving to do the same in their own field. In France the latest word in linguistics was Leonard Bloomfield's distributionalism. Nonetheless it was apparent to Greimas that by extrapolating concepts borrowed from Ferdinand de Saussure and Louis Hjelmslev and forging new methods of investigation, great strides were being made in various domains of the human sciences.

"Comparative Mythology," chapter 1 in this volume, was written in 1962 and owes a great deal to Lévi-Strauss and Roman Jakobson in its methodological and theoretical underpinnings. Greimas's point of departure is that the investigation of meaning is by definition a metalinguistic activity that paraphrases and translates words and utterances by other words and utterances. It therefore follows that the first step in describing signification resides in the transposition of one level of language into another level, of one language into another language. Since meaning can be described as this very possibility of transcoding, the next step is to develop a new terminology and construct an adequate metalanguage that can account for the object in question. Thus, to uncover the "mythological signified," Greimas endeavors to work out a rigorous methodology based on objective criteria of analysis partially adopted from structural linguistics, which, as we noted, had at the time more or less abandoned research into signification. Dumézil's work on myth, considered in chapter 1 as the translation of "mythological language into ideological language," is "overanalyzed" much in the same way Lévi-Strauss overanalyzed the Oedipus myth. In short, a new formulation of Dumézil's analysis is proposed by which the study of myth and the structural methodology borrowed from the social sciences are used to examine the superstructures of social ideologies. This is indeed a major development from a semiotic point of view, since in Hjelmslev's terms a "connotative semiotics" is transformed into a "denotative semiotics" that is a precondition for an adequate description of a text.

By reducing the problem of meaning to its minimal dimensions, that is to say, to the transcoding of significations, scientific activity in this domain consists in establishing techniques of transposition. The main feature in the analysis of Dumézil's work can be found in the conversion of the syntagmatic manifestation of myth into paradigmatic relations, or, in other words, in the setting up of correlations between a limited number of units of the mythic signified distributed throughout the narrative. As a first important methodological step a level of pertinence is defined and a discourse, based on the principle of interdefinition, is constructed on the mythological object. However, it should be noted that this new formulation of Dumézil's text does not correspond *stricto sensu to* formalization as defined for example by logicians in formal theory, since, from the outset, semiotics is not considered a formal language per se but rather an intermediary stage toward explanation, toward giving a scientific account of meaning.

Yet, in spite of the real gains made in adopting the preceding methodological perspective, the conclusions of this study clearly point to the insufficiencies of Lévi-Strauss's paradigmatic definition of myth as a correlation of two pairs of units of the signified that are in significant opposition to each other and that exclude any syntagmatic relation. Indeed, Greimas does use methodological procedures borrowed from structural anthropology and even refines major constituent units by breaking them down into distinctive features called semes, or semic categories and archilexemes (sets of semic categories constituting pairs of lexemic oppositions making up the elementary structures of myth). Yet he also makes a case for the need to investigate syntagmatic structures that could be rounded in discourse analysis.

"Toward a Semiotics of the Natural World," chapter 2 of this volume, was written after *Sémantique structurale* (1966), which sketched out the initial model of the elementary structure of signification and for the first time presented a syntactic and semantic (actantial) theory of discourse (for a detailed account of this seminal work, see Fredric Jameson, *The Prison House of Language*, 1972, and Ronald Schleifer's introduction to Greimas, *Structural Semantics*, 1983b). Chapter 2 raises further questions of a metasemiotic and theoretical nature by exploring the possibilities of the description or the apprehension of signification in systems not dependent on natural languages. Paraphrasing Hjelmslev, Greimas (1970) defines semiotics as "a hierarchy that *can* be subjected to analysis and the elements of which can be determined by reciprocal relations (and by commutation)" (p. 22). In other words, a semiotics exists only as a possibility of description and the system of relations described does not depend on the nature of the signs by which the external or internal world is manifested. Description is thus thought of as the construction of a network of relations by the identification and naming of both the observed relations and their points of intersection or disjunction.

This investigation of the gestural domain of the natural world through the description of pertinent features at the level of content, which are at the same time distinctive and significative, brings to the fore the anthropological dimension of Greimas's semiotics. "Comparative Mythology," as we have noted, focuses on the paradigmatic organization of text, whereas chapter 2 investigates the syntagmatic dimension of gesture, considered both as a "discoursive structure" because it appears within the context of the subject/object relation and as an "utterance" constructed by the human subject and deciphered by another subject. The semiotic status of gestural signs, which are defined in terms of the semiotic relation between expression and content, is studied in conjunction with the fundamental problem of identifying what actually constitutes gestural units. Human beings, as bodies, are first of all viewed as figures of the world and then as complex mechanisms that, through mobility, produce differential (positional) gaps at the level of the signifier by which signification can take place. Gestural activity is explored within the framework of the project defining it. Consequently a programmed gestural project can be said to constitute the signified of gestural activity, whereas the gestural sequence can be equated with its signifier. This enables Greimas to define the semiosis of a gestural program as the relation between a sequence of gestural figures taken as the signified and the gestural project considered as the signifier. Yet when all is said and done, the analysis of gestuality raises problems as to the functional nature of gestural semiotics. In chapter 2, Greimas identifies the need to work out a level of analysis dealing specifically with the organization of content and which would be part of a general functional semiotics also encompassing the semantic dimension of natural languages and hints at the possible form it could take.

3. NARRATIVE GRAMMAR

Chapters 3 and 4, the last two programmatic essays we translated from *Du sens*, lay the groundwork for what will become the cornerstone of Greimas's semiotics. These two works openly acknowledge a debt both to Vladimir Propp, who provided the syntactic component for the deep semio-narrative grammar, and to Lévi-Strauss, who furnished the idea for the semantic component. After Propp's thirty-one functions (designating syntagmatic units that remain constant despite the diversity of narratives, and whose ordered sequence makes up the structure of folktale) were redefined in terms of a limited number of actants, it then became possible to conceive of a principle of organization underlying whole classes of narratives. And thus deep structures were posited as being the principle of organization, not only of figurative discourses, but also of abstract discourses (philosophical, political, scientific, etc.) as well as of other semiotic systems not necessarily expressed through natural languages (cinema, figurative painting, architecture, advertising, etc.). Moreover, following Jean Petitot-Cocorda (1985) we would like to suggest that these structures are lived existentially in human passions, ideology, actions, and dreams and that semio-narrative structures, to borrow a phase from Gilbert Durand, can be thought of as "the anthropological structures of the imaginary." This being so, for Greimas it became of the utmost importance to work out a means, or a grammar, that could account for such structures. Indeed, the semio-narrative grammar he elaborated establishes a specific relation between syntax and semantics, which Petitot-Cocorda describes as "the projection (or conversion) of the paradigmatic axis onto the syntagmatic axis, the understanding of which constitutes one of the central problems of structuralism, perhaps even its most central problem" (1985, pp. 48-49).

The semantic universe defined as the set of the systems of values can be apprehended as meaningful only if it is articulated or narrativized. Thus, any discourse presupposes a semantic universe hypothetically made up of the totality of significations, postulated as such prior to its articulation, and which it actualizes in part. This microsemantic universe, at the fundamental level, articulates elementary axiological structures such as life/death (individual universe) and nature/culture (collective universe). These basic structures situated at the deep semantic level are considered as ad hoc universals that serve as starting points for the analysis of semantic universes, be they individual or collective. Their meaning is never apprehensible as such, but rather only when they are manifested in the form of an articulated signification, or in other words, when they are converted into actantial structures. Petitot-Cocorda (1985) clearly perceives the theoretical import of Greimas's semiotics when he situates the semio-narrative structures within an anthropological framework: "The deep semantic categories are universals of the imaginary. We are not unconscious of them, and they exist only because they are axiologized and ideologically invested in object-values, the quest for which governs the actions (narrative programs in Greimassian terminology) of the subject actants. It is only through the circulation of object-values governed by actantial syntax that they can be apprehended. In other words, they cannot be subjectivized as such but instead only by means of a logic of actions. The role of actantial syntax is therefore to *convert into a narrative doing* the fundamental semantics that constitute the message of narrative and determine its anthropological function. This syntax enables one to grasp, through the simulacrum of a 'scene' that dramatizes them, the unconscious crystallising processes of subjectivity" (1985, pp. 50-51).

Chapter 3, "The Interaction of Semiotic Constraints," suggests the possibility of a generative trajectory, beginning with a fundamental semiotic level that is then converted into an actantial syntax before ultimately being manifested through discoursivization, but focuses especially on the first domain of the global trajectory. The main object of the theory of the semiotic square is to articulate the substance of the content (in Hjelmselv's terms) and therein constitute the form of content. This elementary structure should be considered "on the one hand, as a concept uniting the minimal condition for the apprehension and/or the production of signification, and, on the other hand, as a model containing the minimal definition of any language (or, more generally, of any semiotic system or process) and of any semiotic unit" (Greimas and Courtés, 1982, p. 314). Prior to any semantic investment whatsoever, the elementary structure appears as a complex binary semic category that correlates two contrary semes by means of a relation of junction (conjunction/disjunction) and by a relation of reciprocal presupposition. Yet, as Petitot-Cocorda (1985) remarks, "As a simple logical form formalized in terms of Boolean elementary set logic, the semiotic square is trivial, and of little interest, since it only reformulates logical squares going back to Aristotle. But if we see it as a structure in the strong sense of the term, then everything changes, since it becomes an 'organic' and 'self-regulating' system of interdependent and founding relations that do not define terms, but rather in much the same way as in a phonological paradigm, *positional values*, places that are defined in a purely relational fashion." The constituent relations of contrariety and contradiction of the semiotic square, it is argued, are not logical in nature, but in the Jakobsonian sense are 'qualitative oppositions and privative oppositions and must be treated as such.' The formal characteristics of the semiotic square are founded on a dynamic topology of places and connections and not upon a static logic of terms and connections (pp. 51-52).

Chapter 4, "Elements of a Narrative Grammar," sets in place the various components and the interrelationships of the first two levels of the theory of narrativity, represented graphically in their entirety under the heading of Generative Trajectory in Greimas and Courtés (1982); see the accompanying schema.

The main theoretical problem that arises in this model of narrativity concerns the passage (conversion) on the one hand from a taxonomic morphology, or paradigmatic relation, to an operative syntax or syntagmatic one, and on the other, the passage (conversion) from a fundamental abstract syntax to a narrative anthropomorphic surface-syntax, and ultimately to a discoursive-figurative syntax. We should note, however, that there exist in the theory two types of conversions; "vertical" conversions (having to do with the relations between levels) and "horizontal" conversions (dealing with the relations between the syntactic and semantic components of each level) (See Petitot-Cocorda, 1982, p. 5). At the deep level, horizontal conversion, or the passage from the elementary morphology constituted by fundamental relations to an operative syntax, is ensured by the introduction of an actant subject: "Signification, to the extent that one seeks to find in it an object, appears as an articulation of stable fundamental relations; it can also be represented dynamically, if one considers it as an apprehension or production of meaning by a subject." In short, equivalences are established between the fundamental constituent relations of the taxonomic model and the projections of the same relations or operations by means of a horizontal anthropomorphic conversion at the deep level. And thus the relation of contradiction at the taxonomic level as a contradictory operation at the syntactic level will negate one of the terms and at the same time affirm its contradictory term.

Generative Trajectory			
		Syntactic Component	Semantic Component
Semiotic and narrative structures	Deep level	FUNDAMENTAL SYNTAX	FUNDAMENTAL SEMANTICS
	Surface levels	SURFACE NARRATIVE SYNTAX	NARRATIVE SEMANTICS
Discoursive structures		DISCOURSIVE SYNTAX Discoursivization Actorialization Temporalization Spatialization	DISCOURSIVE SEMANTICS Thematization Figurativization

In this transpositional model the problem of vertical conversion, or the passage from the fundamental syntax to the surface anthropomorphic narrative syntax, is resolved by the setting up of procedures that establish equivalences between these two levels. It should be noted that the equivalence posited here does not correspond to identity but rather is founded on the presupposition that "two or more syntactic forms (or two or more semantic formulations) can be referred to a constant topic" (Greimas and Courtés, 1982, p. 62). In addition, insofar as a meaning is transformed into signification when articulated, each new articulation is an enrichment or increase in meaning, so that in proceeding from the deep level to the surface levels the surface must be considered as richer than the deep level: "Consequently any conversion must be viewed as equivalence and as a surplus of signification" (ibid.). As Greimas reiterates in an interview with Ruprecht (1984), conversion is homotopic and heteromorphic; that is to say, "the forms pass from the deep structures (where operations take place on the semiotic square) to the semionarrative level (where there exists a surface narrative grammar); both of these levels are concerned with the same thing but in a different way" (p. 14).

The conversion of the deep level into the surface level is ensured by the establishment of equivalences between syntactic operations at the fundamental level and syntactic doing at the surface level. Thus syntactic doing, having been converted from syntactic operation that was itself converted from taxic relation, provides the necessary mediation for the generation of a narrative utterance that is the major component of narrative grammar. The utterance $NU = F(A)$ is seen as a process that is composed of a function, in the Proppian sense, and an actant. Conversion thus rests on the equivalence between the syntactic operation and syntactic doing on the one hand, and between syntactic doing and an elementary utterance of the actantial doing, on the other.

The anthropomorphic actantial dimension establishes relations between subjects and objects, subjects and anti-subjects, subjects and senders and receivers. The first relation, founded on the institution of the subject as a wanting subject and the object as an object of value, can be described in terms of modal utterances. *Wanting* is the first of a series of determined semantic restrictions that specify actants as virtual operators of a doing. Other semantic restrictions, the introduction of the modalities of *being-able-to* and *knowing*, constitute the being or the doing of the actant subject. The relation of subject and object is, furthermore, syntactically describable in terms of utterances of state that are junctive in nature. The second relation between subject and anti-subjects is considered as the conversion of the paradigmatic relation of contradiction at the deep level, into an anthropomorphic syntagmatic series at the surface level. In addition, the transformation of contents, which at the surface level appear as a series of confrontations and struggles constituting the narrative units, results from operations of contrariety (negation) and

147

presupposition (assertion). Negation is reformulated as domination and assertion as attribution, whereas performance is formulated as a syntagmatic, ordered, series of confrontation, domination, and attribution.

The third relation between subject and sender, subject and receiver, is reformulated in terms of a general structure of exchange. The attribution of an object of value is here seen as a disjunctive operation (privation) and a conjunctive one (attribution). This reformulation makes it possible to represent the previous operations as places of transfers of objects of value from one location to another and thereby to establish a topological syntax of objective values, which, since it follows the logical operations at the level of deep grammar, organizes narration as a process creating values. However, by changing focus and examining the relation between operators, subject and sender or receiver, we can see that topological syntax governs the transfer both of the subject's capacity to do, and of the values. Also, by manipulating subjects and endowing them with the virtuality of doing, the topological syntax governs the institution of syntactic operators. In a later, more complete version of the theory, the subject and sender will be characterised by a dual contractual relation, since not only will the subject actant have a contractual relation with the manipulating operator actant (sender) that institutes it as an operator subject, but also performance will be sanctioned by a final sender, whose absolute competence is presupposed.

Greimas has always claimed, and rightly so, that semiotics was not a science but rather a scientific project, still incomplete, and that what he had attempted to do was to establish theoretical principles that needed to be completed and transformed. However, we should not minimize the import of the theoretical problems related to the issue of conversion and that are due to the generative conceptualisation of the model according to which various components are linked together along a trajectory that proceeds from the simplest to the most complex, from the most abstract to the most concrete. The problem of conversion and equivalences is raised on numerous occasions by Greimas himself, beginning with "Elements of a Narrative Grammar." In an interview with Frédéric Nef (1976) the author admits, "A theoretical construct, no matter how satisfying it appears at first view, runs the risk of remaining hypothetical as long as the problem of *equivalences* between different levels of depth is not clearly posed, as long as the procedures of *conversion* from one level to another have not been elaborated" (p. 24). Again, in a special issue of *Le Bulletin* (1981) devoted to the semiotic square, Greimas once more states that one of the urgent tasks facing semioticians is to undertake research on conversion, to conceive of and construct procedures for passing from the deep level of semantic categorizations to the more surface ones of anthropomorphic narrative syntax and of its investments (pp. 45-46). The same awareness of the possible weak point in the theory is demonstrated in Greimas and Courtés (1982): "As can be expected, the elaboration of conversion rules will be one of the fundamental tests of the coherence of semiotic theory" (p. 62).

It is especially on this very issue of conversion and equivalences within the framework of the narrative grammar we have just sketched, that Paul Ricoeur (1983) puts forth reservations about the actual coherence of the theory. Ricoeur basically takes issue with the model on three counts. The first concerns the conversion of contradiction at the deep level, into polemic at the surface level; that is to say, polemical negativity cannot be derived either from the taxonomic relations of contradiction-contrariety, or from the syntactic operation of negation. The second is related to the fact that there exist syntagmatic supplements at the surface level that cannot be obtained from the conversion of the fundamental grammar to the surface grammar. The third is that the praxic-pathic dimension of narrative sets into play a semantics of action that activates a syntax whose very intelligibility is mixed, since it is both phenomenological and linguistic (see Petitot-Cocorda, 1985, p. 268). In his truly original and brilliant work on the morphogenesis of meaning, Petitot-Cocorda (in a highly innovative and insightful discussion of the legitimacy of schematising the structural categoriality of the semio-narrative structures elaborated by Greimas in terms of catastrophe theory) argues that for Ricoeur's critique to be truly pertinent, the implicit phenomenology of the praxic-pathic semantics of action would have to be formalized so that it could be integrated into a formal model. He also argues that polemical negativity can be schematized in terms of catastrophe theory, and thus a reformulation of fundamental grammar, starting from the schema of conflict, should be able to overcome the difficulty encountered because of its logical conception. He then concludes that the hypothesis of a syntagmatic supplement that is irreducible to the paradigmatic is tenable only if one forces Greimas's thought and views conversion as a simple equivalence between metalanguages, and this is far from being the case (p. 268). In the final analysis, the real problem in the theory that must be addressed is the one

Greimas himself has raised all along, namely, the need to establish the actual procedures of conversion.

Instead of being a simple *aide-mémoire*, the generative trajectory presented earlier provides us with a useful schematization within which we can situate the essays published in *Du sens II*, and which further refines the global semiotic model. Within this specific generative approach, each work reexamines and develops the relations between the various levels, components, and subcomponents of the trajectory.

In surface narrative grammar, the object is one of the terms of the elementary utterance that, when inscribed in a junctive relation with the subject, guarantees the latter's semiotic existence. However, the object, while "remaining unknowable in itself," exists semiotically as "a locus of fixation, a locus of circumstantial clustering of the value determinations." Values invested in the object can only be accounted for syntactically, and it is in this "syntagmatic unfolding that syntax joins semantics." Furthermore, it is only when they are converted from semantic into syntactic structures that values can be apprehended as signification. Subsequently, conversion makes it possible both to define narrativization as the syntagmatic emplacement of values and to perceive it as a discursive organization that manipulates the constitutive elements of the elementary utterance. Moreover, two broad categories of values—descriptive (consumable or storable objects, states and feelings) and modal (wanting, being-able-to, knowing-how-to-be/to-do)—can be distinguished. In turn, descriptive values can be divided further into subjective (essential values) and objective (accidental values), and, in narrative programs, base values can be distinguished from instrumental ones (see Greimas and Courtés, 1982, p. 365).

Since narrative at the surface level was defined as the transformation of a series of utterances of state (junctive utterances) by a metasubject operator (utterance of doing), this syntactic organization makes it possible to represent narrative as a series of virtualizations and actualizations of values. Values inscribed within a given axiological universe circulate in two ways. In the case of constant values between subjects in an isotopic and closed universe, they circulate in the mode of conflictual-polemic confrontation, whereas in the case of exchange, the presence of two objects of value is required, and this structure constitutes a new virtualization and a new actualization of the subject. Simple exchange can then be considered as a complex mode of value transfer at the level of surface syntax. Nonetheless, for such an operation to take place in the case where exchange values are not identical requires their preliminary identification by subjects, who, by fixing the exchange value of the said objects of value, establish a fiduciary contract between themselves. When the objects of value are objects of knowing, or messages being communicated, and when the subjects in question are competent but unequally modalized, then the polemic-contractual, which is one of the fundamental organizing structures of narrative grammar, is transposed into the very core of intersubjectivity, where, as Greimas (1983a) notes, "It seems to be able to account for the fiduciary, troubling and groping, but, at the same time, cunning and dominating, nature of communication" (p. 11).

In participatory communication the contractual dimension of exchange within a closed universe is ensured by a sender that guarantees the circulation of values, the latter corresponding to a mediating domain between an immanent universe and a transcendent universe that are manifested through the presence of actants at the surface level syntax. The sender, who is the source of the contract in discourse, is the disengaged representative of the paradigmatic system of the invested contents, or the values that are the taxonomic constituents of the fundamental grammar (Courtés, 1976, p. 99). From this it follows that the internalization of the conversion of the paradigmatic dimension in the narrative is constituted by the relation between the contractual sequence and the performance sequence. If the contractual sequence is accepted by the subject-receiver as a narrative program, it is transformed into a performing subject: "(on the condition that it acquire a modal competence) that ensures the mediation between system (paradigmatic) and process (syntagmatic), and realizes virtual values" (Petitot-Cocorda, 1985, p. 240).

Insofar as it guarantees the semiotic existence of actants, the "narrative organization of values continues to be the foundation of narrativity." The object of value, which is one of the terms of the elementary utterance previously defined as a semiotic simulacrum, representing our relation to the world in the form of a scene, is also a syntactic concept. The distinction between actants (considered initially as simple supports and then progressively invested by values through junctive relations) and actors (which can syncretize several actants) enables us to explore the relations between elementary narrative structures and discursive structures (see chapter 6).

As an actant progresses through its narrative trajectory it can assume a certain number of narrative states or actantial roles that are defined by its position within the narrative trajectory (syntactic definition) and its modal investment (morphological definition). As a necessary step toward performance, the subject actant will be endowed successively with the modalities of competence, and in this case the "subject assumes those actantial roles which manifest the subject in terms of wanting, the subject in terms of knowing, and the subject in terms of being able to do, and which then indicate the three states in the acquisition of its modal competence" (Greimas and Courtés, 1982, p. 6). Actantial roles, because they are defined morphologically by their modal content, and syntactically by the position of the actant in the narrative trajectory, are situated within narrative syntax. However, when associated with "thematic roles (which structure the semantic component of the discourse), they allow for the construction of actors as loci where narrative and discoursive structures converge and are invested" (ibid.).

What first of all distinguishes an actantial role from an actor is that at the level of discourse "an actor's semantic content is defined by the presence of the semes that are (1) *figurative entity* (anthropomorphic, zoomorphic order), (2) *animated*, and (3) *subject to individuation*." At the same level the actantial role is "manifested, as a qualification, as an attribute of the actor. From a semantic point of view, this qualification is no more than the denomination subsuming a field of functions (that is to say behaviors actually noted in the narrative, or simply implied). Consequently, the minimal semantic content of *role* is identical to the concept of actor, despite the *exception of a seme of individuation*, which the former does not possess. The role is an animated figurative entity, albeit anonymous and social. In turn, the actor is an *individual* integrating and assuming one or several roles" (Greimas, 1970, pp. 255-56). From this it follows that there are three distinct levels of narrative interplay: roles, which are elementary actantial units corresponding to coherent functional domains, are related to actants (elements of the narrative) and to actors (units of discourse) (ibid., p. 256).

The actor is thus seen as the point of investment of both syntactic and semantic components. To be designated as an actor, a lexeme must have both an actantial and a thematic role. And thematic roles in turn, "in order to realize their virtualities, call into play the lexematic level of language and are manifested in the form of figures that are extended into discoursive configurations." Thus the figurative level of discourse, which is the final domain of the narrative trajectory, is characterised by the investment of themes and values in figures. Figures, defined as "figures of content which correspond to the figures of the expression plane of the natural semiotic system" (Greimas and Courtés, 1982, p. 120), when strung over sequences, constitute their discursive configurations. The procedures of figurativization, the first of which can be described as figuration and the second as iconization, invest these figures with specificities that produce a referential illusion. And one of the basic components of figurativization is the onomastic one. Figurativization specifies and particularizes abstract discourse "insofar as it is grasped in its deep structures and by the introduction of anthroponyms (corresponding respectively, on the plane of discursive syntax, to the three procedures constitutive of discoursivization: actorialization, spatialization, and temporalization) that can be inventoried as going from the generic ("king," "forest," "winter") to the specific (proper nouns, spatio-temporal indices, dates, etc.)" (Greimas and Courtés, 1982, p. 119).

4. Toward a Grammar of Modality

The semiotic square and the actantial model worked out in *Du sens* have often attracted the attention of critics who have been quick to seize the import of their heuristic value without necessarily being aware of the general structure of this hypothetico-deductive theory of narrativity. In Greimas's own words, the third phase of his semiotic project, while continuing to evolve a theory of narrativity, focused on constructing a semio-narrative grammar developed as a modal and aspectual grammar. Sensing the need to construct a better-articulated elementary syntax, he abandoned the Proppian formulation of narrative in order to free the theory from concepts that remained too close to the manifest level of discourse.

The first step consisted in reformulating surface narrative syntax in terms of modalities (chapter 7). Starting with the definition of modality as "that which modalizes a predicate of an utterance," modalization is then considered as the production of a "modal utterance which over-determines a descriptive utterance" (Greimas and Courtés, 1982, p. 193). Defined in terms of the structure of the elementary utterance whose end terms are actants, utterances of doing or utterances of state can be considered as the transformation of a junctive state. However, a reformulation of the act as "that which causes to be" permits its redefinition as a hypotactic structure combining competence and performance, with performance presupposing competence, but not vice versa.

Transitive relations defining the descriptive predicate between the subject and the utterance of doing are distinguished both from veridictory relations established by a subject and an utterance produced by another subject, and from factitive relations between the subject and object that are already an utterance of doing. These last two relations, which appear between two hierarchical, distinct subjects—a cognitive subject and a pragmatic subject—constitute the simple modal structure. The advantage of reformulating the act in these terms is that a theory of performance can be developed in the direction of a semiotics of manipulation (or the manipulation of the subject by the sender), a semiotics of action (the acquisition of competence by the subject), and a semiotics of sanction (judgments on self and on other subjects).

When considered at the level of the organization of pragmatic competence, four fundamental modalities were identified: the modalities of having and wanting, which virtualize the process, and the modalities of being able and knowing, which actualize it. Yet the fact that this canonical representation of competence does not always correspond to what happens at the level of manifestation pointed to the need to construct a model that could account for the fundamental modal structure by subsuming its diverse articulations through a series of interdefinitions: "The criteria of interdefinition and classification of modalities should be simultaneously syntagmatic and paradigmatic; each modality would be defined on the one hand as a hypotactic modal structure and, on the other hand, as a category which could be represented on the semiotic square" (Greimas and Courtés, 1982, p. 195).

After having analyzed the modality of doing, Greimas turns in chapter 8 to the modality of being. As Coquet (1985) notes, this analysis completes the study of the actions of the subject (modal competence) with the study of their passions (modal existence) within the context of a modal grammar reformulated along the lines of surface narrative syntax (p. lxxviii). Thymic space, which at the deep level represents the elementary manifestations of a living being in relation to its environment (animated), at the surface level is converted into modal space appearing as an overarticulation of the thymic (human) category. Yet, in any utterance, the subject's semiotic existence is determined by its relation to the *object of value* and the modalising of being considered as the "modifications of the status of the *object of value*. The modalities affecting the object (or rather the value invested therein) [are] said to be constituents of the subject of state's *modal existence*." A taxonomic network for modal syntax is elaborated by projecting the modal utterances onto the semiotic square (wanting-to-be [desirable for the subject of state] having-to-be [indispensable], being-able-to-be [possible], knowing-how-to-be [genuine]). The same interrelations discovered when analyzing the modalization of doing are encountered here and a syntax of modalized values is suggested, based on elementary narrative syntax.

It has been shown that thymic values are converted from the deep level when invested with syntactic objects defined by junctive relations with subjects. As Parret and Ruprecht perceptively remark, this conversion profoundly affects value by placing it under subjectivity and its intentionality. As a theoretical consequence of this the possibility for the pragmatization of Greimas's semiotics by the introduction of *tensivity* and *graduality* in the deep structures themselves is opened up, "thus freeing us from the notion that at the deep level values are economical (in the Saussurian sense) and at the surface level they are graduated and tensive" (p. xlvii). In this way the introduction of modality theory and the working out of conversion procedures constitute decisive steps toward an integrated theory of narrativity.

We have suggested that the problematics of passions are linked to the study of the modal existence of the subject, and more precisely to the modal component of the actantial structures. Whether the object of investigation happens to be a lexeme-passion such as anger—considered as a virtual narrative trajectory—or, on the contrary, passional stories that are realized narrative syntagms, as Landowski (1979) remarks, the exploration of the "passional field" closely involves "all of the levels of the articulations of the theory of narrativity: not only the semio-narrative structures proper (instances of passions being identifiable by their underlying modal and actantial structures), not only the discursive structures (aspectualization, actorialization, semantization of the underlying syntagms), but also the deep level abstract structures" (p. 8).

In contradistinction to action, which can be defined as a syntagmatic organization of acts (Greimas and Courtés, 1982, p. 6), passions (chapter 9) can be considered as the syntagmatic organization of states of mind, or the discoursive aspect of the modalized being of narrative subjects (Greimas and Courtés, 1986, p. 162). Passions, which are either simple or complex (a syntagmatic intertwining of states and of doing), are expressed through actors and, along with actions, determine the roles (actantial and thematic) they realize. Thus the opposition between action and passion represents the "conversion on the discoursive level of the deeper and more abstract opposition between *being* and *doing*, or more specifically between modalized being and modalized doing" (ibid.).

The being of the subject, whether, for example, in simple or in fiduciary expectation, is first of all modalized by the modality of wanting, which actualizes (wanting-to-be-conjoined) in order then to be realized (i.e., to be conjoined with the object of value). It is this very conjunction that guarantees the subject's semiotic existence. Whether at the semiotic or at the discoursive level the notion of value, which we also saw with regard to the doing of the subject, is at the very heart of the theory. Thus, parallel to the trajectory of the subject of doing made up of the acquisition of competence and the accomplishment of performances, there exists a comparable trajectory of the subject of state, presented as successions of "feeling states" made up of highs and lows. Consequently the modalization of the being of the subject has an essential role in the constitution of the competence of syntactic subjects, and the concept of passion is closely linked to the concept of actor. Passion thus becomes "one of the elements that contribute to actorial individuation, able to offer denominations for recognizable thematic roles ('the miser,' 'the quick-tempered,' 'the unconcerned,' etc.)" (Greimas and Courtés, 1986, pp. 162-63). Moreover, the linking of passions to actors and the investigation of relations between thematic roles and actantial roles have opened up a new domain of research into passional typologies.

Another area of investigation mapped out within the confines of a theory of modalities is related to procedures leading to the epistemic act (chapter 10). When situated at the level of surface narrative (manipulation, action, sanction) both persuasive and interpretative doing are defined as cognitive procedures "that, in the first case, end up as causing-to-believe and, in the second, as an act of believing, that is, as an epistemic act." The epistemic act is then defined as a transformation that, when articulated on the semiotic square (to affirm, to refuse, to admit, to doubt), at the level of surface syntax is manifested as a series of hierarchically linked narrative programs. Epistemic modalizations can also be represented as modalities and junctive operations, and before becoming act, or operation (which is of the order of doing), a modal competence or the being of the doing is presupposed on the part of the subject. A further step is taken after noting that since transactions engage the subjects in a fiduciary contract, communication can be defined in terms of contract propositions, which in fact is a presupposition to communication. Situated within a semiotics of manipulation and sanction, cognitive space becomes the locus for a manipulation according to knowing, in which a subject transforms another into a convinced subject, and submits it to judging epistemic activity on the part of a final subject.

However, since the initial definition of epistemic act converted the elements of the square onto the surface syntax, not as contradictions, but as linear gradations, Coquet (1985) notes that "this type of semiotic square represents an important development of 'syntagmatic rationality'" (p. lxxxii). Technical thinking, of an algorithmic nature "founded on objective modal necessity (= on a /not-being-able-to-not-be/)," is opposed to practical thinking, "of a stereotypical nature [which] depends on the co-occurrence, in temporal contiguity, of acts—or the utterances that describe them—whose successivity can be considered predictable and therefore plausible or even necessary ('subjectively,' according to the mode of /having-to-be/)." At the surface level of discourse causal reason, or syntagmatic rationality, is further defined in terms of technical thinking and practical thinking. Yet, parallel thinking leads us to discover a bi-isotopic nature of discourse based on the seeming of the implicit characterizing figurative discourses that, when dereferentialized, create a new referent or thematic level. Parallel discourse, by projecting a double reference ("one that *moves deeper* and creates a more abstract thematic isotopy, and one that moves *laterally* and develops a new parallel figurative isotopy"), constitutes an original type of syntagmatic articulation. Figurative models such as parables, allusive in nature, are given as an example of figurative reasoning. These models, projected by the sender, fiduciary by definition and of the order of subjective /having-to-be/, are opposed to homological thinking, which "introduces mathematical proportion into the evaluation of the relations between isotopies that are presumed to be parallel." Thus, in this chapter, further refining the theoretical foundations of modal grammar, the relations between the fiduciary and the logical within a cognitive universe defined as a network of formal semiotic relations from among which the "epistemic subject selects equivalences it needs in order to receive veridictory discourse" and thereby demonstrates that believing and knowing "are part of the same cognitive universe" are outlined.

5. SEMIOTICS AND SOCIAL SCIENCES

Although modal grammar does constitute a breakthrough in the theory of narrativity, we have pointed out that this grammar was a reformulation and a refinement of the general semiotic grammar worked out in chapter 4, "Elements of a Narrative Grammar." We also have noted that at all levels this grammar sets in place refined significative articulations that correspond to an augmentation or increase in the production of meaning, since signification is indeed defined as articulated meaning. Moreover it has been argued that meaning can be grasped only when articulated or narrativized, narrativity being "the very organizing principle of all discourse, whether narrative (identified in the first instance, as figurative discourse) or non-narrative" (Greimas and Courtés, 1982, p. 209). The theoretical task of semiotics, considered as the science of signification, was to set in place models that could account for the articulation of content and for the trajectory of meaning, from the fundamental domains where semantic substance receives its first articulations, to the final domain where the signification manifests itself through discourse. This has led to the elaboration of hierarchized fundamental and surface semantics and grammar (taxonomy and syntax) establishing formal models able to organize and manipulate contents.

The essays translated from *Sémiotique et sciences sociales* (1976) must be situated within the preceding theoretical context and can be seen as different formulations, different instances, of the fundamental problematics posited by Greimas from the very outset. Specifically, what are the conditions for the production of meaning and how can the transformation of meaning into signification be described? In itself this would have remained trivial had Greimas not defined his project in terms of the elaboration of a scientific discourse, starting from a limited number of concepts (*relation, description, system, process, conversion*) and the construction of models that are hypothetical representations that can be confirmed, invalidated, or falsified within a general semiotic theory controlling their homogeneity and coherence.

Greimas has stated on numerous occasions that semiotics and, in this particular case, a semiotics of the social sciences, cannot claim to have the status of a science that might be described in terms of a "completed organization of knowledge" (Greimas, 1976. p. 9). Knowledge about human beings is so uncertain and contested that at best a semiotics of the social sciences could be characterised as a scientific project in the process of elaborating a scientific discourse. If this is the case, it is legitimate to investigate the scientific status of such discourse by examining its modes of manifestation and "the conditions of its production, as well as the criteria that distinguish it from other forms of knowledge" (ibid.). Such a stance amounts to abandoning the idea that science is a system and adopting the notion that it is a process; that is, in the domain under investigation, science in fact corresponds to a scientific doing.

In chapters 11 through 14, the same procedures are adopted, beginning with an investigation of the claims to "scientificness" of four important disciplines in the social sciences (communication, sociolinguistics, history, and ethnology). This is followed by a reformulation of each discoursive practice, within a coherent theory of narrativity. The purpose here is not only to describe criteria for scientific discourse in general but also to describe scientific doing and thereby investigate how each discipline in question, which does indeed claim to have some sort of scientific status, might better evaluate its own practice and more rigorously organize its doing within a global theory of narrativity. The constructed subject of such discourse, totally independent from its ontological status, as a syntactic actant is described in terms of its virtual and actualizing role as manipulating operator. The taxonomic and syntactic components of this linguistic doing can be examined, the function of the veridictory apparatus can be founded on coherence, and the knowing of the subject can be described. The referentialization of this discourse, the enunciative contract, and the actantial structure of scientific communication, are seen as dominant features of such discourse, which is said to be objective in nature. It is also recognized that "the ideological model of the social sciences—some of which do not seem to have gone beyond the doxological state" (Greimas, 1976, p. 38)—because they are defined by their scientific project and by a scientific doing exercised in the name of this project, is inevitable, "since this project, like any human project, can only be ideological" (ibid.).

Starting from the observation that most definitions of media, or communication, are concerned with means rather than articulated contents,

Greimas argues in chapter 11 that the traditional communication model, sender-code-receiver, does not offer any guarantees of methodological homogeneity. Sender and receiver constitute an interpersonal structure and are endowed with emissive and receptive competencies needed to control performance. Approaching communication from the angle of media necessitates the introduction of channels and codes. This makes analysis unduly complex and, indeed, the only way to confer a homogeneous status on research in the cultural dimension of societies is to posit the unicity of signification manifested through the codes used. One should not lose sight of the fact that the reason for research into this domain is to study the relation between society and individuals. This being so, the interpersonal verbal-exchange model is adapted to the social dimension of semiotic phenomena.

The opposition language (coextensive with grammar)/speech (free use of the lexical thesaurus), leads to the positing of a common language, a common semantic store between members of a linguistic community. The lexemes of this common thesaurus, which is of a metaphorical and axiological nature, constitutes a fundamental semantics that the individual manipulates as a necessary condition for participating in language communities. Social groups are defined semiotically, on the one hand as restricted groups characterised by the competence of all individuals in the group, and on the other, in terms of a typology of a semantic universe and socialized discourses such that "the same individual can participate in several *semiotic* groups and take on as many *sociosemiotic* roles as there are groups into which he or she is integrated." The figurative dimension of discourse is considered as the level at which the involvement of individuals of a society manifests their general adhesion to the ensemble of value systems making up their culture. Greimas proposes a discursive sociosemiotics able to "take on all social discourses, independently of all substances, the channels, or *media* through which they appear (television, film, collective sports, entertainment, picture books, etc.), if only because they all refer back to the very same signifying universe and because their forms of discursive organization are comparable," and suggests specificity criteria for distinguishing between narrative objects produced by social discourse (i.e., relative nonintervention of a narrator, absence of semantic codes).

In chapter 12, "On Theoretical Models in Sociolinguistics," Greimas defines the area of study that focuses on languages having social connotations as being part of the broader field of a socioeconomics delineated in chapter 11, which includes the investigation of the social connotations of nonlinguistic semiotic systems (gestural, alimentary, dress semiotics, etc.). In an attempt to describe natural languages from a sociolinguistic perspective, Greimas explores scientific and ethnological taxonomies, and since they cannot account for how languages are inscribed in their social contexts, he discards them in favor of sociolinguistic taxonomies, which, contrary to the typology of cultural spheres, can indeed be said to establish methodological boundaries within a single domain of investigation.

For sociolinguistics to become a scientific project of a general nature it is necessary to postulate a homogeneous level of research and description. Consistent with the theoretical program elaborated for the analysis of sociosemiotic discourse, Greimas proposes a general model that is both hypothetical and operational. It has three types of connotative categories and taxonomical models that could embrace the domain of sociolinguistics: proxemic, morphological, and functional. These categories and models can be used to distinguish archaic societies from industrial ones. In addition to morphological models, a sociolinguistic syntax, along the lines of a strategy of communication, completes this sociolinguistic grammar, which, as such, could account for the hitherto ill-defined domain of social connotations.

The thrust of chapter 13, "On Evenemential History and the Deep Structures of Historiography," is both to demonstrate the need to construct general models that could account for the production of history and to elaborate the conditions under which a historical knowing-how-to-do, scientific in nature, could be set in place. True to procedures worked out in his general theory of narrativity, Greimas establishes a fundamental deep level where taxonomic organizations and structural transformations take place, a mediating intermediate domain organized by means of surface narrative syntax, and a surface dimension where historicity is manifested. The need to set up such a global, integrated, hierarchical model stems from the nature of historical studies on the whole. Although, for instance, the *Annales* School and Marxist tradition have proposed adequate models for the analyses of deep structures, no coherent models, as such, exist that could link these deep structures to the "conjectural structures of historicity" made up of an "infinite number of microevents happening together at each moment and everywhere."

The deep structures (taxonomic component) would be part of a sort of grammar of history having restrictive rules as well as "rules governing the

161

organization of the syntactic strings that can be inscribed in historical discourse." The intermediate surface syntax would organize the events of history, and it is at this level that procedures for recognizing historical events from among daily facts would be established. It is at this intermediate level that the utterance of doing enables the formulation of all historical events in a univocal manner. However, the specificity of historical discourse necessitates the introduction of the concept of the collective subject considered as the agent of a programmed doing and defined as a modalized actant governed by presupposed virtualizing and actualizing modalities. In addition to the preceding preconditions, the historical collective subject is not a collective actant as such, but a hyponymic subject, for example, a social class. To avoid giving the historical project an intentional ideology, historical syntax, when establishing strings of utterances, should start from "the ends and not the beginnings of historical programs" and make use of "a logic of presuppositions that would found the constituent relations of the strings."

Questioning the aims of ethnology is not a trivial matter since in chapter 14, "Reflections on Ethnosemiotic Objects," Greimas suggests that the identification of specific objectives can bring about not only a reevaluation of approaches but also the elaboration of new methods for bringing together poetic, musical, and gestural facts within a given culture. If considered from a discursive perspective, then these heterogeneous facts can be seen as complex semiotic objects of a syncretic nature. Extrapolating the schema elaborated in investigating sociolinguistic categories (archaic societies with morphologically stable "languages" vs. modern societies with a mobile sociolinguistic syntax) and applying the same principle of transformation, "complex semiotic objects, recognizable at the level of ethnosemiotics, break apart and give rise to a stylistics of multiple variation at the sociosemiotic level."

To study the passage of societies from an ethnosemiotic state (archaic) to a sociosemiotic state (developed) corresponds to analyzing the passage from a "global discourse to disjoined and autonomous discourses (poetry, music, dance), from a discourse having a sacred function, to discourses having ludic or aesthetic functions; from a collective dimension, to an individual dimension" (Coquet, 1985, p. lxv). Thus, for instance, the passage from sacred poetry (collective axiological system) to folk poetry (absence of a specific semantic code) can be considered as a form of desemantization, whereas the passage from the latter to modern poetry (individual values) could be characterised as a reactivation of signification (reintegration of semanticism within its formal structures). When situated within the context of communication, at the ethnosemiotic level, mythical objects are addressed by a sender to a mythical receiver and not to a passive human listener as is the case within the sociosemiotic context where poetry is recited, music heard, and ballet seen. Ethnosemiotic communication, which is a making-to-do and never a making-to-see, has a cohesive function, since it integrates the individual subject within the group by constituting the social group as a collective subject. It is these very integrative social systems of communication that are seen as one of the main features underlying participatory folk manifestations.

Throughout this introduction, in which we have traced the salient features of Greimas's semiotic from a developmental or historiconotional perspective, we have attempted to stress the constructed and hypothetico-deductive aspect of a theory in which concepts are interdefined and hierarchically ordered. We also have emphasized the anthropomorphic dimension of the global theory, conceived of as an ongoing scientific project founded on internal coherence as a precondition to formalization. Further, we have identified three major phases: formulation, narrative grammar, and modal and aspectual grammar. We also have identified the manner in which research began on deep structures, then explored semio-narrative structures, before concentrating on surface (discursive and figurative) structures. However, we should not conclude that the transpositional semiotic theory presented here is in any way a fully completed theory, since research is currently being carried out on the pathemic, ethical, and aesthetic dimensions of discourse. This should complete the construction of the semio-narrative grammar, and further work on aspectualities should lead to the development of an integrated and complementary discourse grammar. As Greimas himself says, "These two tasks should occupy the next generation of semioticians."

REFERENCES

Coquet. J.-C. 1982. *Sémiotique—l'École de Paris*. Paris: Hachette.

———. 1985. "Éléments de bio-bliographie," In *Recueil d'hommages Pour/Essays in Honor of Algirdas Julien Greimas*. Edited by H. Parret and H. G. Ruprecht. Amsterdam: John Benjamins.

Courtés, J. 1976. *Introduction à la sémiotique narrative et discursive*. Paris: Hachette.

Culler. J. 1975. *Structural Poetics*. London: Routledge & Kegan Paul.

Greimas, A. J. 1956. "L'actualité du saussurisme." *Le Français Moderne* 3.

———. 1966. *Sémantique structurale*. Paris: Larousse.

———. 1970. *Du sens*. Paris: Le Seuil.

———. 1976. *Sémiotique et sciences sociales*. Paris: Le Seuil.

———. 1981. "Contre-note." *Le carré sémiotique. Le Bulletin du groupe de recherches sémio-linguistiques* 17:42-46.

———. 1983a. *Du sens II*. Paris: Le Seuil.

———. 1983b. *Structural Semantics*. Introduction by R. Schleifer. Translated by D. McDowell, R. Schleifer, and A. Velie. Lincoln and London: University of Nebraska Press.

———. 1984. "Universaux et narrativité," unedited paper presented at a colloquium on the universals of narrativity. University of Toronto.

Greimas, A. J., and Courtés, J. 1982. *Semiotics and Language: An Analytical Dictionary*. Translated by L. Crist, D. Patte, and others. Bloomington: Indiana University Press.

———. 1986. *Sémiotique: dictionnaire raisonné de la théorie du langage*, II. Paris: Hachette.

Greimas, A. J., and Landowski, E. 1979. *Introduction à l'analyse du discours en sciences sociales*. Paris: Hachette.

Jameson, F. 1972. *The Prison House of Language*. Princeton: Princeton University Press.

Landowski. E. 1979. *Introduction. Sémiotique des Passions. Le Bulletin du groupe de recherches sémio-linguistiques* 9:3-8.

Nef. F., ed. 1976. "Entretien avec A. J. Greimas." In *Structures élémentaires de la signification*. Brussels: Ed. Complexe.

Parret, H., and Ruprecht, H. G., eds. 1985. *Recueil d'hommages pour/Essays in Honor of Algirdas Julien Greimas*. Amsterdam: John Benjamins.

Patte, D. 1982. "Greimas' Model for the Generative Trajectory of Meaning in Discourses." *American Journal of Semiotics* 1:59-78.

Petitot-Cocorda, J. 1982. "Introduction." *Aspects de la conversion. Actes sémiotiques: Le Bulletin du groupe de recherches sémio-linguistiques* 24:5-7.

————. 1985. *Morphogenèse du sens I*. Paris: PUF.

Ricoeur, P. 1983. "Greimas' Narrative Grammar." In *Paris School Semiotics*, P. Perron, ed. Toronto Semiotic Circle Publications 3: 91-114.

Ruprecht, H. G. 1984. "Ouvertures meta-sémiotiques: Entretien avec A. J. Greimas." *Recherches Sémiotiques/Semiotic Inquiry* 4:1-23.

7

DISCURSIVE AND PRESENTATIONAL FORMS

Susanne K. Langer

The logical theory on which this whole study of symbols is based is essentially that which was set forth by Wittgenstein, some twenty years ago, in his *Tractatus Logico-Philosophicus*:

"One name stands for one thing, and another for another thing, and they are connected together. And so the whole, like a living picture, presents the atomic fact. (4.0311)

"At the first glance the proposition—say as it stands printed on paper—does not seem to be a picture of the reality of which it treats. But neither does the musical score appear at first sight to be a picture of a musical piece; nor does our phonetic spelling (letters) seem to be a picture of our spoken language . . . . (4.015)

"In the fact that there is a general rule by which the musician is able to read the symphony out of the score, and that there is a rule by which one could reconstruct the symphony from the line on a phonograph record and from this again—by means of the first rule—construct the score, herein lies the internal similarity between the things which at first sight seem to be entirely different.

Susanne K. Langer. *Philosophy in a New Key*. Cambridge, Mass.: Harvard University Press, 1979. Reprinted with permission from Harvard University Press.

And the rule is the law of projection which projects the symphony into the language of the musical score. It is the rule of translation of this language into the language of the gramophone record." (4.0141)

"Projection" is a good word, albeit a figurative one, for the process by which we draw purely *logical* analogies. Geometric projection is the best instance of a perfectly faithful representation which, without knowledge of some logical rule, appears to be a misrepresentation. A child looking at a map of the world in Mercator projection cannot help believing that Greenland is larger than Australia; he simply *finds* it larger. The projection employed is not the usual principle of copying which we use in all visual comparisons or translations, and his training in the usual rule makes him unable to "see" by the new one. It takes sophistication to "see" the relative sizes of Greenland and Australia on a Mercator map. Yet a mind educated to appreciate the projected image brings the eye's habit with it. After a while, we genuinely "see" the thing as we apprehend it.

Language, our most faithful and indispensable picture of human experience, of the world and its events, of thought and life and all the march of time, contains a law of projection of which philosophers are sometimes unaware, so that their reading of the presented "facts" is obvious and yet wrong, as a child's visual experience is obvious yet deceptive when his judgment is ensnared by the trick of the flattened map. The transformation which facts undergo when they are rendered as propositions is that the relations in them are turned into something like *objects*. Thus, "A killed B" tells of a *way* in which A and B were unfortunately combined; but our only means of expressing this way is to *name* it, and presto!—a new entity, "killing," seems to have added itself to the complex of A and B. The event which is "pictured" in the proposition undoubtedly involved a *succession* of acts by A and B, but not the succession which the proposition seems to exhibit—first A, then "killing," then B. Surely A and B were simultaneous with each other and with the killing. But words have a linear, discrete, successive order; they are strung one after another like beads on a rosary; beyond the very limited meanings of inflections, which can indeed be incorporated in the words themselves, we cannot talk in simultaneous bunches of names. We must name one thing and then another, and symbols that are not names must be stuck between or before or after, by convention. But these symbols, holding proud places in the chain of names, are apt to be mistaken for names, to the detriment of many a metaphysical theory. Lord

Russell regrets that we cannot construct a language which would express all relations by analogous relations; then we would not be tempted to misconstrue language, as a person who knows the meaning of the Mercator map, but has not used one freely enough to "see" in its terms, misconstrues the relative sizes of its areas.

"Take, say, that lightning precedes thunder," he says. "To express this by a language closely reproducing the structure of the fact, we should have to say simply: 'lightning, thunder,' where the fact that the first word precedes the second means that what the first word means precedes what the second word means. But even if we adopted this method for temporal order, we should still need words for all other relations, because we could not without intolerable ambiguity symbolize them by the order of our words."

It is a mistake, I think, to symbolize things by entities too much like themselves; to let words in temporal order represent things in temporal order. If relations such as temporal order are symbolized at all, let the symbols not be those same relations themselves. A structure cannot include as *part of a symbol* something that should properly be *part of the meaning*. But it is unfortunate that names and syntactical indicators look so much alike in language; that we cannot represent objects by words, and relations by pitch, loudness, or other characteristics of speech.

As it is, however, all language has a form which requires us to string out our ideas even though their objects rest one within the other; as pieces of clothing that are actually worn one over the other have to be strung side by side on the clothesline. This property of verbal symbolism is known as *discursiveness*; by reason of it, only thoughts which can be arranged in this peculiar order can be spoken at all; any idea which does not lend itself to this "projection" is ineffable, incommunicable by means of words. That is why the laws of reasoning, our clearest formulation of exact expression, are sometimes known as the "laws of discursive thought."

There is no need of going further into the details of verbal symbolism and its poorer substitutes, hieroglyphs, the deaf-and-dumb language, Morse Code, or the highly developed drum-telegraphy of certain jungle tribes. The subject has been exhaustively treated by several able men, as the many quotations in this chapter indicate; I can only assent to their findings. The relation between word-structures and their meanings is, I believe, one of logical analogy, whereby, in Wittgenstein's phrase, "we make ourselves pictures of facts." This philosophy of language lends itself, indeed, to great technical development, such as Wittgenstein envisaged:

"In the language of everyday life it very often happens that the same word signifies in different ways—and therefore belongs to two different symbols—or that two words, which signify in different ways, are apparently applied in the same way in the proposition. (3.323)

"In order to avoid these errors, we must employ a symbolism which excludes them, by not applying the same sign in different symbols and by not applying signs in the same way which signify in different ways. A symbolism, that is to say, which obeys the rules of *logical* grammar—of logical syntax.

"(The logical symbolism of Frege and Russell is such a language, which, however, does still not exclude all errors.)" (3.325)

Carnap's admirable book, *The Logical Syntax of Language*, carries out the philosophical program suggested by Wittgenstein. Here an actual, detailed technique is developed for determining the *capacity for expression* of any given linguistic system, a technique which predicts the limit of all combinations to be made in that system, shows the equivalence of certain forms and the differences among others which might be mistaken for equivalents, and exhibits the conventions to which any thought or experience must submit in order to become conveyable by the symbolism in question. The distinctions between scientific language and everyday speech, which most of us can feel rather than define, are clearly illumined by Carnap's analysis; and it is surprising to find how little of our ordinary communication measures up to the standard of "meaning" which a serious philosophy of language, and hence a logic of discursive thought, set before us.

In this truly remarkable work the somewhat diffuse apprehension of our intellectual age, that *symbolism* is the key to epistemology and "natural knowledge," finds precise and practical corroboration. The Kantian challenge: "What can I know?" is shown to be dependent on the prior question: "What can I ask?" And the answer, in Professor Carnap's formulation, is clear and direct. I can ask whatever language will express; I can know whatever experiment will answer. A proposition which could not, under any (perhaps ideal, impracticable) conditions, be verified or refuted, is a pseudo-proposition, it has no literal meaning. It does not belong to the framework of knowledge that we call logical conception; it is not true or false, but *unthinkable*, for it falls outside the order of symbolism.

170

Since an inordinate amount of our talk, and therefore (we hope) of our cerebration too, defies the canons of literal meaning, our philosophers of language—Russell, Wittgenstein, Carnap, and others of similar persuasions—are faced with the new question: What is the true function of those verbal combinations and other pseudo-symbolic structures that have no real significance, but are freely used as though they meant something?

According to our logicians, those structures are to be treated as "expressions" in a different sense, namely as "expressions" of emotions, feelings, desires. They are not symbols for thought, but symptoms of the inner life, like tears and laughter, crooning, or profanity.

> "Many linguistic utterances," says Carnap, "are analogous to laughing in that they have only an expressive function, no representative function. Examples of this are cries like 'Oh, Oh,' or, on a higher level, lyrical verses. The aim of a lyrical poem in which occur the words 'sunshine' and 'clouds,' is not to inform us of certain meteorological facts, but to express certain feelings of the poet and to excite similar feelings in us . . . . Metaphysical propositions—like lyrical verses—have only an expressive function, but no representative function. Metaphysical propositions are neither true nor false, because they assert nothing . . . . But they are, like laughing, lyrics and music, expressive. They express not so much temporary feelings as permanent emotional and volitional dispositions."

Lord Russell holds a very similar view of other people's metaphysics:

> "I do not deny," he says, "the importance or value, within its own sphere, of the kind of philosophy which is inspired by ethical notions. The ethical work of Spinoza, for instance, appears to me of the very highest significance, but what is valuable in such a work is not any metaphysical theory as to the nature of the world to which it may give rise, nor indeed anything that can be proved or disproved by argument. What is valuable is the indication of some new way of feeling toward life and the world, some way of feeling by which our own existence can acquire more of the characteristics which we must deeply desire."

And Wittgenstein:

> "Most propositions and questions, that have been written about philosophical matters, are not false, but senseless. We cannot, therefore, answer questions of this kind at all, but only state their senselessness. Most questions and propositions of the philosophers result from the fact that we do not understand the logic of our language. (4.003)"
>
> "A proposition presents the existence and non-existence of atomic facts. (4.1)
>
> "The totality of true propositions is the total of natural science (or the totality of the natural sciences). (4.11)
>
> "Everything that can be thought at all can be thought clearly. Everything that can be said can be said clearly." (4.116)

In their criticism of metaphysical propositions, namely that such propositions are usually pseudo-answers to pseudo-questions, these logicians have my full assent; problems of "First Cause" and "Unity" and "Substance," and all the other time-honored topics, are insoluble, because they arise from the fact that we attribute to the world what really belongs to the "logical projection" in which we conceive it, and by misplacing our questions we jeopardize our answers. This source of bafflement has been uncovered by the philosophers of our day, through their interest in the functions and nature of symbolism. The discovery marks a great intellectual advance. But it does not condemn philosophical inquiry as such; it merely requires *every philosophical problem to be recast*, to be conceived in a different form. Many issues that seemed to concern the *sources* of knowledge, for instance, now appear to turn partly or wholly on the *forms* of knowledge, or even the forms of expression, of symbolism. The center of philosophical interest has shifted once more, as it has shifted several times in the past. That does not mean, however, that rational people should now renounce metaphysics. The recognition of the intimate relation between symbolism and experience, on which our whole criticism of traditional problems is based, is itself a metaphysical insight. For metaphysics is, like every philosophical pursuit, a study of *meanings*. From it spring the special sciences, which can develop their techniques and verify their propositions one by one, *as soon as their initial concepts are clear enough to allow systematic handling*, i.e. as soon as the philosophical work behind them is at least tentatively accomplished. Metaphysics is not itself a science with fixed presuppositions, but progresses from problem to problem rather than from premise to consequence. To suppose that we have outgrown it is to suppose that all "the sciences" are finally established, that human language is complete, or at least soon to be completed, and additional facts are all we lack of the greatest knowledge ever possible to man; and though this knowledge may be small, it is all that we shall ever have.

This is, essentially, the attitude of those logicians who have investigated the limits of language. Nothing that is not "language" in the sense of their technical definition can possess the character of symbolic expressiveness (though it may be "expressive" in the symptomatic way). Consequently nothing that cannot be "projected" in discursive form is accessible to the human mind at all, and any attempt to understand anything but demonstrable fact is bootless ambition. The knowable is a clearly defined field, governed by the requirement of discursive projectability. Outside this domain is the inexpressible realm of feeling, of formless desires and satisfactions, immediate experience, forever incognito and incommunicado. A philosopher who looks in that direction is, or should be, a mystic; from the ineffable sphere nothing but nonsense can be conveyed, since language, our only possible semantic, will not clothe experiences that elude the discursive form.

But intelligence is a slippery customer; if one door is closed to it, it finds, or even breaks, another entrance to the world. If one symbolism is inadequate, it seizes another; there is no eternal decree over its means and methods. So I will go with the logisticians and linguists as far as they like, but do not promise to go no further. For there is an unexplored possibility of genuine semantic beyond the limits of discursive language.

This logical "beyond," which Wittgenstein calls the "unspeakable," both Russell and Carnap regard as the sphere of subjective experience, emotion, feeling, and wish, from which only *symptoms* come to us in the form of metaphysical and artistic fancies. The study of such products they relegate to psychology, not semantics. And here is the point of my radical divergence from them. Where Carnap speaks of "cries like 'Oh, Oh,' or, on a higher level, lyrical verses," I can see only a complete failure to apprehend a fundamental distinction. Why should we cry our feelings at such high levels that anyone would think we were *talking*? Clearly, poetry means more than a cry; it has reason for being articulate; and metaphysics is more than the croon with which

173

we might cuddle up to the world in a comfortable attitude. We are dealing with symbolisms here, and what they express is often highly intellectual. Only, the form and function of such symbolisms are not those investigated by logicians, under the heading of "language." The field of semantics is wider than that of language, as certain philosophers—Schopenhauer, Cassirer, Delacroix, Dewey, Whitehead, and some others—have discovered; but it is blocked for us by the two fundamental tenets of current epistemology, which we have just discussed.

These two basic assumptions go hand in hand: (1) That *language is the only means of articulating thought*, and (2) That *everything which is not speakable thought, is feeling*. They are linked together because all genuine thinking is symbolic, and the limits of the expressive medium are, therefore, really the limits of our conceptual powers. Beyond these we can have only blind feeling, which records nothing and conveys nothing, but has to be discharged in action or self-expression, in deeds or cries or other impulsive demonstrations.

But if we consider how difficult it is to construct a meaningful language that shall meet neo-positivistic standards, it is quite incredible that people should ever say anything at all, or understand each other's propositions. At best, human thought is but a tiny, grammar-bound island, in the midst of a sea of feeling expressed by "Oh-oh" and sheer babble. The island has a periphery, perhaps, of mud—factual and hypothetical concepts broken down by the emotional tides into the "material mode," a mixture of meaning and nonsense. Most of us live the better part of our lives on this mudflat; but in artistic moods we take to the deep, where we flounder about with symptomatic cries that sound like propositions about life and death, good and evil, substance, beauty, and other nonexistent topics.

So long as we regard only scientific and "material" (semi-scientific) thought as really cognitive of the world, this peculiar picture of mental life must stand. And *so long as we admit only discursive symbolism as a bearer of ideas, "thought" in this restricted sense must be regarded as our only intellectual activity*. It begins and ends with language; without the elements, at least, of scientific grammar, conception must be impossible.

A theory which implies such peculiar consequences is itself a suspicious character. But the error which it harbors is not in its reasoning. It is in the very premise from which the doctrine proceeds, namely that all articulate symbolism is discursive. As Lord Russell, with his usual precision and directness, has stated the case, "it is clear that anything that can be said in an inflected language can be said in an uninflected language; therefore, anything that can be said in language can be said by means of a temporal series of uninflected words. This places a limitation upon what can be expressed in words. It may well be that there are facts which do not lend themselves to this very simple schema; if so, they cannot be expressed in language. Our confidence in language is due to the fact that it . . . shares the structure of the physical world, and therefore can express that structure. But if there be a world which is not physical, or not in space-time, it may have a structure which we can never hope to express or to know . . . . Perhaps that is why we know so much physics and so little of anything else."

Now, I do not believe that "there is a world which is not physical, or not in space-time," but I do believe that in this physical, space-time world of our experience there are things which do not fit the grammatical scheme of expression. But they are not necessarily blind, inconceivable, mystical affairs; they are simply matters which require to be conceived through some symbolistic schema other than discursive language. And to demonstrate the possibility of such a non-discursive pattern one needs only to review the logical requirements for any symbolic structure whatever. Language is by no means our only articulate product.

Our merest sense-experience is a process of *formulation*. The world that actually meets our senses is not a world of "things," about which we are invited to discover facts as soon as we have codified the necessary logical language to do so; the world of pure sensation is so complex, so fluid and full, that sheer sensitivity to stimuli would only encounter what William James has called (in characteristic phrase) "a blooming, buzzing confusion." Out of this bedlam our sense-organs must select certain predominant forms, if they are to make report of *things* and not of mere dissolving sensa. The eye and the ear must have their logic—their "categories of understanding," if you like the Kantian idiom, or their "primary imagination," in Coleridge's version of the same concept. An object is not a datum, but a form construed by the sensitive and intelligent organ, a form which is at once an experienced individual thing and a symbol for the concept of it, for *this sort of thing*.

A tendency to organize the sensory field into groups and patterns of sense-data, to perceive forms rather than a flux of light-impressions, seems to be inherent in our receptor apparatus just as much as in the higher nervous centers with which we do arithmetic and logic. But this unconscious appreciation of forms is the primitive root of all abstraction, which in turn is the keynote of rationality; so it appears that the conditions for rationality lie deep in our pure animal experience—in our power of perceiving, in the elementary functions of our eyes and ears and fingers. Mental life begins with our mere physiological constitution. A little reflection shows us that, since no experience occurs more than once, so-called "repeated" experiences are really *analogous* occurrences, all fitting a form that was abstracted on the first occasion. *Familiarity* is nothing but the quality of fitting very neatly into the form of a previous experience. I believe our ingrained habit of hypostatizing impressions, of seeing *things* and not sense-data, rests on the fact that we promptly and unconsciously abstract a form from each sensory experience, and use this form to *conceive* the experience as a whole, as a "thing."

No matter what heights the human mind may attain, it can work only with the organs it has and the functions peculiar to them. Eyes that did not see forms could never furnish it with *images*; ears that did not hear articulated sounds could never open it to *words*. Sense-data, in brief, would be useless to a mind whose activity is "through and through a symbolic process," were they not *par excellence* receptacles of meaning. But meaning, as previous considerations have shown, accrues essentially to forms. Unless the *Gestalt*-psychologists are right in their belief that *Gestaltung* is of the very nature of perception, I do not know how the hiatus between perception and conception, sense-organ and mind-organ, chaotic stimulus and logical response, is ever to be closed and welded. A mind that works primarily with meanings must have organs that supply it primarily with forms.

The nervous system is the organ of the mind; its center is the brain, its extremities the sense-organs; and any characteristic function it may possess must govern the work of all its parts. In other words, the activity of our senses is "mental" not only when it reaches the brain, but in its very inception, whenever the alien world outside impinges on the furthest and smallest receptor. All sensitivity bears the stamp for mentality. "Seeing," for instance, is not a passive process, by which meaningless impressions are stored up for the use of an organizing mind, which construes forms out of these amorphous data to suit its own purposes. "Seeing" is itself a process of formulation; our understanding of the visible world begins in the eye.

This psychological insight, which we owe to the school of Wertheimer, Köhler, and Koffka, has far-reaching philosophical consequences, if we take it seriously; for it carries rationality into processes that are usually deemed pre-rational, and points to the existence of forms, i.e. of *possible symbolic material*, at a level where symbolic activity has certainly never been looked for by any epistemologist. The eye and the ear make their own abstractions, and consequently dictate their own peculiar forms of conception. But these forms are derived from exactly the same world that furnished the totally different forms known to physics. There is, in fact, no such thing as the form of the "real" world; physics is one pattern which may be found in it, and "appearance," or the pattern of *things* with their qualities and characters, is another. One construction may indeed preclude the other; but to maintain that the consistency and universality of the one brands the other as *false* is a mistake. The fact that physical analysis does not rest in a final establishment of irreducible "qualities" does not refute the belief that there are red, blue, and green things, wet or oily or dry substances, fragrant flowers, and shiny surfaces in the real world. These concepts of the "material mode" are not approximations to "physical" notions at all. Physical concepts owe their origin and development to the application of *mathematics* to the world of "things," and mathematics never—even in the beginning—dealt with qualities of objects. It measured their proportions, but never treated its concepts—triangularity, circularity, etc.— as qualities of which *so-and-so much* could become an ingredient of certain objects. Even though an elliptical race-track may approximate a circle, it is not to be improved by the addition of more circularity. On the other hand, wine which is not sweet enough requires more sweetening, paint which is not bright enough is given an ingredient of more white or more color. The world of physics is essentially the real world construed by mathematical abstractions, and the world of sense is the real world construed by the abstractions which the sense-organs immediately furnish. To suppose that the "material mode" is a primitive and groping attempt at physical conception is a fatal error in epistemology, because it cuts off all interest in the developments of which sensuous conception is capable, and the intellectual uses to which it might be put.

These intellectual uses lie in a field which usually harbors a slough of despond for the philosopher, who ventures into it because he is too honest to ignore it, though really he knows no path around its pitfalls. It is the field of "intuition," "deeper meaning," "artistic truth," "insight," and so forth. A

177

dangerous-looking sector, indeed, for the advance of a rational spirit! To date, I think, every serious epistemology that has regarded mental life as greater than discursive reason, and has made concessions to "insight" or "intuition," has just so far capitulated to *unreason*, to mysticism and irrationalism. Every excursion beyond propositional thought has dispensed with thought altogether, and postulated some inmost soul of pure feeling in direct contact with a Reality unsymbolized, unfocused, and incommunicable (with the notable exception of the theory set forth by L. A. Reid in the last chapter of his *Knowledge and Truth*, which admits the facts of non-propositional conception in a way that invites rather than precludes logical analysis).

The abstractions made by the ear and the eye—the forms of direct perception—are our most primitive instruments of intelligence. They are genuine symbolic materials, media of understanding, by whose office we apprehend a world of *things*, and of events that are the histories of things. To furnish such conceptions is their prime mission. Our sense-organs make their habitual, unconscious abstractions, in the interest of this "*rei*fying" function that underlies ordinary recognition of objects, knowledge of signals, words, tunes, places, and the possibility of classifying such things in the outer world according to their kind. We recognize the elements of this sensuous analysis in all sorts of combinations; we can use them imaginatively, to conceive prospective changes in familiar scenes.

Visual forms—lines, colors, proportions, etc.—are just as capable of *articulation*, i.e. of complex combination, as words. But the laws that govern this sort of articulation are altogether different from the laws of syntax that govern language. The most radical difference is that *visual forms are not discursive*. They do not present their constituents successively, but simultaneously, so the relations determining a visual structure are grasped in one act of vision. Their complexity, consequently, is not limited, as the complexity of discourse is limited, by what the mind can retain from the beginning of an apperceptive act to the end of it. Of course such a restriction on discourse sets bounds to the complexity of speakable ideas. An idea that contains too many minute yet closely related parts, too many relations within relations, cannot be "projected" into discursive form; it is too subtle for speech. A language-bound theory of mind, therefore, rules it out of the domain of understanding and the sphere of knowledge.

But the symbolism furnished by our purely sensory appreciation of forms is a *non-discursive symbolism*, peculiarly well suited to the expression of ideas that defy linguistic "projection." Its primary function, that of conceptualizing the flux of sensations, and giving us concrete *things* in place of kaleidoscopic colors or noises, is itself an office that no language-born thought can replace. The understanding of space which we owe to sight and touch could never be developed, in all its detail and definiteness, by a discursive knowledge of geometry. Nature speaks to us, first of all, through our senses; the forms and qualities we distinguish, remember, imagine, or recognize are symbols of entities which exceed and outlive our momentary experience. Moreover, the same symbols—qualities, lines, rhythms—may occur in innumerable presentations; they are abstractable and combinatory. It is quite natural, therefore, that philosophers who have recognized the symbolical character of so-called "sense-data," especially in their highly developed uses, in science and art, often speak of a "language" of the senses, a "language" of musical tones, of colors, and so forth.

Yet this manner of speaking is very deceptive. Language is a special mode of expression, and not every sort of semantic can be brought under this rubric; by generalizing from linguistic symbolism to symbolism as such, we are easily led to misconceive all other types, and overlook their most interesting features. Perhaps it were well to consider, here, the salient characteristics of true language, or discourse.

In the first place, *every language has a vocabulary and a syntax*. Its elements are words with fixed meanings. Out of these one can construct, according to the rules of the syntax, composite symbols with resultant new meanings.

Secondly, in a language, some words are equivalent to whole combinations of other words, so that most meanings can be expressed in several different ways. This makes it possible *to define the meanings of the ultimate single words*, i.e., to construct a dictionary.

Thirdly, there may be alternative words for the same meaning. When two people systematically use different words for almost everything, they are said to speak different languages. But the two languages are roughly equivalent; with a little artifice, an occasional substitution of a phrase for a single word, etc., the propositions enunciated by one person, in his system, may be *translated* into the conventional system of the other.

179

Now consider the most familiar sort of non-discursive symbol, a picture. Like language, it is composed of elements that represent various respective constituents in the object; but these elements are not units with independent meanings. The areas of light and shade that constitute a portrait, a photograph for instance, have no significance by themselves. In isolation we would consider them simply blotches. Yet they are faithful representatives of visual elements composing the visual object. However, they do not represent, item for item, those elements which have *names*; there is not one blotch for the nose, one for the mouth, etc.; their shapes, in quite indescribable combinations, convey a total picture in which nameable features may be pointed out. The gradations of light and shade cannot be enumerated. They cannot be correlated, one by one, with parts or characteristics by means of which we might *describe* the person who posed for the portrait. The "elements" that the camera represents are not the "elements" that language represents. They are a thousand times more numerous. For this reason the correspondence between a word-picture and a visible object can never be as close as that between the object and its photograph. Given all at once to the intelligent eye, an incredible wealth and detail of information is conveyed by the portrait, where we do not have to stop to construe verbal meanings. That is why we use a photograph rather than a description on a passport or in the Rogues' Gallery.

Clearly, a symbolism with so many elements, such myriad relationships, cannot be broken up into basic units. It is impossible to find the smallest independent symbol, and recognize its identity when the same unit is met in other contexts. Photography, therefore, *has no vocabulary*. The same is obviously true of painting, drawing, etc. There is, of course, a technique of picturing objects, but the law governing this technique cannot properly be called a "syntax," since there are no items that might be called, metaphorically, the "words" of portraiture.

Since we have no words, there can be no dictionary of meanings for lines, shadings, or other elements of pictorial technique. We may well pick out some line, say a certain curve, in a picture, which serves to represent one nameable item; but in another place the same curve would have an entirely different meaning. It has no fixed meaning apart from its context. Also, there is no complex of other elements that is equivalent to it at all times, as "2+2" is equivalent to "4." Non-discursive symbols cannot be defined in terms of others, as discursive symbols can.

180

If there can be no defining dictionary, of course we have no translating dictionary, either. There are different media of graphic representation, but their respective elements cannot be brought into one-to-one correlation with each other, as in languages: "*chien*" = "*dog*", "*moi*" = "*me*," etc. There is no standard key for translating sculpture into painting, or drawing into ink-wash, because their equivalence rests on their common *total reference*, not on bit-for-bit equivalences of parts such as underlie a literal translation.

Furthermore, verbal symbolism, unlike the non-discursive kinds, has primarily a *general* reference. Only convention can assign a proper name— and then there is no way of preventing some other convention from assigning the same proper name to a different individual. We may name a child as oddly as we will, yet we cannot guarantee that no one else will ever bear that designation. A description may fit a scene ever so closely, but it takes some known proper name to refer it without possible doubt to one and only one place. Where the names of persons and places are withheld, we can never *prove* that a discourse refers—not merely applies—to a certain historic occasion. In the non-discursive mode that speaks directly to sense, however, there is no intrinsic generality. It is first and foremost a direct *presentation* of an individual object. A picture has to be schematized if it is to be capable of various meanings. In itself it represents just one object—real or imaginary, but still a unique object. The definition of a triangle fits triangles in general, but a drawing always presents a triangle of some specific kind and size. We have to abstract from the conveyed meaning in order to conceive triangularity in general. Without the help of words this generalization, if possible at all, is certainly incommunicable.

It appears, then, that although the different media of non-verbal representation are often referred to as distinct "languages," this is really a loose terminology. Language in the strict sense is essentially discursive; it has permanent units of meaning which are combinable into larger units; it has fixed equivalences that make definition and translation possible; its connotations are general, so that it requires non-verbal acts, like pointing, looking, or emphatic voice-inflections, to assign specific denotations to its terms. In all these salient characters it differs from wordless symbolism, which is non-discursive and untranslatable, does not allow of definitions within its own system, and cannot directly convey generalities. The meanings given through language are successively understood, and gathered into a whole by the process called discourse; the meanings of all other symbolic elements that compose a larger, articulate symbol are understood only through the meaning of the whole, through their relations within the total structure. Their very functioning as symbols depends on the fact that they are involved in a simultaneous, integral presentation. This kind of semantic may be called "presentational symbolism," to characterise its essential distinction from discursive symbolism, or "language" proper.

The recognition of presentational symbolism as a normal and prevalent vehicle of meaning widens our conception of rationality far beyond the traditional boundaries, yet never breaks faith with logic in the strictest sense. Wherever a symbol operates, there is a meaning; and conversely, different classes of experience—say, reason, intuition, appreciation—correspond to different types of symbolic mediation. No symbol is exempt from the office of logical formulation, of *conceptualizing* what it conveys; however simple its import, or however great, this import is a *meaning*, and therefore an element for understanding. Such reflection invites one to tackle anew, and with entirely different expectations, the whole problem of the limits of reason, the much-disputed life of feeling and the great controversial topics of fact and truth, knowledge and wisdom, science and art. It brings within the compass of reason much that has been traditionally relegated to "emotion," or to that crepuscular depth of the mind where "intuitions" are supposed to be born, without any midwifery of symbols, without due process of thought, to fill the gaps in the edifice of discursive, or "rational," judgment.

The symbolic materials given to our senses, the *Gestalten* or fundamental perceptual forms which invite us to construe the pandemonium of sheer impression into a world of things and occasions, belong to the "presentational" order. They furnish the elementary abstractions in terms of which ordinary sense-experience is understood. This kind of understanding is directly reflected in the pattern of *physical reaction*, impulse and instinct. May not the order of perceptual forms, then, be a possible principle for symbolization, and hence the conception, expression, and apprehension, of impulsive, instinctive, and sentient life? May not a nondiscursive symbolism of light and color, or of tone, be formulative of that life? And is it not possible that the sort of "intuitive" knowledge which Bergson extols above all rational knowledge because it is supposedly not mediated by any formulating (and hence deforming) symbol is itself perfectly rational, but not to be conceived through language—a product of that presentational symbolism which the mind reads in a flash, and preserves in a disposition or an attitude?

This hypothesis, though unfamiliar and therefore somewhat difficult, seems to me well worth exploring. For, quite apart from all questions of the authenticity of intuitive, inherited, or inspired knowledge, about which I do not wish to cavil, the very idea of a *non-rational source* of any knowledge vitiates the concept of mind as an organ of understanding. "The power of reason is simply the power of the whole mind at its fullest stretch and compass," said Professor Creighton, in an essay that sought to stem the great wave of irrationalism and emotionalism following the World War. This assumption appears to me to be a basic one in any study of mentality. Rationality is the essence of mind, and symbolic transformation its elementary process. It is a fundamental error, therefore, to recognize it only in the phenomenon of systematic, explicit reasoning. That is a mature and precarious product.

Rationality, however, is embodied in every mental act, not only when the mind is "at its fullest stretch and compass." It permeates the peripheral activities of the human nervous system, just as truly as the cortical functions.

"The facts of perception and memory maintain themselves only in so far as they are mediated, and thus given significance beyond their mere isolated existence . . . . What falls in any way within experience partakes of the rational form of the mind. As mental content, any part of experience is something more than a particular impression having only the attributes of existence. As already baptized into the life of the mind, it partakes of its logical nature and moves on the plane of universality . . . .

"No matter how strongly the unity and integrity of the mind is asserted, this unity is nothing more than verbal if the mind is not in principle the expression of reason. For it can be shown that all attempts to render comprehensible the unity of the mental life in terms of an alogical principle fail to attain their goal."

The title of Professor Creighton's trenchant little article is "Reason and Feeling." Its central thesis is that if there is something in our mental life besides "reason," by which he means, of course, discursive thinking, then it cannot be an alogical factor, but must be in essence cognitive, too; and since the only alternative to this reason is feeling (the author does not question that axiom of epistemology), feeling itself must somehow participate in knowledge and understanding.

All this may be granted. The position is well taken. But the most crucial problem is barely broached: this problem is epitomized in the word "somehow." *Just how* can feelings be conceived as possible ingredients of rationality? We are not told, but we are given a generous hint, which in the light of a broader theory of symbolism points to explanation.

"In the development of mind," he says, "feeling does not remain a static element, constant in form and content at all levels, but . . . is transformed and disciplined through its interplay with other aspects of experience . . . . Indeed, the character of the feeling in any experience may be taken as an index of the mind's grasp of its object; at the lower levels of experience, where the mind is only partially or superficially involved, feeling appears as something isolated and opaque, as the passive accompaniment of mere bodily sensations . . . . In the higher experiences, the feelings assume an entirely different character, just as do the sensations and the other contents of mind."

The significant observation voiced in this passage is that *feelings have definite forms, which become progressively articulated.* Their development is effected through their "interplay with the other aspects of experience"; but the nature of that interplay is not specified. Yet it is here, I think, that cogency for the whole thesis must be sought. What character of feeling is "an index of the mind's grasp of its object," and by what tokens is it so? If feeling has articulate forms, what are they like? For what these are *like* determines by what symbolism we might understand them. Everybody knows that language is a very poor medium for expressing our emotional nature. It merely names certain vaguely and crudely conceived states, but fails miserably in any attempt to convey the ever moving patterns, the ambivalences and intricacies of inner experience the interplay of feelings with thoughts and impressions, memories and echoes of memories, transient fantasy, or its mere runic traces, all turned into nameless, emotional stuff. If we say that we understand someone else's feeling in a certain matter, we mean that we understand why he should be sad or happy, excited or indifferent, in a general way; that we can see due cause for his attitude. We do not mean that we have insight into the actual flow and balance of his feelings, into that "character" which "may be taken as an index of the mind's grasp of its object." Language is quite inadequate to articulate such a conception. Probably we would not impart our actual, inmost feelings even if they could be spoken. We rarely speak in detail of entirely personal things.

184

There is, however, a kind of symbolism peculiarly adapted to the explication of "unspeakable" things, though it lacks the cardinal virtue of language, which is denotation. The most highly developed type of such purely connotational semantic is music. We are not talking nonsense when we say that a certain musical progression is significant, or that a given phrase lacks meaning, or a player's rendering fails to convey the import of a passage. Yet such statements make sense only to people with a natural understanding of the medium, whom we describe, therefore, as "musical." Musicality is often regarded as an essentially unintellectual, even a biologically sportive trait. Perhaps that is why musicians, who know that it is the prime source of their mental life and the medium of their clearest insight into humanity, so often feel called upon to despise the more obvious forms of understanding, that claim practical virtues under the names of reason, logic, etc. But in fact, musical understanding is not hampered by the possession of an active intellect, nor even by that love of pure reason which is known as rationalism or intellectualism; and *vice versa*, common-sense and scientific acumen need not defend themselves against any "emotionalism" that is supposed to be inherent in a respect for music. Speech and music have essentially different functions, despite their oft-remarked union in song. Their original relationship lies much deeper than any such union (of which more will be said in a subsequent chapter), and can be seen only when their respective natures are understood.

The problem of meaning deepens at every turn. The longer we delve into its difficulties, the more complex it appears. But in a central philosophical concept, this is a sign of health. Each question answered leads to another which previously could not be even entertained: the logic of symbolism, the possible types of representation, the fields proper to them, the actual functions of symbols according to their nature, their relationships to each other, and finally our main theme, their integration in human mentality.

Of course it is not possible to study every known phenomenon in the realm of symbolism. But neither is this necessary even in an intimate study. The logical structures underlying all semantic functions, which I have discussed in this chapter, suggest a general principle of division. Signs are logically distinct from symbols; discursive and presentational patterns show a formal difference. There are further natural divisions due to various ways of using symbols, no less important than the logical distinctions. Altogether, we may group meaning-situations around certain outstanding types, and make these

185

several types the subjects of individual studies. Language, ritual, myth, and music, representing four respective modes, may serve as central topics for the study of actual symbolisms and I trust that further problems of significance in art, in science or mathematics, in behavior or in fantasy and dream, may receive some light by analogy, and by that most powerful human gift, the adaptation of ideas.

8

THE POSTMODERN ETHOS

Stanley J. Grenz

Postmodernism was born in St. Louis, Missouri, on July 15, 1972, at 3:32 P.M.

When it was originally built, the Pruitt-Igoe housing project in St. Louis was hailed as a landmark of modern architecture. More importantly, it stood as the epitome for modernity itself in its goal of employing technology to create a utopian society for the benefit of all. But its unimpressed inhabitants vandalized the buildings. Government planners put a lot of effort into attempts to renovate the project. But finally, having sacrificed millions of dollars to the project, the government planners gave up. On that fateful afternoon in mid-July 1972, the building was razed with dynamite. According to Charles Jenkes, who has been reviled as the "single most influential proponent of architectural postmodernism,"[1] this event symbolizes the death of modernity and birth of postmodernity.[2]

Our society is in the throes of a cultural shift of immense proportions. Like the Pruitt-Igoe housing project, the edifice that housed thought and culture in the modern era is crumbling. As modernity dies around us, we appear to be entering a new epoch—postmodernity.

Stanley J. Grenz. "The Postmodern Ethos." In *A Primer on Postmodernism*, ©1996 Wm. B. Eerdmans Publishing Co. Used by permission; all rights reserved.

The postmodern phenomenon encompasses many dimensions of contemporary society. At the core of them all, however, is an intellectual flood or outlook, an "ism"—"postmodernism."

Scholars disagree among themselves as to what postmodernism involves, but they have reached a consensus on one point: this phenomenon marks the end of a single, universal worldview. The postmodern ethos resists unified, all-encompassing, and universally valid explanations. It replaces these with a respect for difference and a celebration of the local and particular at the expense of the universal.[3] Postmodernism likewise entails a rejection of the emphasis on rational discovery through the scientific method, which provided the intellectual foundation for the modern attempt to construct a better world. At its foundation, then, the postmodern outlook is anti-modern.

But the adjective *postmodern* describes more than an intellectual mood. The postmodern rejection of the focus on rationality characteristic of the modern era finds expression in various dimensions of contemporary society. In recent years, the postmodern mind-set has been reflected in many of the traditional vehicles of cultural expression, including architecture, art, and theater. In addition, postmodernism has increasingly become embodied in the broader society. We can detect a shift away from the modern toward the postmodern in pop culture ranging from disjunctive music videos to the new *Star Trek* series and even in the day-to-day aspects of contemporary life, such as the new quest for spirituality in the marketplace and the juxtaposing of different styles in the clothes many people wear.

Postmodernism refers to an intellectual mood and an array of cultural expressions that call into question the ideals, principles, and values that lay at the heart of the modern mind-set. *Postmodernity*, in turn, refers to an emerging epoch, the era in which we are living, the time when the postmodern outlook increasingly shapes our society. Postmodernity is the era in which postmodern ideas, attitudes, and values reign—when postmodernism molds culture. It is the era of the postmodern society.

Our goal in this chapter is to look more closely at the broader postmodern phenomenon and understand something of the ethos of postmodernity. What characterizes the cultural expressions and the broader day-to-day dimensions of the world of the "next generation"? What evidence is there that a new intellectual mind-set is shaping life in our society?

THE POSTMODERN PHENOMENON

Postmodernism refers to the intellectual mood and cultural expressions that are becoming increasingly dominant in contemporary society. We are apparently moving into a new cultural epoch, postmodernity, but we must pinpoint in greater detail what the postmodern phenomenon entails.

The Postmodern Consciousness

The early evidences of the basic ethos of postmodernism have been largely negative. This ethos flows from a radical rejection of the Enlightenment mind-set that gave rise to modernity. We can find traces of the postmodern ethos everywhere in our society. Above all, however, it pervades the consciousness of the emerging generation, and it constitutes a radical break with the assumptions of the past.

The postmodern consciousness has abandoned the Enlightenment belief in inevitable progress. Postmoderns have not sustained the optimism that characterized previous generations. To the contrary, they evidence a gnawing pessimism. For the first time in recent history, the emerging generation does not share the conviction of their parents that the world is becoming a better place in which to live. From widening holes in the ozone layer to teen-on-teen violence, they see our problems mounting. And they are no longer convinced that human ingenuity will solve these enormous problems or that their living standard will be higher than that of their parents.

The postmodern generation is also convinced that life on the earth is fragile. They believe that the Enlightenment model of the human conquest of nature, which dates to Francis Bacon, must quickly give way to a new attitude of cooperation with the earth. They believe that the survival of humankind is now at stake.

In addition to its dark pessimism, the postmodern consciousness operates with a view of truth different from what previous generations espoused.

The modern understanding linked truth with rationality and made reason and logical argumentation the sole arbiters of right belief. Postmoderns question the concept of universal truth discovered and proved through rational endeavors. They are unwilling to allow the human intellect to serve as the sole determiner of what we should believe. Postmoderns look beyond reason to nonrational ways of knowing, conferring heightened status on the emotions and intuition.

The quest for a cooperative model and an appreciation of nonrational dimensions of truth lend a holistic dimension to the postmodern consciousness. Postmodern holism entails a rejection of the Enlightenment ideal of the dispassionate, autonomous, rational individual. Postmoderns do not seek to be wholly self-directed individuals but rather "whole" persons.

Postmodern holism entails an integration of all the dimensions of personal life—affective and intuitive as well as cognitive. Wholeness also entails a consciousness of the indelible and delicate connection to what lies beyond ourselves, in which our personal existence is embedded and from which it is nurtured. This wider realm includes "nature" (the ecosystem), of course. But in addition it involves the community of humans in which we participate. Postmoderns are keenly conscious of the importance of community, of the social dimension of existence. And the postmodern conception of wholeness also extends to the religious or spiritual aspect of life. Indeed, postmoderns affirm that personal existence may transpire within the context of a divine reality.

The conviction that each person is embedded in a particular human community leads to a corporate understanding of truth. Postmoderns believe that not only our specific beliefs but also our understanding of truth itself is rooted in the community in which we participate. They reject the Enlightenment quest for universal, supracultural, timeless truth in favor of searching out truth as the expression of a specific community. They believe that truth consists in the ground rules that facilitate personal well-being in community and the well-being of the community as a whole.

In this sense, then, postmodern truth is relative to the community in which a person participates. And since there are many human communities, there are necessarily many different truths. Most postmoderns make the leap of believing that this plurality of truths can exist alongside one another. The postmodern consciousness, therefore, entails a radical kind of relativism and pluralism.

Of course, relativism and pluralism are not new. But the postmodern variety differs from the older forms. The relativistic pluralism of late modernity was highly individualistic; it elevated personal taste and personal choice as the be-all and end-all. Its maxims were "To each his/her own" and "Everyone has a right to his/her own opinion."

190

The postmodern consciousness, in contrast, focuses on the group. Postmoderns live in self-contained social groups, each of which has its own language, beliefs, and values. As a result, postmodern relativistic pluralism seeks to give place to the "local" nature of truth. Beliefs are held to be true within the context of the communities that espouse them.

The postmodern understanding of truth leads postmoderns to be less concerned than their forebears to think systematically or logically. Just as some people feel comfortable mixing elements of what traditionally has been considered incompatible clothing styles, postmoderns feel comfortable mixing elements of what have traditionally been considered incompatible belief systems. For example, a postmodern Christian may affirm both the classic doctrines of the church and such traditionally non-Christian ideas as reincarnation.

Nor are postmoderns necessarily concerned to prove themselves "right" and others "wrong." They believe that beliefs are ultimately a matter of social context, and hence they are likely to conclude, "What is right for us might not be right for you," and "What is wrong in our context might in your context be acceptable or even preferable."

When did this postmodern consciousness, with its pessimism, holism, communitarianism, and relativistic pluralism, arise?

The Birth of Postmodernity

In a sense, postmodernity has undergone a long incubation period. Although scholars disagree as to who originally coined the term,[4] there is a general consensus that it likely first appeared sometime in the 1930s.[5]

One leading proponent of postmodernism, Charles Jencks, claims that the genesis of the concept lies in the work of the Spanish writer Federico de Onis. In his *Antologia de la poesia espanola e hispanoamericana* (1934) de Onis apparently introduced the term to describe a reaction within modernism.[6]

More often cited as the first use of the epithet is its appearance in Arnold Toynbee's monumental multivolume *Study of History*.[7] Toynbee was convinced that a new historical epoch had begun, although he apparently changed his mind as to whether it was inaugurated by World War I or had emerged already in the 1870s.[8]

In Toynbee's analysis, the postmodern era is marked by the end of Western dominance and the decline of individualism, capitalism, and Christianity. He argues that the transition occurred as Western civilization drifted into irrationality and relativism. When this occurred, according to Toynbee, power shifted from the West to non-Western cultures and a new pluralist world culture.

Although the term was coined in the 1930s, postmodernism as a cultural phenomenon did not gain momentum until three or four decades later. It appeared first on the fringes of society. During the 1960s, the mood that would characterize postmodernism became attractive to artists, architects, and thinkers who were seeking to offer radical alternatives to the dominant modern culture. Even theologians got in the act, as William Hamilton and Thomas J. J. Altizer invoked the ghost of Nietzsche to proclaim the death of God.[9] These varied developments led "culture watcher" Leslie Fiedler in 1965 to affixed the label "postmodern" to the radical counterculture of the day.[10]

During the 1970s, the postmodern challenge to modernity infiltrated further into mainstream culture. By mid-decade it produced one of its most articulate defenders, Ihab Hassan, acclaimed as the "most consistent promoter of the idea of the 'postmodern turn.'"[11] This self-proclaimed spokesperson for postmodernism tied the phenomenon to experimentalism in the arts and ultratechnology in architecture.[12]

But the postmodern ethos was rapidly expanding beyond these two realms. University professors in various humanities departments began to speak about postmodernism, some even becoming infatuated with postmodern ideas.

Eventually, the adoption of the new ethos became so widespread that the designation "postmodern" crystallized as the overarching label for a diverse social and cultural phenomenon. The postmodern storm swept through various aspects of culture and several academic disciplines, most notably influencing literature, architecture, film, and philosophy.[13]

In the 1980s, the move from fringe to mainstream came to completion. Increasingly, the postmodern mood invaded pop culture and even the day-to-day world of the larger society. Postmodern ideas became not only acceptable but popular: it was "cool" to be postmodern. Consequently, culture critics could speak of the "unbearable lightness of being postmodern."[14] When postmodernism became an accepted part of the culture, postmodernity was born.

The Progenitor of Postmodernity

Between 1960 and 1990 postmodernism emerged as a cultural phenomenon. But why? How can we account for the meteoric rise of this ethos in our society? Many observers link the transition to changes that occurred in society during the second half of the twentieth century. No factor, however, looms more significant than the arrival of the information era. In fact, the spread of postmodernism parallels and has been dependent on the transition to an information society.[15]

Many historians label the modern era "the industrial age," because the period was dominated by manufacturing. Focusing as it did on the production of goods, modernity produced the industrial society, the symbol of which was the factory. The postmodern era, in contrast, focuses on the production of information. We are witnessing a transition from an industrial society to an information society, the symbol of which is the computer.

Job statistics offer clear evidence that we are experiencing a shift from an industrial society to an information society. In the modern era, the vast majority of nonagricultural employment opportunities centered in the manufacturing sector of the economy and involved the production of goods. By the late 1970s, however, only 13 percent of American workers were involved in the manufacture of goods, whereas a full 60 percent were engaged in the "manufacture" of information.[16] As fewer and fewer workers are needed to stand at the assembly line, training for careers related to information—whether as a data processor or a consultant—has become almost essential.

The information society has produced a whole new class of persons. The proletariat has given place to the "cognitariat."[17] And for business, the emergence of the postmodern society has meant a shift from the modern technique of centralized control to the new model of "networking." Hierarchical structures have been replaced by a more decentralized, participatory form of decision making.

The information age has not only altered the work we do but brought the world together in a manner never before possible. The information society functions on the basis of an organized communication network that spans the globe. The efficiency of this integrated system is astounding. In the past, information could spread no faster than human beings could travel. But now information can transverse the globe at the speed of light. More important than the modern ability to travel around the world relatively quickly and painlessly is the postmodern capability to gain information from almost anywhere on earth almost instantaneously.

As a consequence of the global communication system, we now have at our fingertips access to knowledge of events throughout the world. In this sense, we do indeed inhabit a global village.

The advent of the global village has produced seemingly self-contradictory effects. The mass culture and global economy that the age of information is creating are uniting the world into what one droll observer has called "McWorld."[18] But at the same time that the planet is coming together on one level, it is falling apart on another. The advent of postmodernity has fostered simultaneously both a global consciousness and the erosion of national consciousness.

Nationalism has diminished in the wake of a movement toward "retribalization," toward increased loyalty to a more local context. This impulse is found not only in the countries of Africa but also in such unlikely places as Canada, which is repeatedly plagued by threats of secession by the largely French-speaking province of Quebec and by feelings of alienation among its Western provinces. People are increasingly following the new dictum: "Think globally, act locally."

The advent of the postindustrial information society as the successor to the modern industrial society provides the foundation for the postmodern ethos.[19] Life within the global village imbues its citizens with a vivid awareness of the cultural diversity of our planet—an awareness that seems to be encouraging us to adopt a new pluralist mind-set. This new mind-set embraces more than just tolerance for other practices and viewpoints: it affirms and celebrates diversity. The celebration of cultural diversity, in turn, demands a new style—eclecticism—the style of postmodernity.

The information society has also witnessed a shift from mass production to segmented production. The repetitive manufacture of identical objects has given way to the fast-changing production of many different objects. We are moving away from the mass culture of modernity, which offered a few styles that changed with the seasons, toward a fragmented "taste culture," which offers an almost endless variety of styles. High school students, who once defined themselves in terms of a relatively few social categories, such as jocks and nerds, now think in terms of as many as a dozen different categories, reflecting differing tastes and styles.

The Uncentered Realm of Postmodernism

These characteristics indicate that in an important sense the postmodern ethos is centerlessness. No clear shared focus unites the diverse and divergent elements of postmodern society into a single whole. There are no longer any common standards to which people can appeal in their efforts to measure, judge, or value ideas, opinions, or lifestyle choices. Gone as well are old allegiances to a common source of authority and a commonly regarded and respected wielder of legitimate power.

As the center dissolves, our society is increasingly becoming a conglomerate of societies. These smaller social units have little in common apart from geographic proximity.

> The postmodern condition . . . manifests itself in the multiplication
> of centres of power and activity and the dissolution of every kind
> of totalizing narrative which claims to govern the whole complex
> field of social activity and representation.
> Steven Connor, *Postmodernist Culture*
> (Oxford: Basil Blackwell, 1989), p. 9.

The postmodern philosopher Michel Foucault offers a name for this centerless postmodern universe: "heterotopia."[20] Foucault's designation underlines the monumental shift away from modernity that we are witnessing. The Enlightenment belief in inevitable progress provided the motivation for the utopian vision of modernity. The architects of modernity sought to design the one perfect human society in which peace, justice, and love would reign— utopia. Postmoderns no longer dream of utopia. In its place they can offer only the incommensurable diversity of the postmodern heterotopia, the "multiverse" that has replaced the universe of the modern quest.

POSTMODERNISM AS A CULTURAL PHENOMENON

The loss of centeredness introduced by the postmodern ethos has become one of the chief characteristics of our contemporary situation. It is perhaps most evident in the cultural life of our society.[21] The arts have undergone a profound transition as we have moved from modernity to postmodernity.

The Postmodern Celebration of Diversity

The central hallmark of postmodern cultural expression is pluralism. In celebration of this pluralism, postmodern artists deliberately juxtapose seemingly contradictory styles derived from immensely different sources. This technique not only serves to celebrate diversity but also offers a means to express a subtle rejection of the dominance of rationality in a playful or ironic manner. Postmodern cultural works are often "double-coded," carrying meaning on two levels. Many postmodern artists have employed features of older styles specifically in order to reject or ridicule certain aspects of modernity.

One widely used juxtaposing technique is the *collage*, which offers the artist a natural means of bringing together incompatible source materials. At the same time, by allowing for obvious confiscation, quotation, or repetition of existing images, the collage heightens the postmodern critique of the myth of the single, creating author. A related juxtaposing tactic is *bricolage*, the reconfiguration of various traditional objects (typically elements from previous stages in the tradition of the artistic medium) in order to achieve some contemporary purpose or make an ironic statement.

> Post-Modernism is fundamentally the eclectic mixture of any tradition with that of the immediate past: it is both the continuation of Modernism and its transcendence. Its best works are characteristically doubly-coded and ironic, making a feature of the wide choice, conflict and discontinuity of traditions, because the heterogeneity most clearly captures our pluralism.
>
> Charles Jencks, *What Is Post-Modernism?* 3d ed.
> (New York: St. Martin's Press, 1989), p. 7.

The postmodern artist's use of diverse styles means that postmodern works often reflect an eclecticism that draws from many historical eras. Purists consider this sort of juxtaposition abominable, on the grounds that it violates the integrity of historical styles for the sake of making an impression in the present. These critics fault the postmodern form of expression for moving beyond history to a flat present without depth or extension, in which styles and histories circulate interchangeably.[22] They find postmodernism lacking in originality and crassly devoid of style.

But there is a deeper principle operative in postmodern cultural expressions. The intent of postmodern works is not necessarily tastelessness. Rather, postmoderns often seek to undermine the concept of the powerful originating author. They attempt to destroy what they see as the modernist ideology of style, replacing it with a culture of multiple styles. To achieve this end, many postmodern artists confront their audience with a multiplicity of styles, a seemingly discordant polyphony of decontextualized voices. This technique— lifting elements of style from their original historical context—is what their critics denounce as the dislocation and flattening of history.[23]

Regardless of the opinions of these critics, however, postmodernism is exerting a powerful influence on contemporary Western culture. The juxtaposition of styles, with an accompanying emphasis of diversity and deemphasis of rationality, has become a hallmark of our society and is evident in a wide range of contemporary cultural expressions.

Postmodern Architecture

In architecture, as in other aspects of culture, modernism dominated until the 1970s. Modernist architects throughout the West developed what came to be known as the International Style. As an expression of the wider modernist ethos, this architectural movement was guided by faith in human rationality and the hope of constructing a human utopia.

Imbued with modern utopianism, architects constructed buildings according to the principle of unity. Frank Lloyd Wright set the pace for many others when he claimed that the modern edifice should be an organic entity. He declared that a building should be "one great thing" instead of a "quarrelling collection" of many "little things."[24] Each building should express one unified, essential meaning.

The modern commitment to the principle of unity produced an architecture characterized by what Charles Jencks calls "univalence." Modern buildings display simple, essential forms typified by the nearly universal pattern of glass-and-steel boxes. Architects attain simplicity of form by allowing one theme to dominate the construction, which they usually achieve by a device known as "repetition." At the same time, by their approximation to geometrical perfection, modern buildings exemplify a type of otherworldliness.

197

As it developed, the central stream of modern architecture became a universalizing movement. It promoted the program of industrialization and demoted the variety characteristic of local expression. As a consequence, the expansion of modern architecture often destroyed the existing urban fabric. It virtually decimated everything that stood in the way of the bulldozer, the chief tool of the modern quest for "progress."[25]

Some modernist architects were not satisfied to limit the modern vision to their own discipline. They believed that architecture should become the visible expression of a new unity of art, science, and industry.

> Together let us desire, conceive, and create the new structure of the future, which will embrace architecture and sculpture and painting in one unity and which will one day rise toward heaven from the hands of a million workers like the crystal symbol of a new faith.
> Walter Gropius, "Programme of the staatliches Bauhaus in Weimar" (1919), in *Programmes and Manifestoes on Twentieth-Century Architecture*. ed. Ulrich Conrads, trans. Michael Bullock (London: Lund Humphries, 1970), p. 25.

Postmodern architecture emerged in response to certain tendencies in modernist architecture. Instead of the modern ideal of univalence, postmoderns celebrate "multivalence." Postmodern architects reject as too austere the modernist requirement that buildings be designed to reflect an absolute unity. Their works, in contrast, purposely explore and display incompatibilities of style, form, and texture.

The rejection of modern architecture is evident in several features of the postmodern reaction. For example, in response to the modernist contempt for anything unessential or superfluous, postmodern buildings give place to ornamentation. Further, where modernist architects sought to demonstrate an absolute break with the past by rigorously purging from their designs any relics of earlier eras, postmodernist architects retrieve historical styles and techniques.

Lying behind the postmodern rejection of modernist architecture is a deeper principle. Postmoderns claim that all architecture is inherently symbolic. All buildings, including modern structures, speak a kind of language. In their quest for pure functionality, many modernist architects sought to banish this dimension. But after the modern scalpel has cut away everything that does not conform to the utility principle, postmoderns claim, all that is left is the technique of building. Eliminated is the artistic dimension that allows a structure to represent an imaginary world or to convey a story. Postmoderns complain that none of the architectural wonders of the past, such as the great cathedrals, which point to another realm, could have been built during the reign of modernism.

> A building itself has the power, by having been built right or wrong or mute or noisy, to be what it wants to be, to say what it wants to say, which starts us looking at buildings for what they are saying rather than just accepting their pure existence in the Corbusian manner.
>
> Charles Moore, in *Conversations with*
> *Architects*, ed. John Cook and Heinrich Klotz
> (New York: Praeger, 1973), p. 243.

Through such devices as the addition of ornamentation, postmoderns are attempting to restore what they call the "fictional" element to architecture. They want to rescue the discipline from its captivity to pure utility and reinstitute its role in creating "inventive places."[26]

But the postmodern critique of modernist architecture is even more extensive. Postmoderns challenge modernism's claims to universality and its assertions of transhistorical value. They argue that, contrary to the assertions of the modernists, their archictectual accomplishments were less expressions of reason or logic than they were articulations of a language of power. Modern buildings derive their language from the industrial forms and materials of the modern era and the industrial system they served.[27] These forms and materials give expression to the brave new world of science and technology.[28]

Postmodernists want to abandon this language of power to which modernist architects are seemingly oblivious. They want to move away from what they see as the dehumanizing uniformity of an architecture that speaks the language of standardized mass production. In its place, postmoderns seek to explore new hybrid languages that incorporate the postmodern concepts of diversity and pluralism.

Postmodern Art

Postmodern architecture was born out of a rejection of the principles of the predominant modernist architecture of the twentieth century. Postmodernism has made its presence felt in the world of art in a similar manner.

Modernist architecture seeks to rid itself of all remnants of preceding styles. Art theorists such as Clement Greenberg define modernist art in similar terms.[29] Modernism becomes what it is by engaging in self criticism in order to purge itself of what it is not; modern artists engage in this sort of self-criticism in order to render their art "pure."[30] Thus, the expression of modernism in art, like its expression in architecture, follows the univalence impulse. One of the great virtues for modernist artists, then, is stylistic integrity.

Postmodernist art, in contrast, moves from an awareness of the connectedness between what it acknowledges as its own and what it excludes. For this reason, it embraces stylistic diversity, or "multivalence." It chooses "impurity" rather than the "purity" of modernism.

Many postmodern artists conjoin diversity with the typically postmodern technique of juxtaposition. As we have already noted, one of their favorite forms of composition is the collage. In fact, Jacques Derrida, who has been called "the 'Aristotle' of montage," considers the collage to be the primary form of postmodern discourse.[31] A collage naturally draws the viewer into the production of its meaning, and the inherent "heterogeneity" of the collage ensures that the meaning it elicits can be neither univocal nor stable. It continually invites the viewer to find new meaning in its juxtaposition of images.

> At root Post-Modern art is neither exclusionary nor reductive but synthetic, freely enlisting the full range of conditions, experiences, and knowledge beyond the object. Far from seeking a single and complete experience, the Post-Modern object strives toward an encyclopedic condition, allowing a myriad of access points, an infinitude of interpretive responses.
>
> Howard Fox, "Avant-Garde in the Eighties," in
> *The Post-Avant-Garde: Painting in the Eighties*, ed. Charles
> Jencks (London: Academy Editions, 1987), pp. 29-30.

Pressed to its limits, artistic juxtaposition becomes what is sometimes termed *pastiche*. The goal of this tactic, which has been employed in both high-culture and pop-culture contexts (e.g., MTV videos), is to barrage the viewer with incongruous, even clashing images that call into question any sense of objective meaning. The disjointed, unharmonious design of pastiche with its gaudy color schemes, discordant typography, and the like, has moved beyond the world of avant-garde art into the everyday realm of book jackets, magazine covers, and mass advertising.

Postmodern artists don't view stylistic diversity merely as a means to grab attention. The attraction is deeper than that. It's part of a more general postmodern attitude, a desire to challenge the power of modernity as invested in institutions and canonical traditions. Postmodern artists seek to challenge the modernist focus on the stylistic integrity of the individual work and undermine what they see as the modernist "cult" of the individual artist. They seek ways of purposely denying the singleness of works of art. Through methods such as obvious confiscation, quotation, excerption, accumulation, and repetition of already existing images, they attack the "fiction" of the creating subject.[32]

An example of this radical postmodern critique can be found in the work of the photographic artist Sherrie Levine. For one exhibition, Levine rephotographed well-known artistic photographs of Walker Evans and Edward Weston and presented them as her own. Her act of art piracy was so obvious that she could not be charged with simple plagiarism. Her goal was not to fool anyone into believing that someone else's work was her own but rather to call into question the idea of a distinction between an "original work" and its public reproduction.[33]

Postmodern Theater

In a sense, the theater is perhaps the most appropriate artistic venue for the expression of the postmodern rejection of modernism. The modernist movement saw a work of art as transcending time, as expressing timeless ideals. The postmodern ethos, in contrast, celebrates transience—and transience is inherent in performance.[34] Postmoderns view life, like the story told on the stage, as an assemblage of intersecting narratives. That being the case, what better way to depict transience and performance than through the cultural medium that is intrinsically dependent on these two features.

Despite this close connection, obviously not every theatrical production is an expression of the postmodern ethos. Many scholars date postmodern theater to the upsurge of performance art during the 1960s.[35] Its roots lie further back, however, in the work of the French writer Antonin Artaud in the 1930s.

Artaud challenged artists—especially dramatists—to become protesters who would destroy what he considered to be the idolatry of classical art. He advocated replacing the traditional stage and the production of theatrical masterpieces with a "theater of cruelty." He called for the abandonment of the older script-centered style and an exploration of the language intrinsic to theater, which includes light, color, movement, gesture, and space.[36] In addition, Artaud advocated transcending the distinctions between actors and observers and drawing the audience into the dramatic experience. It was Artaud's intent to force the audience to confront the primal reality of life that lies beyond all social convention.[37]

In the 1960s, aspects of Artaud's dream began to become a reality. As theorists rethought the nature of theatrical expression, they called for the freeing of performance from its subservience to what they saw as the repressive power of the traditional authorities.

Some of the new theorists concluded that this repressive power was exercised by the underlying script or text.[38] To solve the problem, they eliminated the script and made each performance immediate and unique. Once performed, each work would truly disappear forever.[39]

Other theorists attributed the repressive power to the director.[40] They sought to solve the problem by emphasizing improvisation and group authorship. And, moving against all classical conventions, they celebrated the resulting loss of the concept of the theatrical work as a unified production.

Postmodern theatrical performance builds on these earlier experiments. It sets in opposition different constituents of performance, such as sound, light, music, language, setting, and movement. In this manner, postmodern theater displays a specific theory of performance—an "aesthetics of absence" in contrast to the older "aesthetics of presence."[41] The aesthetics of absence rejects the idea that a performance ought to evidence a sense of underlying, permanent truth. It maintains that the sense of presence that the performance evokes can be no more than an "empty presence." In keeping with the postmodern ethos generally, the meaning of the performance can be only transient, dependent on the situation or context in which it occurs.

> The stage will no longer operate as the repetition of a present, will
> no longer *re*-present a present that would exist elsewhere and prior
> to it, a present whose plenitude would be older than it, absent from
> it, and rightfully capable of doing without it: the being-present-to-
> itself of the absolute Logos, the living present of God.
>
> Jacques Derrida, *Writing and Difference*, trans. Alan Bass
> (Chicago: University of Chicago Press, 1978), p. 237.

Postmodern Fiction

The influence of the postmodern ethos on literature is particularly difficult to assess. Literary critics continue to debate exactly what it is that distinguishes postmodern fiction from its predecessors. Nevertheless, this style of writing reflects the central characteristics evidenced in the other artistic genres we have surveyed.[42]

Following the general postmodern style, postmodern fiction employs the tactic of juxtaposing. Some postmodern authors have brought together traditional forms in displaced ways in order to provide ironic treatments of otherwise perennial themes.[43] Others have juxtaposed the real and the fictitious.

This juxtaposition may involve the characters themselves. Some postmodern author-narrators draw attention to the fictitiousness of the characters and their actions at one point and present the same characters as participants in a kind of history at another point, thereby evoking from the reader the same sort of moral or emotional response evoked in traditional realistic fiction.

Some postmodern authors juxtapose the real and the fictitious by interjecting themselves into the work. They may even discuss the problems and processes involved in the act of narration. Through this paradoxical device, the author blurs the distinction between the real and the fictional. The tactic also underlines the close connection between author and fictional work. Insofar as the fiction is the vehicle through which the author speaks, the author's voice is no longer separable from the fictional story

Postmodern fiction repeatedly juxtaposes two or more pure, autonomous worlds. When this occurs, the characters who inhabit the literature are often confused as to which world they are in and uncertain about how they should act in this "close encounter."

As is the case in the use of this postmodern technique in other genres, juxtaposition is used in literature with a specific, antimodernist purpose. The goal of the modernist writer was to gain a handle on the meaning of a complex but nevertheless singular reality. Postmoderns, in contrast, raise questions about how radically different realities can coexist and interpenetrate.

Like other postmodern cultural expressions, postmodern literary works focus on contingency and temporality, implicitly denying the modern ideal of an atemporal, universal truth.[44] Postmodern fiction also heightens the focus on temporality in order to dislodge the reader from his or her attempt to view the world from a vantage point outside time. Postmodern authors want to leave the reader naked in a world devoid of eternal essences that are unaffected by the flow of time and the contingencies of temporal context.[45]

> And need one say that the more nakedly the author appears to reveal himself in such texts, the more inescapable it becomes, paradoxically, that the author as a *voice* is only a function of his own fiction, a rhetorical construct, not a privileged authority but an object of interpretation?
>
> David Lodge, "Mimesis and Diegesis in Modern Fiction,"
> in *The Post-Modern Reader*, ed. Charles Jencks
> (New York: St. Martin's Press, 1992), pp. 194-95.

Postmodern authors sometimes achieve the same effect by incorporating language that breaks closed thought structures or calls into question the standard canons of reason as a means of denying that any discourse is ultimately capable of presenting an account of the real.[46]

Perhaps the best representative of modernist fiction was the detective story. Fictional works such as the adventures of Sherlock Holmes take the reader on a quest to uncover the hidden truth that lies beneath the perplexing surface of reality. Despite what appears to be an insufficient number of clues, master detectives always manage to solve the mystery in the end. They will often then almost condescendingly show the audience (represented by some awed observer in the text, such as Dr. Watson in the Holmes mysteries) how the application of human powers of observation and reason to the facts of the situation lead inevitably and logically to the correct conclusion. In this manner, the seemingly disjointed narrative becomes a unified whole.

One typically postmodern fictional form is the spy novel.[47] Although set in the context of the contemporary "real" world, this type of narrative in fact juxtaposes two radically different worlds. The most obvious is the realm of appearance, which seems to reflect the real but soon turns out to be an illusion. Operative beneath and within the realm of appearance is a second realm, which is somewhat sinister and is generally more authentic than the "real" world.

By juxtaposing these two realms, the story holds the reader in a continual state of uncertainty. Is anyone truly who he or she appears to be? What is actually real and true, and what is deception and danger?

The spy story leads us to raise the same questions about our own world. Are we also living between two juxtaposed realms? Are people and events around us truly what they appear to be?

Science fiction is a less subtle postmodern genre.[48] It more obviously presents a rejection of the modern quest. Typically, science fiction stories are less interested in uncovering timeless truth than in exploring otherness. They bring other worlds or other realities into our vision in order to highlight the disparities between them.

Science fiction leads us to ask the central philosophical questions about our world: What is reality? What is possible? What forces are really at work?

POSTMODERNISM AS A PHENOMENON IN POPULAR CULTURE

Most of us have likely had our most direct contact with postmodernism through science fiction and spy stories, for these have penetrated deeply into the popular culture of our day. But through our immersion in our world, we are constantly and often unconsciously exposed to—even bombarded with—the postmodern ethos.

In a sense, exposure to the postmodern ethos through popular culture is itself characteristically postmodern. The refusal to set "high art" above "pop" culture is a defining feature of postmodernity.[49] Postmodernism is unique among avant-garde movements in that it appeals not to an artistic elite but to all those engaged in the activities of daily life through popular culture and the mass media.

To this end, postmodern works often display another type of double coding. They speak a language and use elements that are accessible to nonprofessionals as well as professional artists and architects. In this manner, postmodern expressions bring the professional and the popular realms together.[50]

Filmmaking as the Foundation for Postmodern Culture

Certain technological developments have facilitated postmodernism's penetration into the most influential dimensions of popular culture. One of the most significant of these is the development of the film industry.

Filmmaking technology fits the postmodern ethos in that its products— films—give the illusion of being what they are not. The film may appear to be a unified narrative presented by a specific group of performers, but in fact it is a technological artifact assembled by a variety of specialists from a range of materials and with a range of techniques that are seldom evident in the film itself. In this sense, the unity of a film is largely an illusion.

For example, a film is different from a theatrical production in that it is almost never the record of a single performance by a group of actors. What the viewer sees as a continuous, unified performance is actually a kind of residue that emerges from a sequence of events—the making of the film—that was disjointed in both time and space.

The scenes themselves participate in the "hoax." What appears to be a continuous narrative moving from start to finish is actually a compilation of events filmed at various times and in various locations. Indeed, the sequence in which the scenes appear in the film seldom reflects the order in which they were filmed. What unity there is in the film is imposed by the editor, who assembles the footage into the finished product.

Nor are the characters necessarily represented by the same actors throughout the film. Filmmakers have long employed stunt doubles in the filming of hazardous scenes, for example. And new technologies make possible the editing of individual frames of the film to insert duplicate images of an actor, actors from old films into new productions, and even wholly computer-generated images.

In the end, the film we view is the product of technology. Different teams use photography and other methods to assemble an accumulation of materials that the editor then combines (with the help of other techniques to preserve the illusion) to produce what seems to the viewer to be a unified whole. But, in contrast to a theatrical production, a film derives its unity from technology rather than from the contribution of the human actors.[51]

Because the unity of a film lies in the techniques of the filmmaking process rather than in the narrative as such, filmmakers have considerable freedom to fracture and manipulate the story in various ways. They are able, for instance, to juxtapose scenes depicting incompatible topics and themes drawn from footage shot at spatially or temporally separated locations without compromising the unity of the whole.

Postmodern filmmakers delight in collapsing space and time into an eternal here-and-now. Their efforts in this regard are facilitated by the growing body of previously produced film on which they can draw in various ways to augment fresh footage. Thus we see Humphrey Bogart in scenes of *The Last Action Hero* and Groucho Marx in a Diet Pepsi commercial. New technology promises to make possible even more disjunctive mergers of the "real world" with other realities, along the lines of the juxtaposition of cartoon and human characters in the box office hit *Who Framed Roger Rabbit?*

The ability to juxtapose diverse pieces of footage into what for the viewer becomes a unified whole gives the filmmaker a unique opportunity to blur distinctions between "truth"' and "fiction," "reality" and "fantasy." Postmodern filmmakers have exploited these capabilities to express the postmodern ethos. For example, postmodern films treat the purely fictitious and fantastic with the same seriousness as the real (e.g., in *Groundhog Day*). They endow a purely fictional story with the air of a documentary (e.g., in *The Gods Must Be Crazy*). They intermix bits of the historical record with speculation and pass the whole off as historically accurate (e.g., in *JFK*). And they use filmmaking techniques to juxtapose totally incongruent worlds inhabited by characters unsure of which is truly real (e.g., in *Blue Velvet*).[52]

Living in a postmodern society means inhabiting a film-like world—a realm in which truth and fiction merge. We look at the world in the same way we look at films, suspicious that what we see around us may in fact be illusion. Despite a film's disjunctions, however, the viewer can at least be certain that it expresses something about the minds that produced it; the filmmaker provides an often unattended center to the world the film creates. Looking at the world, on the other hand, postmoderns are no longer confident that any Mind lies behind it.

Television and the Dissemination of Postmodern Culture

Filmmaking technology may have provided the foundation for postmodern pop culture, but television proved a more efficient vehicle for disseminating the postmodern ethos throughout society.

Viewed from one perspective, television is merely the most effective means to date for transmitting "film" from its creators to the public. Much of television programming simply consists of broadcasting what a multitude of filmmakers produce in a variety of formats ranging from the short commercial to the miniseries. Television is a medium through which film invades the day-to-day lives of millions of people, and in this sense it can be viewed simply as an extension of the film industry.

But beyond its connection with film, television displays characteristics uniquely its own. There are ways in which television is more flexible than film. A film is a static finished product. Television can go beyond this to offer live broadcasting. The television camera can give viewers a picture of events as they are happening almost anywhere in the world.

This ability to provide the viewer with a live picture of an event leads many people to believe that television presents actual events in themselves—without interpretation, editing, or commentary. For this reason, television has quickly become the "real world" of postmodern culture, and television reporting has emerged as the new test for being real. Many viewers don't think something is really important unless it shows up on CNN, *Sixty Minutes*, or a made-for-TV miniseries. Anything not submitted to the "ontological test" of being aired on television is relegated to the periphery of life in contemporary society.[53]

Television has the ability both to offer live broadcasting of the "facts" happening in our world and to disseminate the products of the filmmaker's creativity. This double ability endows television with a unique power. It has the ability to juxtapose "truth" (what the public perceives as actual event) with "fiction" (what the public perceives as never having actually happened in the "real" world) in ways that film cannot. And, indeed, contemporary television performs this feat incessantly. It happens, for example, every time a live telecast is interrupted for "a word from our sponsor."

Television exceeds the capacity of film to realize the postmodern ethos in another sense as well. As a matter of course, commercial television broadcasting presents the viewer with an ongoing variety of incompatible images. A typical evening newscast, for example, will bombard the viewer with a series of unrelated images in quick succession—a war in a remote country, a murder closer to home, a sound bite from a political speech, the latest on a sex scandal, a new scientific discovery, highlights from a sporting event. This collage is interspersed with advertisements for better batteries, better soap, better cereal, and better vacations. By giving all these varied images—news stories and commercials alike—roughly equal treatment, the broadcast leaves the impression that they are all of roughly equal importance.[54]

The news broadcast is followed by a plethora of prime-time programs that seek to attract and hold an audience by focusing on action, scandal, violence, and sex. The evening's sitcoms and dramas seem to be invested with the same weight as the earlier news stories. In this manner, television blurs the line between truth and fiction, between the truly earth-shattering and the trivial.

And as though a single channel's programming did not supply the viewer with enough discordant images, contemporary television offers the viewer dozens—soon to be hundreds—of different channels. Cable and direct satellite broadcasts supply an incredible variety of viewing options, and, armed with remote control, a viewer can shuttle through the wasteland perpetually in search of something interesting—a news update, a boxing match, a financial report, an old movie, a weather forecast, a stand-up comedian, a documentary, an infomercial, or anything from the vast sea of sitcoms, cop shows, westerns, soap operas, medical dramas, and other reruns of more than four decades of network programming.

By offering its collage of images, television unintentionally juxtaposes the irreconcilable. But in addition, it obliterates spatial and temporal distinctions. It merges the past and the present, the distant and the local, bringing all together into one perpetual here-and-now—the "present" of the television viewer. In this manner, television intrinsically displays what some critics see as two central characteristics of postmodern texts: it effaces the boundary between past and present, and it locates the viewer in a perpetual present.[55]

Many social observers speak of television as representing the postmodern psychological and cultural condition. It presents a multitude of images that are readily detached from their reference to reality, images that circulate and interact in a ceaseless, centerless flow.[56]

And film and television have been joined by a newer and increasingly popular conduit of information—the personal computer.

The advent of "the screen"—whether the movie, the television, or the computer screen—epitomizes the postmodern blurring of the traditional contrast between the subjective self and the objective world. The screen is not merely an external object that we look at. What happens on the screen is neither wholly "out there" (merely on the screen), nor wholly in us; rather, it seems to occur in some space between the two.[57] The screen brings us into its world just as it enters into ours. As what happens on the screen becomes an extension of ourselves, we become an extension of it. The screen thus becomes an embodied form of our psychic worlds.

Living in the postmodern era means inhabiting a world created by the juxtaposition of diverse images. The world of the screen blurs undifferentiated images into a fragmented present, and postmoderns who are wedded to this world remain unsure that it is anything more than a blur of images.

> The disappearing ego [is] the victory sign of postmodernism . . . .
> The self is transformed into an empty screen of an exhausted, but hyper-technical culture.
>
> Arthur Kroker, Marilouise Kroker, and David Cook,
> "Panic Alphabet," in *Panic Encyclopedia: The Definitive
> Guide to the Postmodern Scene* (Montreal: New
> World Perspectives, 1989), p. 16.

Other Expressions of Postmodernism in Pop Culture

Film may have made postmodern popular culture possible, and television may have disseminated that culture, but rock music is probably the most representative form of postmodern pop culture.[58] The lyrics of many rock songs reflect postmodern themes, but the connection between rock music and postmodern pop culture runs deeper. Rock music embodies a central hallmark of postmodernity: its dual focus on the global and the local.

Contemporary rock music now enjoys a global audience, endowing it with world-unifying capabilities. We need only remind ourselves of the international following that allows popular rock figures to embark on highly profitable "world tours." At the same time, though, rock music retains a local flavor. In the offerings of the big stars and the small-town bands alike, rock reflects a plurality of styles borrowed from local and ethnic musical forms.

Equally significant as an embodiment of the postmodern ethos is the connection to electronic production that rock music shares with television and filmmaking. A crucial dimension of the rock culture is the live performances of its most popular stars. But today's "live" experience no longer takes the traditional form of an intimate concert in which the performer seeks to communicate directly with audience. Far more often it consists of what some observers call "manufactured mass closeness."[59]

Today's rock concert is typically a mass event, involving audiences numbering in the tens of thousands. Most fans in attendance are simply too far away to see the performers on the stage clearly. Even so, they still manage to "experience" the event. The performance is brought to them through the use of enormous video screens that relay closeups of the performer throughout the location. This technique both abolishes and re-emphasizes the actual distance between performer and audience. Jubilant fans feel close to their hero despite the fact that the performer's presence is artificial, mediated by a screen. Technology transforms the intimacy of a "live performance" into a mass gathering of fans who watch "live" videos together while being bombarded with special effects.

Technology also blurs the distinction between the original performance and its reproduction. It breaks down the distinction between the "live" and the reproduced dimensions of the musical experience. In fact, the performance is no longer a separate reality lying behind the particular context in which it occurs. Rather, it is a blend of what the performers do and a technological reproduction of their actions. The performance is enmeshed in the technology that delivers it to the audience.

Perhaps more subtle than the interplay between postmodernism and rock music is the presence of the postmodern ethos in contemporary clothing styles. Postmodern fashions reveal the same tendencies found in other pop cultural expressions. We see it in the popularity of clothes that prominently display trademarks and product labels, for example, a feature that blurs the distinction between fashion and advertising.

Above all, the postmodern outlook is evident in what is called "bricolage." In pointed defiance of the traditional attempt to coordinate individual pieces of clothing in a unified look, the postmodern style intentionally juxtaposes incompatible or heterogeneous elements, such as garments and accessories from each of the preceding four decades.

As in other expressions of postmodernism, the juxtaposition of traditionally incompatible fashion elements is not merely random. It may be calculated to produce an ironic effect or to parody modern fashion norms or perhaps the modern fashion industry as a whole.[60]

> From rock music to tourism to television and even education, advertising imperatives and consumer demand are no longer for goods, but for experiences.
>
> Steven Connor, *Postmodernist Culture*
> (Oxford: Basil Blackwell, 1989), p. 154.

The pop culture of our day reflects the centerless pluralism of postmodernity and gives expression to the antirationalism of postmodernism. As evidenced in the clothes they wear and the music they listen to, postmoderns are no longer convinced that their world has a center or that human reason can perceive any logical structure in the external universe. They live in a world in which the distinction between truth and fiction has evaporated. Consequently, they become collectors of experiences, repositories of transitory, fleeting images produced and fostered by the diversity of media forms endemic in postmodern society.

Postmodernism assumes various forms. It is embodied in certain attitudes and expressions that touch the day-to-day lives of a broad diversity of people in contemporary society. Such expressions range from fashions to television and include such pervasive aspects of popular culture as music and film. Postmodernism is likewise incarnated in a variety of cultural expressions including architecture, art, and literature. But postmodernism is above all an intellectual outlook.

Postmodernism rejects the very idea of the solitary scholar born of the Enlightenment. Postmoderns denounce the pretense of those who claim to view the world from a transcendent vantage point from which they are able to speak imperiously to and on behalf of all humankind. Postmoderns have replaced this Enlightenment ideal with the belief that all claims to truth—and ultimately even truth itself—are socially conditioned.

NOTES

[1] Steven Connor, *Postmodernist Culture* (Oxford: Basil Blackwell, 1989), p. 69.

[2] Jencks, *The Language of Post-Modern Achitecture*, 4th ed. (London: Academy Editions, 1984), p. 9. See also Jencks, "The Post-Modern Agenda," in *The Postmodern Reader*, ed. Charles Jencks (New York: St. Martin's Press, 1992), p. 24.

[3] Jencks, "The Post-Modern Agenda," p. 11.

[4] For a helpful discussion of the origins of the term, see Margaret Rose, "Defining the Post-Modern," in *The Post-Modern Reader*, pp. 119-36.

[5] Already in the 1930s it served as the designation for certain developments in the arts. Craig Van Gelder, "Postmodernism as an Emerging Worldview," *Calvin Theological Journal* 26 (November 1991): 412.

[6] Jencks, *What is Post-Modernism?* 3d ed. (New York: St. Martin's Press, 1989), p. 8.

[7] Steven Connor, *Postmodernist Culture* (Oxford: Basil Blackwell, 1989), p. 65.

[8] For a discussion of Toynbee's use of the term and its meaning, see Rose, "Defining the Post-Modern," pp. 122-24. See also Margaret A. Rose, *The Post-Modern and the Post-Industrial: A Critical Analysis* (Cambridge: Cambridge University Press, 1991), pp. 9-11.

[9] Thomas J. J. Altizer and William Hamilton, *Radical Theology and the Death of God* (Indianapolis: Bobbs-Merrill, 1961). For a short discussion of this movement, see Stanley J. Grenz and Roger E. Olson, *Twentieth-Century Theology: God and the World in a Transitional Age* (Downers Grove, Ill.: InterVarsity Press, 1993), pp. 156-61.

[10] Fiedler, "The New Mutants," in *The Collected Essays of Leslie Fiedler*, vol. 2 (New York: Stein & Day, 1971), pp. 382, 389.

[11] Connor, *Postmodern Culture*, p. 204.

[12] Hassan, "The Question of Postmodernism," in *Romanticism, Modernism, Postmodernism*, ed. Harry R. Garvin (Toronto: Bucknell University Press, 1980), pp. 117-26.

[13] Connor, *Postmodernist Culture*, p. 6.

[14] Gary John Percesepe, "The Unbearable Lightness of Being Postmodern," *Christian Scholar's Review* 20 (December 1990): 18.

[15] See, e.g., Paolo Portoghesi, "What Is the Postmodern?" in *The Post-Modern Reader*, p. 211.

[16] Jencks, *What Is Postmodernism?* p. 44.

[17] Jencks, *What Is Postmodernism?* p. 44.

[18] Benjamin Barder, "Jihad vs. McWorld," *Atlantic Monthly*, March 1992, p. 53.

19 For a discussion of major works that herald the advent of a postindustrial age, see Rose, *The Post-Modern and the Post-Industrial*, pp. 21-39.

20 Foucault, *The Order of Things: An Archaeology of the Human Sciences* (New York: Pantheon Books, 1970), p. xviii.

21 For a detailed study, see Steven Connor, *Postmodernist Culture* (London: Basil Blackwell, 1989).

22 Fredric Jameson, "Postmodernism and Consumer Society," in *The Anti-Aesthetic: Essays on Postmodern Culture*, ed. Hal Foster (Port Townsend, Wash.: Bay Press, 1983), pp. 114, 115-16, 125.

23 For examples, see Jameson, "Postmodernism and Consumer Culture," pp. 116-17.

24 Wright, "Organic Architecture" (excerpt, 1910), in *Programmes and Manifestoes on Twentieth-Century Architecture*, ed. Ulrich Conrads, trans. Michael Bullock (London: Lund Humphries, 1970), p. 25.

25 Jencks, "The Post-Modern Agenda," p. 24.

26 Heinrich Klotz, "Postmodern Architecture," in *The Post-Modern Reader*, pp. 241-42.

27 Paolo Portoghesi, *After Modern Architecture*, trans. Meg Shore (New York: Rizzoli, 1982), p. 3.

28 Robert Venturi, *Learning from Las Vegas* (Cambridge: M.I.T. Press, 1977) pp. 135-36.

29 Greenberg is often credited with having provided modernist art with its most influential form of legitimation. See Connor, *Postmodernist Culture*, p. 81.

30 See Clement Greenberg, "Modernist Painting," in *Postmodern Perspectives: Issues in Contemporary Art*, ed. Howard Risatti (Englewood Cliffs, N.J.: Prentice-Hall, 1990), pp. 12-19. See also Greenberg, "Towards a Newer Laocoon," in *Pollock and After: The Critical Debate*, ed. Francis Frascina (London: Harper & Row, 1985), pp. 41-42.

31 David Harvey, "The Condition of Postmodernity," in *The Post-Modern Reader*, p. 308. Gregory L. Ulmer refers to Derrida as the Aristotle of montage in "The Objects of Post-Criticism," in *The Anti-Aesthetic*, p. 87.

32 Douglas Crimp, "On the Museum's Ruins," in *The Anti-Aesthetic*, p. 53.

33 For a discussion of Levine's intent, see Douglas Crimp, "The Photographic Activity of Postmodernism," *October* 15 (Winter 1980): 91-100.

34 Michel Benamou, "Presence as Play," in *Performance in Postmodern Culture*, ed. Michel Benamou and Charles Caramello (Milwaukee: Center for Twentieth Century Studies, 1977), p. 3.

35 See, e.g., Steven Connor, *Postmodernist Culture* (London: Basil Blackwell, 1989), p. 134.

36 Connor, *Postmodernist Culture*, p. 135.

37 Walter Truett Anderson, *Reality Isn't What It Used to Be: Theatrical Politics, Ready-to-Wear Religion, Global Myths, Primitive Chic, and Other Wonders of the Postmodern World* (San Francisco: Harper & Row, 1990), p. 49.

38 E.g., Antonin Artaud; see his essay "The Theatre of Cruelty: Second Manifesto," in *The Theatre and Its Double*, trans. Victor Corti (London: Calder & Boyers, 1970), pp. 81-87.

39 Patrice Pavis, "The Classical Heritage of Modern Drama: The Case of Postmodern Theatre," trans. Loren Kruger, *Modern Drama* 29 (1986): 16.

40 Bernard Dort, "The Liberated Performance," trans. Barbara Kerslake, *Modern Drama* 25 (1982): 62.

41 Henry Sayre, "The Object of Performance: Aesthetics into the Seventies," *Georgia Review* 37 (1983): 174.

42 For a discussion of fiction by an early postmodern literary thinker, see Ihab Hassan, *The Dismemberment of Orpheus: Towards a Postmodern Literature* (New York: Oxford University Press, 1971).

43 John Barth, "The Literature of Replenishment, Postmodernist Fiction," *Atlantic Monthly*, January 1980, pp. 65-71; Umberto Eco, "Postmodernism, Irony, the Enjoyable," in *Postscript to "The Name of the Rose"* (New York: Harcourt Brace Jovanovich, 1984), pp. 65-72.

44 Connor, *Postmodernist Culture*, p. 118.

45 William V. Spanos, "Heidegger, Kierkegaard and the Hermeneutic Circle: Towards a Postmoern Theory of Interpretation as Discourse," in *Martin Heidegger and the Question of Literature: Toward a Postmodern Literary Hermeneutics*, ed. William V. Spanos (Bloomington, Ind.: Indiana University Press, 1979), p. 135.

46 Edith Wyschogrod refers to such techniques using the term *differentiality*. See *Saints and Postmodernism: Revisioning Moral Philosophy* (Chicago: University of Chicago Press, 1990), p. xvi.

47 Anderson, *Reality Isn't What It Used to Be*, pp. 101-2.

48 Brian McHale, *Postmodernist Fiction* (New York: Methuen, 1987), pp. 59-60.

49 Andreas Huyssen, "Mapping the Postmodern," in *The Post-Modern Reader*, p. 66. See also Jameson, "Postmodernism and Consumer Society," p. 112.

50 Jim Collins, "Post-Modernism as Culmination: The Aesthetic Politics of Decentred Culture," in *The Post-Modern Reader*, p. 105.

51 See Walter Benjamin, "The Work of Art in the Age of Mechanical Reproduction," in *Illuminations*, trans. Harry Zohn (London: Fontana, 1970), pp. 219-54.

52 For a discussion of *Blue Velvet* as a postmodern film, see Norman K. Denzin, *"Blue Velvet*: Postmodern Contradictions," in *The Post-Modern Reader*, pp. 225-33.

53 Arthur Kroker and David Cook, *The Postmodern Scene: Excremental Culture and Hyper-Aesthetics* (New York: St. Martin's Press, 1986), p. 268.

54 For a discussion of this situation, see Neil Postman, *Amusing Ourselves to Death: Public Discourse in the Age of Show Business* (New York: Viking Press, 1985); and *Technolopoly: The Surrender of Culture to Technology* (New York: Vintage Books, 1993), pp. 73-82.

55 Jameson, "Post-Modernism and Consumer Society," pp. 111-25.

56 Lawrence Grossberg, "The In-Difference of Television," *Screen* 28 (1987): 28-45.

57 Jean Baudrillard, "The Ecstasy of Communication," in *The Anti-Aesthetic*, pp. 126-34.

58 Connor, *Postmodernist Culture*, p. 186.

59 Connor, *Postmodernist Culture*, p. 151.

60 Connor, *Postmodernist Culture*, p. 191.

9

A NOTE ON ADVERTISING CULTURE

Marcel Danesi

Today's world has often been characterized as a *postmodern* culture; i.e., as a culture that has lost faith in the progressive social and technological achievements that led to the *modern* world's scientific sophistication and self-assurance. Its mode of cognizing has been described by social critics as ironic, nihilistic, surreal. Human actions are not perceived to have some ulterior purpose, but to be essentially meaningless. Lifestyle advertising is, in my view, definable as a form of postmodern communication, a discourse that mirrors how contemporary humans in the mass perceive reality—as a collage of lifestyle images that reflects basic drives, desires, and sexual experiences.

Late-twentieth-century humans have largely abandoned hope in the existence of worlds other than the present one. We appear, by and large, to be sceptical and cynical about the "meaning" of human existence. We feel that there really is nothing "out there," that everything is an illusion, and that life is a momentary state of consciousness on its way to extinction.

But there is, paradoxically, a countervailing force that is also shaping our fractured psyche. On a deeper intuitive level we seem to be constantly and desperately hoping that there is a "plan" to existence, and that our otherwise

Marcel Danesi. *Interpreting Ads: A Semiotic Guide.* Ottawa: Legas Press, 1995.

senseless actions can be tied together in a teleologically meaningful way. Like the six characters in Luigi Pirandello's 1921 play, *Six Characters in Search of an Author*, we seem today to urgently need to continue our search for an author to write us into existence. The search may lead errantly to televangelism, cults, pseudo-meditation sects, and the like, but more often than not it is leading to a profound reevaluation of the meaning of consciousness and particularly of the concept of the human spirit. At a more profound level we seem to sense that there is a spiritual reality that can only be felt, not understood.

The *modern* perspective originated in the Renaissance and was reinforced in the Age of Reason. *Modern* cultures have always put their faith in human reason and in its intellectual offspring—science and logic: i.e., unlike medieval cultures, they have never searched for the design and meaning of reality solely in the words of God, but in the discoveries of science and in the theoretical creations of the logical mind. In other words, the modern mind has always believed that the world is self-contained and can be perfectly well understood by the methods of science without reference to supernatural explanations. But like the medieval mind, modern cultures have never eliminated the need for believing in God, having always felt that God is at the "centre" of the universe, that God is ultimately the "author" of the cosmological and human worlds that the mind seeks to understand through reason.

In the eighteenth century, the dizzying growth of technology and the constantly increasing certainty that science could eventually solve all human problems—perhaps even prolong life indefinitely by discovering the "life principle" and thus conquering death—brought into existence a new form of mentality. By the end of this century, the now famous assertion that "God is dead" by the German philosopher Friedrich Nietzsche (1844-1900) both acknowledged that the modern mind had run its course and that a new world view had crystallized—a world view that had lost its belief in anything beyond the immediate material form of existence.

The term *postmodernism* came out of the field of architecture to describe the eclectic, colourful variety of building styles that urban architects were beginning to design more and more in the seventies. Immediately after it was coined, the term caught on like wildfire in academic circles, and is now used to describe everything from contemporary paintings to the methods of artificial intelligence. *Postmodernism* can be defined simply as the world view of

218

late-twentieth-century urban culture that everything "out there" is a figment of the human mind. That there is no absolute truth in our histories and in our scientific theories. It is, therefore, a term that has come forward to nicely capture the view that all knowledge and history are expressions of the human mind, not "discoveries" made by the mind.

In my view, there is little doubt that the contemporary version of the postmodern mind has been in large part fostered by our advertising-mediated culture. Viewing the world through a television camera or through magazine ads is bound, eventually, to lead to a perspective that Solomon (1988: 212) aptly characterizes as "perceptual montage." This means that we tend at times to gaze upon the world as if it were a TV program or a scene in an ad. Day in and day out these fragmented images of life are bound to influence our overall view that reality is illusory, surreal as in most lifestyle advertising since about the middle part of the twentieth century. Ultimately, we are led to form the view that human actions are a montage of disconnected images, desires, feelings, etc.

Language in the postmodern mind takes on a new modality of representation: it is either imbued with irony or else it is reduced to mere verbal recipes, stock phrases, and the kind of formulaic discourse that ads constantly promulgate. It is not tied to a larger social, religious, or philosophical narrative. It is instantaneous, satisfying immediate desires. The postmodern mind is ahistorical and nihilistic. As the sociologist Zygmunt Bauman (1992: vii-viii) has perceptively remarked, postmodernism is "a state of mind marked above all by its all-deriding, all-eroding, all-dissolving *destructiveness.*"

Traditionally, the religious forms of discourse—gospels, catechisms, sacred books, etc.—have always had, as one of their intents, the promulgation of the "good news" about the origin, development, and destiny of humanity. This is in fact the meaning of the word *gospel.* Today, the good news, as Bachand (1992: 6) aptly claims, "is being announced by advertisers." Advertising now constitutes a form of discourse that celebrates consumption; it is the liturgy of consumerism. But this new catechism has no "divine author" with meaningful "answers to life." Its discourse categories merely announce that: "If you buy this or that, then you will be eternally young, sexy, happy, etc." No wonder, then, that mythic-religious themes pervade modern advertising. What is implicit in the advertising discourse is consumeristic prophecy—a postmodern replacement of eschatological prophecy which once proclaimed the immanence of the afterlife in the present world. As Bachand (1992: 7) eloquently puts it: "The product literally seems like a creation emerging from the depths of formless matter to provide endless satisfaction."

As Spitzer (1978) has noted, it is ironic to contemplate that traditional Protestantism may have been the motivating force behind advertising's evolution and installment, since it has always encouraged the accumulation of goods in the world. As a consequence, it has unwittingly legitimized the contemporary discourse of advertising. The advertiser has, in a basic social sense, taken over the role of the preacher, promulgating the good news and the constant need to improve oneself. As Bachand (1992: 7) states: "There is a sermon in each advertisement; and all advertisers devote themselves to proclaiming their faith and the means of attaining paradise on earth through consumption and, in the meantime, through communication."

How did this all come about? Nietzsche's nihilistic prediction that "God was dead" meant, of course, that everything in human belief systems, including religious beliefs, can be seen by the reflective mind to be no more than constructions of that very mind. By the early part of the twentieth century the view that history had a purpose which was "narrated," so to speak, by a divine source (as, for example, in the Western Bible) was coming increasingly under attack. At mid-century, Western society was starting to become increasingly more "deconstructive," i.e., more inclined to take apart the structures—moral, social, and mental—that had been shaped by this narrative. By the sixties, Western society had become fully entangled in a postmodern frame of mind, believing more and more that human beings fulfil no particular purpose for being alive, that life is a meaningless collage of actions on a relentless course leading back to nothingness.

Now, not everyone in our culture thinks in this way. There are many who, as a matter of fact, react against this kind of outlook. But it is becoming symptomatic of increasingly larger sectors of the culture. And, in my view, advertising has become the discourse form that reflects this cultural "symptomatology." Image-making has now become fully externalized in the form of products manipulated by media specialists. Television and advertising have become the postmodern mind's imagination and language. But the advertiser's imagination and his/her language typically fail to make a distinction between imagery and information on the one side, and true knowledge and wisdom on the other.

Advertising has become a kind of cultural *meta-language*, synthesizing verbal and nonverbal elements into a "compressed" textuality that sends out its message instantly, effortlessly, sensorially. The magazine ad, for instance, can be viewed as contemporary *art* form, given that art of any type is a code-based form of representation that converts sense and feeling structures into signifying cultural texts. Magazine advertising is psychologically powerful because it combines the visual mode of representation (as do the fine arts) with the verbal one (as do the literary arts). As Henri Lefebvre (1968: 202-203) has put it, advertising has become the "poetry" of contemporary society, seizing "art and literature, with all available signifiers and vacant signifieds." As Bachand (1992: 3) also observes, since "ordinary" people today do not engage in "serious" reading or philosophical contemplation by and large, it should come as little surprise to find that advertising has come forward to provide "an opportunity for varied aesthetic experience." This is why the writer Georges Jean (1966: 82) remarked a few decades ago that advertising has come forward to fill the "need for poetry which exists in every human being."

Bachand (1992: 3) puts this whole line of reasoning in perspective as follows:

> Thus advertising reinterprets the elements of semiological heritage in its own way, while taking modern sensibilities into account. It combines and transforms the processes and content of communication and thus participates in the updating and revival of the classical forms of expression.

No wonder, then, that advertising is being acknowledged as art more and more; having even its own category of prize at the Cannes film festival. Although we may superciliously be inclined to condemn its objectives, as an aesthetic-inducing experience we invariably enjoy it. Advertisements convince, please, and seduce. Advertising works aesthetically. And it is adaptive, constantly seeking out new forms of expression reflecting fluctuations in social trends and values. Its forms have even been adapted and coopted by mainstream artists and writers. Some pages of the contemporary writer Jean Marie Gustave Le Clézio, for instance, reveal an amalgam of traditional literary expression and advertising styles and forms. As Bachand (1992: 6) states, in this way "a dialectic of recuperation and diversion is developed, and through it the different semiotic systems that constitute the prevailing social imagination are refracted."

But there is a fundamental difference between the great works of art that all cultures identify as "saying something" about life and advertising. The goal of the great artists has always been to imbue our universal human experience with meaning and sense of purpose. The great works of visual art, the great dramas, the great music of *all* cultures, not just the Western one, are meant to transform the experience of human feelings and events into memorable works that transcend time and culture. Advertising, on the other hand, communicates nothing of any lasting or profound value, but trendy, "cool" attitudes and images. This new artistic vernacular constitutes a means aimed at grabbing the attention of a generation of individuals with seemingly reduced attention spans. Advertising is the art of the trivial, quickly becoming all too familiar and boring.

In this postmodern world, all is not lost, as Nietzsche so glumly predicted. I may be perhaps overly optimistic, but I believe that the human spirit will prevail, and that our postmodern culture will eventually redefine and reconstitute itself. I believe that it is unlikely that people are victimized by advertising, as many psychologists would claim. Children and teenagers are more influenced to act by their families and by their peers than they are by media images. In my opinion, there is no causal link between television violence, for instance, and violence in society in general. Did television engender the wars fought throughout history, including the two devastating world wars in this century? Did it spur Jack the Ripper to slash his victims to death? Was it responsible for all the horrendous crimes perpetrated in the name of religion, nationhood, and the like? Of course it didn't. It makes no sense whatsoever to think of television and advertising as instigators of specific kinds of aberrant behaviours. If that were so, then this principle would apply to all media, codes, and texts, including religious ones. What is more accurate to say is that the general *modus pensandi* and lifestyle models of our culture are reflected in the textuality of advertisements.

Even though we absorb the messages transmitted constantly by ads and commercials, and although these may have some unconscious effects on our behaviour, we accept media images only if they suit our already established preferences. If we complain about the shallowness of our television and advertising culture, we really have no one to blame but ourselves.

It is true, however, that advertising has probably contributed significantly to creating a desire for the lifestyles it portrays in other parts of the world.

When asked about the stunning defeat of Communism in eastern Europe, the Polish leader Lech Walesa was reported by the newspapers as saying that it all came from the television set, implying that television undermined the stability of the Communist world's relatively poor and largely sheltered lifestyle with images of consumer delights seen in Western programs and commercials. Different cultures have indeed been reshaped to the form and contents of television's textuality. Marshall McLuhan's phrase of the "global village" is still an appropriate one—television and advertising have shrunk the world and diminished the interval between thought and action.

Demographic surveys now show consistently that people spend more time in front of television sets than they do working, that watching TV is bringing about a gradual decline in reading, that television's textuality is leading to the demise of the nation state concept as ideas and images cross national boundaries daily through television channels. When the German printer Johann Gutenberg (1400?-1468?) invented movable type to print the Bible, he initiated a veritable revolution in human mental evolution and culture by making ideas readily available to a larger population. Television and advertising have triggered the twentieth century's own "Gutenberg revolution." But rather than homogenizing the world, it is my view that human diversity and ingenuity will lead to a greater variety in television programming and advertising and, therefore, in social textuality. As Solomon (1988: 124-125) aptly puts it, our "craving for variety is nature's way of providing us with an evolutionary edge in the struggle for survival in a constantly changing world."

Advertisements generate a truly interesting and rich array of connotations. These can be deciphered by analyzing the iconic and verbal cues of the surface ad text semiotically. Once the subtext has been decoded, the appeal of the ad seems to vanish, even in the case of highly connotative ads like the ones that Chanel regularly puts out.

Thus, at the risk of sounding élitist, I believe that advertising will never be able to replace the traditional forms of artistic expression. These document humanity's search for meaning; their subtexts are open-ended and profound. Advertising, on the other hand, exploits our need for meaning trivially to enhance sales of a product. Many critics refer to the effects of advertising as *reification*, the process of encouraging people to identify their desires and needs with objects that can be bought and sold. Advertising seems no more just to advertise products, but to promote a way of life through reification. But we must not forget, as Leiss, Kline and Jhally (1990: 33) remind us, that blaming advertising is like blaming the messenger for the message: "Objections directed at advertisements, the industry, and its alleged social impacts are often indirect attacks on the so-called materialistic ethos of industrial society, or on capitalism in general as a social system; these are critiques of society masquerading as critiques of advertising."

In the end, it may be true that advertising may be reshaping the world in more ways than we might think, as some critics suggest. As I look at people shopping, at parties, driving down the road, sitting at an outdoor café sipping coffee, etc., I cannot help but see in their bodily schemas, in the way they wear their clothes, in the discourse they generate, a reenactment of many of the images and scenes created by advertisers. I witnessed a striking example of this a few years ago when I attended a party of young upscale professionals. At a certain point during the evening, I saw an interactional scene that reminded me of a beer commercial that was popular on television at the time. The young men and women were posturing towards each other in ways that were almost identical to those of the actors in the television commercial. A culture mediated so pervasively by advertising images is asking for trouble. What Kubey and Csikszentmihalyi (1990: 199) have to say about the psychosocial effects of television applies, in my view, as well to advertising:

> Because consciousness is necessarily formed by exposure to information, media fare helps define what our most important and salient goals should be. Being an intimate part of the consumer society, television tells us that a worthwhile life is measured in terms of how many desirable material objects we get to own, and how many pleasures we get to feel. To achieve such goals complex skills are unnecessary. Even though some people spend a great deal of attention in trying to find bargains, in monitoring prices and sales, in developing culinary taste and fashion sense, in keeping abreast of new models and new gadgets, for the most part consumption does not require much disciplined effort and therefore does not produce psychological growth.

The answer to the dilemma of advertising is not to be found in censorship or in any form of state control of media and information. Even if it were possible in a consumerist culture to control the contents of advertising, this would invariably prove to be counterproductive. The answer is, in my view, to become aware of the subtexts that ads and commercials generate with the help of semiotic analysis. When the human mind is aware of the hidden codes in texts, it will be better able to fend off the undesirable effects that such texts may cause. As Drummond (1991: 7) has put it, semiotics can help to demystify advertising creativity and make "the process of meaning creation more accessible."

REFERENCES

Bachand, D. (1992). The Art of (in) Advertising: From Poetry to Prophecy. *Marketing Signs* 13: 1-7.

Bauman, Z. (1992). *Intimations of Postmodernity*. London: Routledge.

Drummond, G. (1991). An Irresistible Force: Semiotics in Advertising Practice. *Marketing Signs* 10: 1-7.

Jean, G. (1966). *La poésie*. Paris: Seuil.

Kubey, R. and Csikszentmihalyi, M. (1990). *Television and the Quality of Life*. Hillsdale, N. J.: Lawrence Erlbaum Associates.

Lefebvre, H. (1968). *La vie quotidienne dans le monde moderne*. Paris: Gallimard.

Leiss, W., Kline, S. and Jhally, S. (1990). *Social Communication in Advertising: Persons, Products and Images of Well-Being*. Toronto: Nelson.

Solomon, J. (1988). *The Signs of Our Time*. Los Angeles: Jeremy P. Tarcher.

Spitzer, L. (1978). La publicité américaine comme art populaire. *Critique* 35: 152-171.

10

THE DIALOGICAL PLEASURE OF INTERTEXTUALITY IN *THE NAME OF THE ROSE*

Rocco Capozzi

> A book is made up of signs that speak of other signs,
> which in their turn speak of things.
> (*The Rose*)

I. A LITERARY AND LINGUISTIC PASTICHE

Critics generally agree that after the various labels and classifications (such as metaphysical, mystery, detective story, historical novel, gothic novel, essay novel, *bildungsroman,* etc.) have been tried and applied to *The Name of the Rose*,[1] Umberto Eco's novel proves to be above all a confirmation that texts are made of unlimited semiosis and intertextuality, and that a narrative (a text) is essentially a literary and linguistic pastiche of signs and systems of signs from the universal encyclopedia of literature(s) and language(s). *The Name of the Rose* illustrates the notion that with an aesthetic text the semiotic practice of writing and reading, coding and decoding, constructing and deconstructing (in short: the whole process of signification, communication, and intepretation)

This article is derived from the second chapter of my work in progress, "Eco the Semantic Narrator."

is an "interdisciplinary dissemination" (Eco, 1978) of linguistic and cultural codes and of encyclopedic competence(s), of both authors and readers.

The Rose seems as if it had been written to demonstrate both the Peircean theorization of unlimited semiosis and the Bakhtinian views of the novel as a "developing genre" and as a linguistic and literary hybrid: "The novel permits the incorporation of various genres, both artistic (inserted short stories, lyrical songs, poems, dramatic scenes etc.) and extra-artistic (everyday, rhetorical, scholarly, religious genres and others) (Bakhtin, 1979). In fact, Eco's novel is a perfect example of conscious (and unconscious) "hybridization"; it is a text where many other texts merge, combine, collide, intersect, speak to and illuminate one another—each with its own language (or languages) and "ideologue(s)."[2] *The Rose*, succinctly put, is an ambiguous, polyvalent, encyclopedic, and self-reflexive novel intended to generate multiple meanings. It is a novel that wishes to be: an intersection of textual traces and textures; a dialogue among many texts; and a literary text generated through the processes of writing and reading, recalling and writing, re-writing and re-reading, etc.

In terms of possible influences I would like to reiterate my earlier reaction to those critics who search in the novel for specific sources in order to identify Eco's eclectic "debts,"[3] such as to William of Occam, Roger Bacon, Jorge L. Borges, Conan Doyle, Michail Bakhtin, Charles S. Peirce, Jury Lotman, Maria Corti,[4] Italo Calvino, Eco himself, and so on. The list can be endless as it depends on the reader's competence to detect overt and hidden quotations, or better, to detect unconscious as well as intentional and playful allusions to other writers and other texts (from both scholarly and popular literature) which are part of Eco's extensive library/encyclopedia. Soon after its appearance the strongest temptation for critics has been to analyze *The Name of the Rose* almost exclusively as an application of Eco's own theories presented in his well known *A Theory of Semiotics* (1976) and *The Role of the Reader* (1979).[5] I certainly followed this rather obvious lead as I focused on William of Baskerville as an *ante litteram* "detective" and "semiotician" (Capozzi, 1982) and in the process did not pay sufficient attention to the fact that in *The Rose* Eco was also expanding his views on intertextuality, rhizomes,[6] "codes," and "dictionaries," within the wider notion of a "universal encyclopedia," in order to explain the endless chain of horizontal and vertical (syntagmatic and paradigmatic) relationships of signs and codes. A notion that encompasses a dynamic interrelationship of history, philosophy, theology, aesthetics, literary tradition, and socio-anthropological culture in general,[7] and which views the "universe of semiosis . . . postulated in the format of a labyrinth"—or of a rhizome (as we see theorized in *Semiotics and the Philosophy of Language*, 1984). Of course, if one wishes to trace Eco's own works in *The Rose*, it is necessary to examine, together with his theoretical writings, his equally stimulating essays and comments on different aspects of modern culture (ranging from cultural phenomena such as Snoopy, Superman, Woody Allen, pin-ball machines, word processors, hyper-realism, and libraries, to major writers and thinkers like Joyce, Manzoni, Marcuse, Barthes, and Huizinga) collected in such works as *Diario minimo, Apocalittici e integrati, Sugli specchi e altri saggi*. Nonetheless, as I have already stated elsewhere, this approach would reduce Eco's application of unlimited intertextuality to a mere question of identifying sources (Capozzi, 1983) and/or "anxiety of influence" (to say it with Harold Bloom). Thus it would undermine the whole strategy of using found manuscripts, quotations, and intertextuality as a foreseen parodic textual strategy for generating other texts, as well as for generating the pleasure of writing, reading, and interpreting. Such a search for debts, influences, and sources would also overlook Eco's intentions of demonstrating how in the act of writing an author undertakes what Maria Corti appropriately calls a "literary journey" (a *viaggio testuale* which envolves author-text and reader; Corti 1978) in the labyrinths of the encyclopedia of literature and culture. Equally important, the question of sources would ignore Eco's Bakhtinian echoes of a text as a re-writing and re-reading of other texts; or as an interrelationship of different discourses and meanings. In fact, for Eco, as for Bakhtin, just as there is no utterance without relations to other utterances—"there is no utterance devoid of intertextual dimension" (Todorov, 1984: 60-62), in the same way there is no literary text (no novel) without relations to other texts which have preceded it (and which will follow it).

With *The Rose* Eco has chosen to conduct a serious and erudite discussion on the nature of narrating and interpreting signs through a most pleasurable and playful fiction. I would add that it is hard to conceive that our *semiotico ludens*—our great observer of cultural phenomena and mass communication, with a well-known great sense of humour—would have not narrated his stimulating "possible world" through a *divertissement* of puns, word play, parody, irony, and winking at the reader, while capturing his interest through a well-developed plot (full of suspense) and through innumerable "inferential walks"[8] in the encyclopedia of literature and culture in general. We would agree that most of Eco's works demonstrate his talent of *docere et delectare*—his basic belief that one can teach and learn while having fun (and perhaps in full agreement with the Freudian theory that much truth can be found in a joke). In terms of narrations Eco feels that "pleasure is a sufficient reason for reading a story" (Eco *Specchi*, 165; my trans.). He has specifically stated about *The Rose*: "I wanted the reader to enjoy himself, at least as much as I was enjoying myself" (*Postscript* 59).

Without embarking on a lengthy discussion of whether laughter (and the truth hiding under it) in Eco's novel is reminiscent of Bakhtin's views on Rabelais and on carnivals, whether it is Pirandellian, or whether it is simply parodic in nature, it may be interesting to know that in 1975, in a review-interview, Domenico Porzio, without knowing, was actually announcing Eco's plans for *The Name of the Rose*. After sharing some news about our semiotician who used to sign his early writings with the name "Dedalus," as a tribute to Joyce, and after reminding us that Eco had written *Filosofi in libertà*—"freed philosophers" (an amusing short text, relatively unknown and extremely hard to find), Porzio quotes our author who plans to publish "in twenty years, maybe . . . a work on the comic," because, Eco explains: "Signs and language . . . are no longer attributes exclusive to man. Ethnology is showing that other animals also use reason and language. The last remaining difference is laughter. Laughter is a mysterious and metaphysical mechanism" (Porzio, 1975; my trans.). The only information missing in this statement is that "laughter" will be at the centre of a "metaphysical" detective novel about a "mysterious" book in a labyrinthine library. Of course we know that it is only five years later, and not twenty, that Eco will publish his unprecedented success in the history of modern Italian literature.

2. A MOSAIC OF BOOKS. UNLIMITED INTERTEXTUALITY AND SEMIOSIS

Literary pastiches (intentional "hybridizations") are obviously assembled in a writer's laboratory/library. *The Rose*, in addition to being viewed as a collage of signs and quotations, or as a literary and linguistic pastiche, generated by Eco's impressive encyclopedic competence, should also be seen in light of parodies,[9] which besides being openly self-reflexive, focus not on "repetitions" in themselves but on the "new" which is inherent to the "differences" of repetitions, while also indirectly focusing on the author who uses them for artistic reasons and as a way of transmitting and repeating other writers' discourses. I should add that by "linguistic and literary pastiche" I intend a "constructed" text which is overtly intra- and intertextual, metaliterary and metalinguistic—precisely as Eco's novel wishes to be (perhaps just short of being a purely self-reflexive and narcissistic divertissement).[10] The linguistic pastiche of *The Rose* is much too obvious as Latin, German, Italian, French, scientific, semiotic, literary, religious, philosophical, architectural, and other verbal "signs" come together in the novel. Needless to say, the many languages spoken by Salvatore's—"Salvatore spoke all languages and no language" (*Rose* 46)—, a humorous esperando *ante litteram*, is in itself a manifestation of a "Babelic" fusion, and "primeval confusion" (47), of languages which can be decoded mainly by those with some linguistic (encyclopedic) competence.[11] This linguistic pastiche complements, most appropriately, the intertextual literary collage of *The Rose*, a novel where—from the opening page to the last, from "genesis" to "apocalypse"—[12] many "voices" and many "echoes" (of ideas and poetics) come together in such a fashion that at times (as undoubtedly carefully planned by Eco) it is difficult to distinguish our author's own words from those of others. And here it is worth remembering that the chains of allusions multiply as the Babelic (con)fusion of languages is linked to J.L. Borges' "The Library of Babel" in which we can find every book including those not yet written.

Eco has repeatedly underlined in interviews, talks, and articles, as well as in *Postscript to The Name of Rose* (1984), that his narrative is a myriad of metafictional indicators and of intertextual traces of Occam, Bacon, Villon, Dante, Manzoni, Borges, Wittgenstein, Peirce, Barthes, Bakhtin, Calvino, Eco, Snoopy etc. Actually, throughout the entire novel Eco reiterates that his is a "tale of books," a "book made of other books," a mosaic of books, "a book about books." We need only to recall one of Adso's conclusions throughout his lessons on reading and interpreting signs (verbal and nonverbal), as well as books and intertextuality, as he states:

> Until then I had thought each book spoke of the things, human or
> divine, that lie outside books. Now I realized that not infrequently
> books speak of books: it is as if they spoke among themselves. In

> the light of this reflection, the library seemed all the more disturbing to me (286).
> The good of books lies in their being read. A book is made up of signs that speak of other signs, which in turn speak of things (396).

On his journey—and it is only appropriate that a "novice," in his gradual formation, should learn through the experience of a journey[13] (one of the key, and most obvious, overcoded symbols of *The Rose*)—Adso learns from William that the nature of books is similar to the nature of "signs." As he loses more and more of his naiveté, Adso learns to accept that when speaking of signs he "can always and only speak of something that speaks . . . of something else"; perhaps without ever arriving at the "final something"—at the "true one" (382). Beginning with the early pages in which William, master in the art of making abductions, guesses from some imprints (traces) not only the type of horse that made those imprints but also the horse's name, Brunello, we see that throughout the novel Eco often discusses different types of signs and icons, and the art of interpreting signs:

> The idea is sign of things, and the image is sign of the idea, sign of sign. But from the image I reconstruct if not the body, the idea that others had of it (317).

In short, in the novel there is a plethora of "traces" of Peirce's concept of signs and unlimited semiosis. Umberto Eco has often quoted, rephrased, and even redefined Peircean notions of semiotics in his own terms, and here it may be worthwhile to recall two of Eco's definitions which are most pertinent to our discussion:

> Unlimited semiosis is above all a notion that refers to the code, not to the message. I mean . . . the fact that every sign, linguistic or otherwise, can be identified and interpreted through other signs, in an infinite circularity [. . .] A text functions (and functions also as an open text) precisely on the basis of the mechanism of unlimited semiosis (Mincu, 61; my translation).
> I might say that a semiotics of unlimited semiosis is based on infinite interpretations, on conjectures and abductions, and on the interrogation of texts as if they were universes and of universes

(including the world of our daily experience and that of science) as
if they were texts (Rosso, 10).

Furthermore, we should recall that in *A Theory of Semiotics* Eco has defined a
sign as something that stands for something else and as "everything that can
be used to lie" (Eco, 1976: 17). All of this falls within the plan of *The Rose* as a
system of signs that stands for other systems of signs (in addition to entering
into a dialogue with other systems), and, just as important, as a possible world
used at the same time to lie and to convey some truths.

I do not feel that there is a need here to dwell at great length on the
definition of intertextuality; critics like Eco, Corti, Kristeva, Todorov, Genette,
and Riffaterre, have all accepted, in one form or another, Mikhail Bakhtin's
suggestion that a literary text is "a mosaic of quotations" and "an absorption
and transformation" of other texts (Roudiez, 66). Nonetheless, I would recall
Kristeva's words as she speaks of a "transposition of one or more *systems* of
signs into another" (Roudiez 15), and of "permutations of texts" whereby "in
the space of a given text, several utterances, taken from other texts, intersect
and neutralize one another" (Roudiez, 36). These words shed additional light
on *The Rose* as a mosaic of books—as a novel of books within books, and of
signs and system of signs within other systems. In fact, Eco's strategy of
using quotations and other books fits very well in Bakhtin's list of the different
ways in which in the Middle Ages writers used other writers' words:

> The relationship to another's word was . . . complex and ambiguous
> in the Middle Ages. The role of the other's word was enormous at
> that time: there were quotations that were openly and reverently
> emphasized as such, or that were half-hidden, completely hidden,
> half-conscious, unconscious, correct, intentionally distorted,
> unintentionally distorted, deliberately reinterpreted and so forth.
> The boundary lines between someone else's speech and one's own
> speech were flexible, ambiguous, often deliberately distorted and
> confused. Certain types of texts were constructed like mosaics out
> of the texts of others (Bakhtin 69).

Considering that Eco is speaking (among many other things) about the
Middle Ages and that he uses most of these forms of quotations, Bakhtin's
words seem to have been written especially for *The Rose*, which is without a

doubt an excellent "orchestration of meaning by means of heteroglossia"[14] (Bakhtin 371). And we certainly agree that in *The Rose* many voices/discourses can be heard/read along Eco's discourse.

3. Palimpsests, archi-texts, and postmodernism

In some circles "palimpsest" seems to have become a household term after *The Rose*. In Italy the term becomes popular before the movie director J.J. Annaud flashes it on the screen in his own "palimpsest" derived from Eco's novel, and even before Genette uses it for a literature which, like parody, is once removed, or, as he puts it, is "to the second power."[15] Speaking of literature "once removed," as we recall Eco's novel is a textual journey "on a fourth level of encasement,"[16] that is, at least four times removed from Adso's experience (and possibly "five times," depending on whether one reads a translation from the Italian). With few exceptions, critics have not pointed out that the term palimpsest appears in the Second Day, when William and Adso discover Venantius' body upside down in a barrel of blood. Looking at the footprints in the snow, around the pool of blood, William comments: "Snow, dear Adso, is an admirable parchment on which men's bodies leave very legible writing. But this palimpsest is badly scraped, and perhaps we will read nothing interesting on it" (105).[17] As we can see from the choice of words William/Eco extends to the reading of nature (to nonverbal signs) the type of reading associated with the act of writing (or rewriting) over traces of previous writings. Naturally *The Name of the Rose*, far from being "badly scraped," is a clear "palimpsest" that allows readers to recognize numerous and various forms of intertextual traces/prints.

The Rose, is an *archi-text*, an *archi-novel*, throughout which many texts, many novels, are intentionally disseminated. From the title of the novel to the Latin verses "*stat rosa pristina nomine, nomina nuda tenemus*"[18] in the last page; or, from the preface, with its own ironic or parodic title "Naturally, A Manuscript,"[19] to the last blatant, or not so blatant, quotation from other texts, *The Rose* is an "infinite circularity" of intra- and intertextual echoes.

Critics, in various degrees, have written on the paradigmatic strategies, on the disseminated and explosive chains of signifiers (Barthes), and on the "inferential walks"—all foreseen (and planted) by the author. I would add that these endless labyrinthine walks, in and outside the text, not only do not tire the reader but are the very essence of the Barthesian *plaisir du texte* (of writing and reading) clearly advocated by Eco. Moreover, these strategic "walks" challenge and satisfy at the same time the reader's encyclopedic competence as he matches it against the author's.

Teresa De Lauretis has best summarized Eco's narrative success stating that *The Rose* is "a narrative *summa*—the novel most novelistic, the mystery most unsolvable, the *Bildungsroman* most picaresque, the text most intertextual, the manuscript found, not just in a bottle but in a Chinese box" (De Lauretis, 1985: 15). To this I would add that the success of *The Rose* as a pleasurable reading experience lies in the fact that it succeeds as an artistic play with language and literature both in its syntagmatic construction, typical of realistic novels (and of detective novels) linked to a logic of cause and effect, and in its paradigmatic construction, as it relies on the associative logic of intertextuality, unlimited semiosis, "dialogical" and multi-voiced discourses, and chains of associations that link the reader's overall encyclopedia to that of the writer.

Among the various semiotic and narrative theories applicable to *The Rose* one must certainly include Eco's manifestastion of literary postmodernism (in both form and content)—as he draws from history [a revival of the Middle Ages with allusions to the present][20] and from literature [an intentional pillaging of other texts and other genres such as the historical novel, philosophical texts, popular literature, literary criticism, semiotics, etc.].[21] Eco has clearly distinguished postmodernism from the *avant-garde*, for the way they differ in their treatment of past and present. The *avant-garde*, Eco reminds us, tends to destroy the past, whereas postmodernism consists of "recognizing that the past—since it cannot really be destroyed, because its destruction leads to silence—must be revisited; but with irony, not innocently" (*Postscript* 67). Giving an example of the ironic pleasure between two lovers who "in an age of lost innocence" can still say "I love you desperately," Eco explains that they are both "playing consciously and with pleasure at the game of irony." Moreover, he states: "Irony, metalinguistic play, enunciation to the second power, these are the characteristics of the postmodern" (Rosso, 3; also in *Postscript* 67-68).

We need only to substitute William and Adso for the "two lovers" to see how Eco is indeed using innumerable quotations, or allusions to other writers, fully aware that between him and his readers, there is no "innocence," instead there is plenty of "conscious play of irony." Needless to say, modern readers, just as Adso, have lost their "innocence" through experience or, vicariously, through readings. Thus the presence (or echoes) of François Villon, Dante, Sherlock Holmes, Wittgenstein, or of anyone else, are conscientious manipulations of well known "clichés"—they are careful assemblages of *déjà-vu* and *déjà-lu*. But clichés, as Eco has well illustrated in his analysis of *Casablanca*, can also be used constructively: "two clichés make us laugh, but a hundred clichés move us because we sense dimly that the clichés are talking among themselves and celebrating a reunion" ("Casablanca" 11). This is exactly what the "hundreds" of books do in *The Rose*: "they talk among themselves and celebrate a reunion." Naturally the dialogic interrelationship of many texts in Eco's novel is reinforced even further, and kept alive, by the reader's intertextual encyclopedic competence.

As Teresa De Lauretis also suggests,[22] if we examine closely Eco's article "*Casablanca*: Cult Movies and Intertextual Collage" we notice that we could easily replace *Casablanca* with *The Rose*, finding many analogies between one of Eco's favourite movies and his novel. Let's examine two quotations from Eco's analysis of *Casablanca*:

> *Casablanca* is a cult movie precisely because all the archetypes are there [. . .] *Casablanca* has succeeded in becoming a cult movie because it is not one movie. It is "the movies" (*Casablanca* 10)
>
> In *Casablanca* one enjoys the quotation even though one does not recognize it, and those who do recognize it feel as belonging to the same clique (11).

It is not difficult to assume that the immortal Bogart film was also used as a model for his own strategies of using quotations and other intertextual frames, and that he may have indeed assembled *The Rose* as an intentional "cult" novel (and why not ?). And I should add that Eco's use of a "Snoopy" phrase[23] or of any other quotation which may border on "extreme banality" (such as the echo of Sherlock Holmes's proverbial: "Elementary, my dear Watson"?) is a calculated technique which overturns kitsch into sublime, exactly as he sees happening to the clichés employed in *Casablanca* where "Just as extreme pain meets sensual pleasure, and extreme perversion borders on mystical energy, so does extreme banality allow us to catch a glimpse of the sublime" (*Casablanca* 11).[24]

If we consider that Eco was one of the original promoters of the "Gruppo '63" (and of the *Neoavanguardia*) we can assume that with *The Rose* (with his revival of the pleasure of narrating) he is also reconciling writers and readers who had been divided for nearly twenty years in Italy. In the sixties and seventies many had spoken of the predominance of *écriture*, of the "writerly text," over the readerly text. Critics such as S. Pautasso at the end of the seventies spoke of a *"rivincita del lettore"* (literally a "revenge of the reader"; see Pautasso, 1979) as they saw a return to more traditional novels and a decrease in meta-linguistic and meta-narrative experiments. Italo Calvino's *If an a Winter Night a Traveler* (1979) actually gave the impression that the reader was suddenly surging as a protagonist. The so-called *"letteratura in laboratorio per gli addetti ai lavori"* [literature made in a laboratory for the experts in the field] appeared to have had its day in Italy. However Calvino's and Eco's novels, postmodern or otherwise, demonstrated that the fascination with "literariness" was not entirely gone. Calvino and Eco demonstrated that their novels could entertain while teaching readers about writing, reading, and decoding narratives which are overtly meta-narrative. Let alone that both *The Name of the Rose* and *If an a Winter Night a Traveler* are clearly two novels in which the authors play cat and mouse with their text and with their readers.

Speaking of readers, when Renato Barilli expressed some concern about possible misinterpretations, by "naive readers," of postmodern writings—a literature made up of quotations (the so called *letteratura tra virgolette*—"literature between quotation marks") (*Sugli Specchi* 113), Eco replies that writers cannot be concerned with "astute" or "naive" readings. Our author had explained in *The Role of the Reader* that at the time of generating ("constructing") a text a writer "constructs . . . [his] own model reader." In other words every writer plants multiple levels of interpretations and multiple levels of pleasure for foreseen multiple readers. In fact, in *The Rose*, fully aware that there will be at least three types of readers: "those who will focus on the story, those who will look for analogies with his own historical time, and those who will chase after intertextual traces" (from the paperjacket of *Il nome della rosa*; 1980),[25] Eco has provided sufficient pleasure for all of them.

4. *The Rose* as a Trans-textual Labyrinth.

The biggest and most important lesson that the reader learns, with the help of Adso, is that "the adventure of writing,"[26] *The Name of the Rose*, is above all a *speculum libri*—a microcosm of semiosis and intertextuality.

Naturally every text to some degree is also a *speculum mundi*, however, we are explicitly warned by Adso that his is "a tale of books, not of everyday worries" (xix).[27] And, to use yet another "textual" neologism, Eco's novel is overtly *trans-textual* in its continuous network, a rhizome,[28] of associative or vertical interrelations with many other texts[29] and with culture in general. I would add that behind every intertextual echo we can easily sense the presence of Eco, winking at us, reminding us that it is time to take another "inferential walk."

Eco's novel, just as the library in the monastery, is structured as a labyrinthine relationship of books which challenges, or threatens, those who enter it. The library, as we are told by Alinardo, is "a great labyrinth, sign of the labyrinth of the world. You enter and you do not know whether you will come out" (158). Alinardo's words actually give us a clue to the reading of *The Rose*—"sign of the labyrinth" of intertextuality, where you enter and come out, depending on your encyclopedic competence of literature, semiotics, philosophy, history, fine arts, etc. The labyrinthine library is undoubtedly the most overcoded symbol of the novel as it alludes not only to Borges' "The Library of Babel" but above all to all the activities of reading, decoding, and interpreting the various textual strategies assembled by Eco. *The Rose* (pun aside) becomes an echo chamber filled with words such as: sign, book, library, and labyrinth[30]—all interrelated.

In *Postscript to The Rose*, our author speaks of the labyrinth as "an abstract model of conjecturality" (*Postscript* 57), reminding us that in detective novels the act of reading is a sequence of conjectures—with one story ramifying into so many other stories. It is easy to see how his notion of labyrinths recalls the labyrinth of intertextuality, and, by extension, the image of a labyrinthine library. I would add that just as the inhabitants of the monastery, the readers of *The Rose* are also dominated by the "library/labyrinth." Libraries and books, however, are supposed to be instruments of knowledge and not prison-labyrinths or impenetrable fortresses. Furthermore, speaking of books we remember that Adso comes to the realization that "Books are not made to be believed, but to be subjected to inquiry" (380) and, more important, that "To know what one book says you must read others." I should add that in addition to this view on the nature of books, Eco is analogously also recalling the Bakhtinian principle that language should not be "conceived as a sacrosanct and solitary embodiment of meaning and truth," but rather as "one of many possible ways to hypothesize meaning" (Bakhtin 370). And most important, in *The Rose*, a perfect fusion of erudition, theories, semiotics, and narrative lies, Eco has masterfully incorporated both Borges' notion of the "Library of Babel" with Bakhtin's theory that "Intentionally or not, all discourse is a dialogue with prior discourses on the same subject, as well as with discourses yet to come, whose reactions it foresees and anticipates" (Todorov x).

5. The ironic last laugh

The theme of laughter is undoubtedly part of the multiple levels of interpretations and one of the many intertextual traces linked not only to the "forbidden" book hidden in the library but also to the theme of irony, parody, and to the many other uses of laughter in general. My conclusion is that since Eco wishes to make the truth of his novel laugh, and since *The Rose* is also a novel about epistemology and how to use knowledge, one of the truths underneath laughter seems to point directly to the idea that man must learn to use books (and knowledge from books) constructively and not as an end to itself. Contrary to Benno's credo: "We live for books" (112), William (Eco) argues for a pursuit of learning which promotes a wider horizon of knowledge. We are in fact reminded that "Aristotele had spoken [in the allegedly lost Second Book of *Poetics*] of laughter as something good and as an instrument of truth" (112).

The treatment of laughter requires a lengthy discussion on the various interpretations of possible truths hiding under Burgos' laughter. I would briefly point out that throughout *The Rose* Eco appears to suggest that today we have lost the art of laughter; pretty much in the same way that Bakhtin suggests that in modern times we have lost the original sense of parody and of laughter as it existed in the Middle Ages (Bakhtin 70-83). But as I come to a close I wish to mention a possible interpretation of a playful truth injected by Jorge da Burgos as he laughs at William and Adso while the library is burning. I find it hard to believe that Eco has not calculated that Burgos's "diabolic" laughter at the end will certainly make us think of the proverb "laughs well he who laughs last." I suspect that it is through this ironic twist of comic relief that Eco also redeems Borges—the great master of libraries, labyrinths, parodies, palimpsests, and fictions—so openly and ironically impersonated by Burgos.[31] And thus in Burgos' swallowing of the poisoned truth Eco appears to kill two birds with one stone. On one hand, Burgos/Borges is symbolically buried with the truth(s) of the book/library. On the other hand, our author continues to play cat and mouse with his readers, suggesting perhaps that just as Burgos swallows the forbidden book/truth, in the same fashion readers (not necessarily all gullible ones) will swallow the story of *The Rose*. In fact, Burgos' diabolic laughter is yet one more way of enticing many critics to embark on generating innumerable pages on the various interpretations and truths assembled (and hidden) in *The Name of the Rose*.[32] But the reader of *The Rose*, just as Adso, through this "textual journey" cannot help but to lose a great deal of his innocence about "books" and to gain an ironic awareness that ultimately, after the reading of a text, or of a novel, *"nomina nuda tenemus."* As we recall Eco closes his novel with one final intertextual quotation in Latin (based on a poem of Bernard de Cluny): I leave this manuscript, I do not know for whom; I no longer know what is about: *stat rosa pristina, nomina nuda tenemus"* (502; literally translated: "the rose of the past remains in its name, we hold empty words").

WORKS CITED

Bakhtin, Mikhail (1981). Ed. by M. Holquist. *The Dialogic Imagination*. Austin: Univ. of Texas Press.

Capozzi, Rocco (1982). "Scriptor et Lector in fabula." *Quaderni d'Italianistica*. III, 2: 219-229.

Capozzi, Rocco (1983). "Intertextuality and Semiosis: Eco's éducation semiotique." *Recherches Semiotiques/Semiotic Inquiry*. III, 3: 284-296. The Italian trans. appears in Saggi su Il nome della rosa. Milano: Bompiani, 1985. Pp. 156-173.

Corti, Maria (1978). *Il viaggio testuale*. Torino: Einaudi.

De Lauretis, Teresa (1985). "Gaudy Rose: Eco and Narcissism." *Substance*, 47: 13-29.

Deleuze, Gilles and Guattari, Felix. (1976). *Rhizome*. Paris: Iditions de Minuit.

Eco, Umberto (1976). *A Theory of Semiotics*. Bloomington: Indiana U. P.

Eco, Umberto (1979). *The Role of the Reader*. Bloomington: Indiana U.P.

Eco, Umberto (1980). *Il nome della rosa*. Milano: Bompiani.

Eco, Umberto (1983). *The Name of the Rose*. Trans. by W. Weaver. N.Y.: Harcourt Brace Jovanovich.

Eco, Umberto (1984a). *Postscript to the Name of the Rose*. N.Y.: Harcourt, Brace Jovanovich.

Eco, Umberto (1984b). *Semiotics and the Philosophy of Language*. Bloomington: Indiana U. P.

Eco, Umberto (1985a). *Sugli specchi e altri saggi*. Milano: Bompiani.

Eco, Umberto (1985b). " 'Casablanca'. A Cult Movie." *Substance*. 47: 1-13.

Eco, Umberto (1993). *La ricerca della lingua perfetta nella cultura europea*. Roma: Laterza. Trans. By J. Fentness. *The Search for the Perfect Language*. Oxford:Backwell Publishers.1995.

Eco, Umberto (1994). *L'isola del giorno prima*. Milano: Bompiani. Trans. By W. Weaver. *The Island of the Day Before*. New York: Harcourt Brace and Co. 1995.

Genette, Gerald (1982). *Palimpsestes. La littérature au second* decré. Paris: Seuil.

Giovannoli, Renato. (1985).Edited by. *Saggi su Il nome della rosa*. Milano: Bompiani.

Hutcheon, Linda (1985). *A Theory of Parody*. N.Y. and London: Metheun.

Kristeva, Julia (1969). *Recherches pour une sémanalyse*. Paris: Seuil.

Kristeva, Julia (1974). *La révolution du langage poétique*. Paris: Seuil.

Mincu, Marina. (1982). Edited by. *La semiotica letteraria italiana*. Milano: Feltrinelli.

Pautasso, Sergio (1979). *Anni di letteratura*. Milano: Rizzoli.

Ponzio, Augusto. Edited by (1977). *Michail Bachtin. Semiotica, teoria della letteratura, e marxismo*. Bari: Dedalo Libri.

Porzio, Domenico (1975). "Il signore dei segni." *Epoca* (Dec. 27) 20.

Ricardou, Jean (1967). *Problèmes du Nouveau Roman*. Paris: Seuil.

Rosso, Stefano (1983). "A correspondence with U. Eco." *Boundary2* (Fall) 1-13.

Roudiez L.S. Ed. and trans. (1980). *Desire in Language. A Semiotic Approach to Literature and Art* by Julia Kristeva. N.Y.:Columbia U. P.

Stephens, Walter E. 1983. "Ec(h)o in Fabula." *Diacritics* 13: 51-64.

Todorov, Tvetzan (1984). *Mikhail Bakhtin. The dialogical principle*. Trans. by Wlad Godzich. Minneapolis: Minnesota Univ. Press.

NOTES

*   This article is derived from the second chapter of my work in progress "Eco the semiotician narrator."

1   *The Name of the Rose* (Trans. by William Weaver). N.Y.: Warner Books, 1984. Hereafter, *The Rose*. All quotations from this edition will be indicated in the text.

2   "The speaking person in the novel is always, to one degree or another, an ideologue, and his words are always *ideologemes*. A particular language in a novel is always a particular way of viewing the world, one that strives for a social significance. It is precisely as ideologemes that discourse becomes the object of representation in the novel, and it is for the same reason novels are never in danger of becoming a mere aimless verbal play (Bakhtin 333).

3   "Debts" is a term that Eco himself has used in *Postscript to The Name of the Rose* in reference to Borges: "I wanted a blind man who garded a library (it seemed a good idea to me), and library plus blind man can only equal Borges, also because debts must be paid" (Eco, 1983: 28).

4   See the various references throughout this paper to Maria Corti's *Il viaggio testuale*. Torino: Einaudi, 1978.

5   *The Role of the Reader*. Bloomington: Indiana University Press. 1929. Hereafter, *Reader*

6   "If texts can be produced and interpreted as I suggested in *The Role of the Reader* . . . it is because the universe of semiosis can be postulated in the format of a labyrinth. The regulative hypothesis of a semiotic universe structured as a labyrinth governs the approach to other classical issues such as metaphor, symbol, and code. *Semiotics and the Philosophy of Language*. Bloomington: Indiana University Press, 1986, p. 2.

7   Thus a dynamic interelationship of various signs from various cultural codes, all mutually dependent, each complementing and explaining the other, and all being part of a writer's (and reader's) "encyclopedia."

8   "...they are elicited by discursive structures and foreseen by the whole textual strategy as indispensable components of the construction of the *fabula*" (*Reader*, 32).

To Eco's definition I would add Corti's allusion to Lotman's "textuality of culture" as she speaks of the journey of the reader in the text and, consequently, of the journey of the text in culture, in society, in history" (Corti, 1978: 14; my trans.). Lotman's "textuality" is also present in her explanation of Eco's "open work" as she distinguishes the "textual journey" of the reader from that of the writer: "while the journey of the author in his text tends to make it structured, closed within itself, and thus closed, the journey of the reader produces the open work" (15).

9   I find befitting to our discussion Linda Hutcheon's definitions and analysis of parody with statements such as: "Parody is one of the major forms of modern self-reflexivity; it is a form of inter-art discourse" (Hutcheon, 1985: 2); "Parody is repetition with critical distance, which marks difference rather than similarity" (6).

10 See Teresa De Lauretis's article "Gaudy Rose: Eco and Narcissism," *Substance*, 47 (1985). For the notion of "self-reflexive and narcissistic" forms of narration see some of the most recent texts on the subject such as Robert Alter's *Partial Magic. The Novel as a Self-Conscious Genre*. Berkeley: Univ. of California Press, 1975; and Linda Hutcheon's *Narcissistic Narrative: The Metafictional Paradox*. N.Y. and London: Metheun, 1984.

11 The discussions on the origin of languages(s) vis-à-vis the Tower of Babel, signs, metaphors, and icons reappear in greater details in Eco's third novel *The Island of*

the Day Before. Moreover, Eco's professional interest in the origins of languages have been published in *The Search of the Perfect Language* (1993).

[12] Beginning with the opening line of the Prologue: "In the beginning was the word..." to the destructive fire in the conclusion, the allusions to "genesis" and "apocalypse" are far too many to be listed here. Nonetheless I should mention that with the terms genesis and apocalypse I intented to focus on the creative (generating) process of the text (including the creation—invention—of the second book of *Poetics*) and on its destruction, when we come to the end of the novel, with the disappointing realization that all we may have is "*nomina nuda.*"

[13] Besides referring to the journey as a metaphor of initiation, knowledge, and awareness—for Adso (and for the reader)—I am also speaking of the metanarrative journey that Eco undertakes in the encyclopedia of literature (and history), and consequently of the reader's journey, of his many "inferential walks," in and outside the text (all demanded by *The Rose*).

"Journey" and "text" are obviously one in *The Rose*; they are combined in the metaphor of the experience of transformation that the reader/traveller (and not just Adso) undertakes in this *viaggio testuale*.

[14] In *The Dialogic Imagination* we find various references to this term. See especially pp.263 and 400. For our discussion I find pertinent the following statement: "the novel must represent all the social and ideological voices of its era, that is, all the era's languages that have any claim to being significant, the novel must be a microcosm of heteroglossia" (411).

[15] See G. Genette. *Palimpsestes. La Littérature au second decré*. Paris: Seuil, 1982.

[16] "So I write the introduction immediately, setting my narrative on a fourth level of encasement, inside three other narratives. I'm saying that Vallet said that Mabillon said that Adso said..." (*Postscript*, 20).

As we recall Eco's 1980 novel comes from a manuscript (received in 1968) which is an Italian translation of a 1842 French translation of an earlier French edition of an original [?] manuscript written in Latin by a German monk around the end of the fourteenth century. I don't think that Eco could have made the parody of the "found manuscript" any more obvious and humorous than this.

[17] Pertinent to our discussion is Eco's other reference to a "palimpsest" as he speaks of the movie *Casablanca*: "it is a great example of cinematic discourse, a palimpsest for the future students of twentieth-century religiosity, a paramount laboratory for semiotic research in textual strategies" ("Casablanca" 3).

[18] As reminded by Eco, this Latin verse is a quotation from *De contemplum mundi*, by a Benedictine monk of the twelfth century. A verse which in turn recalls F. Villons's famous "*oj sont les neiges d'antan?*"

This final intertextual trace in the novel is in fact a *mise en abime* of intertextual echoes on the theme (and overcoded symbol) of the "rose," which naturally sends the reader back to the title of the novel and to a possible rereading of the text. But the Latin verse also leaves us perplexed, as we face the paradox: nominalism and/or realism? Empty, naked, words and/or reality?

[19] This is perhaps Eco's longest wink to his readers as they pause to turn a page and begin to read Adso's preface.

[20] In their juxtaposition both historical periods, Middle Ages and present days become examples of times of political tension, intolerance, dogmatism, and terrorism.

[21] In a postmodern fashion Eco uses (rather than revives) the historical novel, or any past literature, not for nostalgic reasons but rather because they are there to be used by anyone who chooses to do so. For an analysis of Eco's views on postmodernism— before the term becomes over inflated with meanings and much too abused—see in *Postscript* "Postmodernism, Irony, the Enjoyable," 65-72.

[22] See "Gaudy Rose: Eco and Narcissism." *Substance* 47 (1985), pp. 19-29.

[23] We recall that in his *Postscript to The Rose* Eco had explained: "Is it possible to say "It is a beautiful morning at the end of November" without feeling like Snoopy? But what if I had Snoopy say it?...A mask: that was what I needed" (19).

Although I am in full agreement that even Charles Shulz has his intertextual echo in *The Rose*, I would be surprised if our author through Snoopy is not also playing with the famous debates, from the days of the *Nouveau roman*, on whether or not one can still begin novels with a banality like "*La marquise sortit à cinq heures.*"

[24] This makes us think of what Corti calls "sublime *artigianato*" and "technical ability" of the writer on his "journey toward other writers's works throughout the centuries" (Corti, 1978: 12; my trans.).

[25] I would suggest to read W. E. Stephens' translation of the entire paragraph translated from the Italian original that does not appear on book covers of English translations. See Stephen's "Ech(h)o in Fabula," p. 51.

[26] I am using Jean Ricardou's expression from his analysis of Robbe-Grillet, where he states; "...un roman est-il pour nous moins *l'écriture d'une aventure que l'aventure d'une écriture.*" *Problemes du Nouveau Roman*. Paris: Ed. du Seuil, 1967, p.111.

[27] Naturally, this too is a trick; for it smells too much of the proverbial warning in movies or books "...any resemblance to real characters or places is purely coincidental."

[28] Eco has linked labyrinths, encyclopedias, and rhizomes in several of his works and especially in *Semiotics and Philosophy of Language* (1984, see especially pp. 80-84).For the notion of rhizome as defined and explained by Gilles Deleuze and Felix Guattari see *Rhizome* (1976). A translation appears in *A Thousand Plateaus. Capitalism and Schizophrenia* (Minneapolis: Univ. of Minnesota Press, 1987), 3-25.

244

[29]   Hutcheon even speaks of a "trans-contextual" function: "In *The Name of the Rose*, Umberto Eco 'trans-contextualizes' characters, plot, details, and even verbal quotations..." (Hutcheon 12).

[30]   The most overcoded signs—book, library, and labyrinth—appear to focus on the following associations:

      book = microcosm; image and mirror of our world; a network of systems of signs; intertextuality.

      library = encyclopedia; metaphor of research, of knowledge, and of storage of lies and truths; unlimited intertextuality.

      labyrinth = intricate relations of signs (and systems of signs)with other signs; metaphor of journies; structured chaos; a rhizome.

[31]   From the first appearance of Jorge da Burgos the reader is aware that Burgos is a parodistic travesty—a parodistic deformation—of Borges. The deformation is naturally befitting because Borgos' relationship with books, libraries, and labyrinths is completely the opposite of those of the great Borges.

[32]   See *Saggi su "Il nome della rosa"* (Ed. by R. Giovannoli). Milano: Bompiani, 1985; and the special issue on *The Rose, Substance*, 47 (1985). These are only two "books" in a library which will direct us toward other books in our attempt to decode and interpret Eco's novel. But what better way to start our journey in the labyrinth of a library than to begin with *The Role of the Reader*, which reminds us that novels are "machines for generating interpretations."

11

THE WHOLE, FROM AN IMPOSSIBLE VANTAGE

Floyd Merrell

I. GOING TO EXTREMES

To recap by putting many of the above sections rather baldly, medieval painting was an expression of what "reality" in some form or fashion and according to the spirit of the times *was like*. It was a foregrounding of iconicity (Firstness, *qualisignification*), with relatively little relation to the abstract, intellectual makings of the mind; or perhaps better said, the abstract relations inherent in medieval art were primarily dictated by church dogma, there was apparently no need for intellection of the secular sort.

Renaissance painting was in part an attempt to demonstrate that its predecessors actually depicted what *was not*. In this manner the relation between Renaissance works and medieval works and between Renaissance works and the world was presumably that of indexicality (*sinsignification*, Secondness). But, pursuing the Albertian perspective as though they had a window from which objectively to gaze upon the world, these artists went much further. They believed they were truly reduplicating what *actually was*;

Floyd Merrell. *Peirce's Semiotics Now: A Primer*. Toronto: Canadian Scholars' Press Inc., 1995.

through their works they were supposedly holding a mirror up to the world and seeing it in its unmediated purity. This utopian project was an illusion, however. The "vanishing point" turned out to be in certain respects as artificial as an indefinite number of other possible perspectives.

As I have pointed out, since the Renaissance, and prior to Cubism, almost all Western art has been the result of an effort either to depict a specific moment of representation or some timeless ideal—the latter often found in religious themes. In both cases the element of time was ubiquitous, but implicit, whether the time in question was conceived to be transient time—compelling the artist to capture a fleeting moment in a static frame—or eternal time—a contradiction of terms, but the ultimate goal of the artist reaching for the otherworldly realm where the angels tread. With Picasso and Braque the Renaissance images of time came to a screeching halt. Now, time as it was hitherto known simply did not exist. It was swallowed up in space in the artist's attempt to present an object from multiple perspectives simultaneously. There was no viewing a scene now, then later, and then still later, on a series of canvases in the style of Monet and others. Nor was it a matter of viewing a nude woman alongside two men soberly discussing some engrossing topic as if they belonged to two scenes at the same place but at different times. Quite simply, time was spatialized, it became space-time.

Physicist Géza Szamosi (1986:227) denies any direct relation between the space-time of twentieth century science and Cubism:

> Can we say that the space of relativity or quantum theory corresponds in any way to the space of a cubist painting or a constructivist sculpture?
>
> The answer seems to be a qualified "no." The twentieth-century notions of space, . . . did not evolve from direct, immediate sense perceptions, either in science or in the visual arts. These notions were the results of searches into what may be hidden beyond superficial appearances or immediate impressions . . . . The spatial (or, rather, the space-time) notions of relativity evolved logically from the demands posed by the constancy of the speed of light. The problems of cubist artists had nothing to do with this problem or with mathematically formulated logic. The cubist space, . . . tended to be a two-dimensional surface which excluded the third; the mathematics of relativity works in four-dimensional space-

time . . . . [L]ooking for similarities in these two enterprises is quite useless.

I would take issue with Szamosi on one important point: the manner in which the Einsteinian space-time continuum is usually depicted *iconically* (*legisignifyingly*), and its relation in this regard to Cubism. The ordinary Janes and Joes with a university education have at least some vague idea about relativity with respect to four-dimensional space-time—three dimensions of space and one of time. An important point of the new world picture generally goes unacknowledged, however. Einstein's theory entails an imaginary view of the universe from the perspective of a photon of light. According to this perspective, one of the vectors of space dissolves, that of length, and time as a series of instants vanishes. In other words, from a vantage point traveling at the speed of light, objects lose their length and become flattened into a plane, and all instants of time are equally flattened into one monolithic "now." We are left with nothing more than a plane; there are only horizontal and vertical directions. This, I hardly need write, is the ultimate Cubist dream.

Leonard Shlain argues quite effectively that since the Renaissance, artists have commonly struggled to depict four dimensions: three of space and either a temporal moment or different appearances at different moments. Cubism, in contrast, discards the frozen moment as well as Renaissance depth, presenting no more than a flat surface:

> Picasso and Braque eliminated both transient and eternal time. In a Cubist painting time does not exist. The viewer cannot *imagine* any next moment in a Cubist painting because there *is no* next moment. Further, by destroying perspective Cubism eliminates depth. Without time or depth the Cubist painting has been reduced from four dimensiones to two. The genius of Cubism is that it allows the viewer to escape from the system of reference that has three vectors of space and the coordinate of time. Einstein's answer to his original question is that the only place in the universe that would allow for a similar escape would be astride a beam of light. It behooves us to incorporate this view into our thinking. Cubism is a visual aid to this end. (Shlain 1991:200)

We should not let our euphoria regarding a depiction of four dimensions into two and a wedding between the arts and the sciences get the better of us, however. Shlain himself cites various art historians, and even a reported comment by Einstein, suggesting that modern art and the emerging scientific picture of the world have little to nothing in common. Yet Shlain doggedly persists in his argument that parallels are there. As the reader will observe in the pages that follow, I wish by and large to avoid this debate, focusing instead on the relevance of the arts and the sciences to Peirce's categories of Firstness, Secondness, and Thirdness, and his general sign theory, while leaving the idea of structural parallels aside. In order to address myself properly to Cubism in this respect, I must first resort to the most extreme forms of post-Cubist expression: the apparently purposeless art of the likes of Mark Rothko and Jackson Pollock, John Cage's music, and the prose of Samuel Beckett, Alain Robbe-Grillet and others.

Rothko's gigantic canvases marked by large black swaths have stimulated critics to remark on their mysterious, almost spiritual effect on the viewer. The black on white is for all intents and purposes valueless, as if an invisible hand with a giant brush had suddenly made a random streak on a vast expanse. It exists for its own sake, it is the creation of the place of objects—all living organisms included—among other objects of signs among signs, apparently without feeling or thought, sentiment or metaphysics, aesthetics or mathematics, and scraped clean of the past: it is in an eternal "now." Memory, history, knowledge, are apparently abandoned for mere ghosts of that which we would like to feel makes us human. There is an attempt on the part of the painter to divorce himself from memory and history, theory and method, expectations and purpose, and, in a state of cool calculation, slap what is of the stuff of existence on the canvas in one fell-swoop. Once a Rothko painting happens— and indeed, "happens" is perhaps the best term—it is the authentic expression in itself: it simply *is*. This is virtually sheer spontaneity, the possibilities of a form of pre-Firstness, of the semiotic "node" coupled with intellect. Given this element of intellect, however residual, there is definitely a degree of control, yet spontaneity is ubiquitous. In a nondenominational chapel in Houston, Texas, the "Rothko Chapel," there is a circular wall containing some of Rothko's large brooding canvases consisting simply of a few realms of color varying from top to bottom (Barnes 1989). There is hardly any *here* or *there*; there is only a somberly tranquil, pre-*qualisignifying* mood. These are not canvases to think with, but to unthink. They are not there to be analyzed, but silently to be gazed at. Some of their contemplators say they stir feelings of wonder and reverence comparable to those described by astonomers after experiencing the illuminations from nebulae, the vastness of the universe.

Pollock presents an even more spontaneous sense of *semiosis*. Through his visual medium he translates the apparent purposelessness and formlessness of his paintings into a strange new sense of form. Re-construction is for Pollock not a rigorously displayed structural process, like that of the Cubists, but an intangible flow and flux that serves to destroy all conventional notions of content and form. Everything appears mutilated: line, color, pigment, texture, in the dense swirls and tangles of paint dripped from high above the canvas or thrown onto the canvas spread out on the floor from all angles, combine in random or near random fashion. Pollock nimbly dances about his canvases, doing what he does by simply doing what he does. It is to all appearances pure anarchism, this "action painting," though it is not purely accidental or aleatory. It is an expression of relatively unmediated feelings, emotions, sentiments, intuitions, that is, of quasi-immediate sensations of pre-Firstness *par excellence*. At least it is perhaps as close as one can get, outside mystical experiences, to pre-Firstness, to primordial "chaos," to the void, to Peirce's "nothingness." This, in short, is pre-*qualisignification* at its best, or at its most bewildering, depending upon the view.

According to Cage's recipe for creating random—purposeless—music, composers should "give up the desire to control sound," clear their mind of music, and "set about discovering means to let sounds be themselves rather than vehicles for man-made theories or expressions of human sentiments" (Cage 1961:10). In order to accomplish this, composers must find ways and means:

> to remove themselves from the activities of the sounds they make.
> Some employ chance operations derived from sources as ancient as
> the Chinese *Book of Changes* or as modern as tables of random
> numbers used also by physicists in research. Or, analogous to the
> Rorschach tests of psychology, the interpretation of imperfections
> in the paper upon which one is writing may provide a music free
> from one's memory and imagination. (Cage 1961:10)

Sounds should simply emerge as discrete, individual entities evoking raw sensations, without syntax or grammar. The result evinces a static character, a sort of auditory counterpart to Pollock's canvases. The painter goes in no particular direction, and there is no conceivable progress or end in sight. There is no necessary concern with time as a measure of distance from past to future. The composer randomnizes her music, merely implying pitch, tone, time, relationships, textures, often simply in terms of vague, schematic drawings rather than conventional musical scores. The performer, in his turn, has hardly any alternative but to guess what the composer originally had in mind. But that's not really the task, for the composer shouldn't have anything at all in mind. What the performer must do is simply let body and brain do what comes most naturally, that is, randomnly. In this sense, the "signs" on the score, close to Peirce's pre-Firstness or "nothingness," are a quivering, scintillating, tantalizing set of superposed possibilities (*overdetermination*) any of which might spontaneously jump out at a given moment.

Such music and painting are an affirmation of life without parallels or contrasts; they simply *are*—i.e., the *like it* and *not it* have not (yet) emerged. They are not an attempt to bring order out of chaos. They are a "purposeful purposelessness," a "way of waking up to the very life we're living, which is excellent once one gets one's mind and one's desires out of its way and lets it act of its own accord" (Cage 1961:12). In this regard, perhaps one could surmise that this type of art somehow gets at Peircean habit at its deepest levels of natural expression, which is, at the same time, an expression of chaos and of pure order. That is, assuming that what for us appears as pure chaos actually enjoys some underlying ordering principle of which we cannot be aware.[1] In such case, what is totally without order with infinite degrees of freedom is at the same time totally ordered, depending upon the perspective.

Art critic Leonard B. Meyer (1967:70-71) writes that:

> Since complete random or indeterminate music is avowedly and purposefully without any organization, it is impossible to analyze or discuss its form or process . . . . [R]andom procedures are a means to an end and their real significance begins to appear when one asks *why*—for what purpose—they are employed. This distinction between means and ends is also important because in music, as well as in other arts, the same ends have been achieved in different ways. In fact, . . . the aesthetic effects produced by random methods of composition are, paradoxically, the same as

those realized by totally ordered music. Hence it is not surprising
to find that sometimes the same composer writes both kinds.

The natural response to random music or painting tends towards
incredulity at first, then disparagement, with remarks like "An ape could have
done that" or "It takes no talent to throw that garble together." But such an
attitude misses the point entirely. The point is that this *avant garde* art is a
renewed attempt to approach the equivalent of pure *qualisignification*
(Firstness) and at best, pre-*qualisignification*. It involves not what the artist
can do (*sinsignification*, Secondness) or what she *can mean* (*legisignification*,
Thirdness) by her art. It is simply a matter of her *being*. And her work evinces
no climax or point of culmination, there is no purpose or goal, no control
exercised over the addressee; no expectations are aroused, nor are there any
surprises. The work simply *is*. It needs no more justification.

A prime example of the narrative counterpart to purposeless, goalless
music and painting is found in Robbe-Grillet and especially the later work of
Beckett, among other writers at the mid-point of this century. Robbe-Grillet's
Jealousy (1959), for example, is presented practically as a static series of
disconnected sensations, without any perceptible progression towards some
goal or other. It is simply affirmation, without analogies or correspondences;
the words just say themselves. There is no causality or determination regarding
what should come later. There is no character or plot, no meaning. The self is
extinguished, to become hardly more than just another sign among signs; the
narrative becomes depersonalized, insofar as that is possible. This writing, like
Cage's letting sounds be themselves or Pollock's letting the paint drip however
it may, engages in constant struggle against cultural demands that predispose
standards of time and space, and of aesthetics, ethics, and metaphysics.
Personal goals and private, idiosyncratic desires must be eschewed;
preconceptions must be forgotten with a vengeance; expectations must become
indifference. Sadness and joy, anguish and jubilation, wisdom and folly, love
and hate, all lose their charm and their sting, as quiescence pervades (Robbe-
Grillet 1965).

Beckett's fiction suggests a comparable sense of senselessness, but with
even greater impact. In *Waiting for Godot* (1954) the characters are simply on
stage. They talk but say hardly anything. There is virtually no action, nothing
really happens, and for all intents and purposes even time could be standing

still were it not for the limitations of language, tied as it is to sequential unfolding. Much more dramatic in this regard is Beckett's novel, *The Unnamable* (1958), after a reading of which it is difficult to say whether a few minutes have transpired, or a few days, weeks, months, or years. *The Unnamable's* self is shriveled to a dimensionless point; it has lost whatever identity it might have had. He has no voice, yet he cannot stop speaking; he has no expectations of anything, but he is surprised that he is not surprised that nothing happens; nothing troubles him, but he is troubled that nothing troubles him; he longs to do nothing, but he hesitates in his doing nothing. Like the French "new novel," especially that of Robbe-Grillet and Natalie Sarraute, *The Unnamable* consists of language virtually without meaning, commentary, or interpretation; it simply *is*, without judgement, without value (Morrissette 1962).

In this art, there are only signs as unique particulars, with hardly any intentionally constructed lines of resemblance (*qualisignification*) or correspondence or causal connections (*sinsignification*) between them, let alone purpose and interpretation (*legisignification*). They are signs virtually without implication: there is no difference between them that makes a meaningful difference. Relations in space and unidirectional time are nowhere evident.[2] Whitehead (1938:326) has much the same to say about such discrete entities, or "occurrences," as he calls them, in the physical world:

> Suppose that two occurrences may be in fact detached so that one of them is comprehensible without reference to the other. Then all notion of causation between them, or of conditioning, becomes unintelligible. There is—with this supposition—no reason why the possession of any quality by one of them should in any way influence the possession of that quality, or of any other quality, by the other. With such a doctrine the play and inter-play of qualitative succession in the world becomes a blank fact from which no conclusions can be drawn as to past, present, or future, beyond the range of direct observation.

Surprisingly enough, however, Whitehead is writing about the ultimate extrapolation of the "positivist" sciences of his day, which could not legitimately hold any "hopes for the future or regrets for the past."[3] As an approximation to pure *qualisignification*, one might take it that the art of Pollock and Cage, and Beckett and Robbe-Grillet—or detached, selfless, positivist science, depending on the view—is by no means good to think with, as is a Cubist painting, an Escher work, or a Borges, an Italo Calvino, or a Franz Kafka tale. For it is virtually devoid of the stuff thinking is made of: *sinsignification* and especially *legisignification*. Selfless art, like entirely objective positivist science, it might appear, overlap on their most basic points. That is to say, just as the positivist view of science is ideally that of disembodied minds objectively describing a lifeless universe, so also one might conclude that the avant-garde art in question approximates a totally impersonal, selfless expression.

Such an unhappy marriage between avant-garde art and positivist science would miss the mark, however. On the one hand, positivist science, as Whitehead argued so effectively, was dead from the very beginning: it described a *lifeless* universe. "Purposeless" art, on the other hand, makes an effort to exercise an effortless expression of the very essence of the *living* universe. The fundamental difference is that positivism presupposed a detached spectator filling his mind—as if it were an empty bucket—with the "facts" of the world, then giving objective account of them and hence knowing them. This entails chiefly *sinsignification* and *legisignification*. As such, the project is an extension of Renaissance ideals. In contrast, the art of Pollock and Cage and Beckett and Robbe-Grillet, among others of the period, places the artist within the flow of signs and lets them reveal themselves as they may. This is submergence in *qualisignification* and even pre-*qualisignification* with a quietist vengeance.

So regarding the work of these artists, let's take stock of where we are, wherever that may be.

II. OF THE FOLD: OR, ORIGAMI SEMIOTICS ANYONE?

The goalless, purposeless, virtually meaningless art I have addressed is not without its own form of wish fulfillment: it is an effortless, unwilled willing towards what *is*, before it becomes *like it* or *not it*, and by all means before the suggestion of any injunctive *do such-and-such* comes into the picture. It all seems to be a matter of spatial, yet timeless, *becoming*, but *becoming* without discernible purpose, at least for now. This is something entirely new in Western art. In the first place, the timeless, utopian ideal has generally been pitted against corrupted and impoverished human time-bound efforts to reach that divine ideal. Now, whatever might go as timelessness is "nothing," though it makes up the sphere of *becoming*. In the second place, the Western artist has generally taken the canvas as useless emptiness to be filled with well-honed colors; the musician has customarily engaged in a mathematically rigorous construction of sounds out of silence; the writer has set himself the task of molding a well-wrought story of impeccable form on the blank page. In each case, nothing, which is of no consequence, must give way to something, which can reveal its treasures of meaning to she who is in possession of the right key to understanding.

Much Eastern art, music, and writing, in contrast, adopts *nothing* and *nothingness* as essential to the work's very existence. Consider origami art, of the Japanese tradition, for example. The origamist takes a blank sheet of paper and, by folding it according to a predefined set of temporal sequences, constructs a space that contains itself. The "empty" space takes on a definite countenance. This is not a Western painter carefully and intentionally adding color to the canvas, the musician controlling sounds, the writer beating language into proper shape. Origami space of no-*thing* folds itself into some-*thing*. It is an even more "abstract" counterpart to Pollock's leaving paint to drip on its own, Cage's allowing sounds to do their own thing, Beckett's passively letting words pour out of the Unnamable's mouth. In spite of the obvious differences between the origamist and the avant-garde Western artists I have placed under the spotlight, I wish to use origami as a paradigm case for illustrating Peircean *semiosis* further. The reason for my doing so is this: at the heart of *semiosis*, that is, at the "node" in Figure 5, lies Peirce's "nothingness," which is in certain ways more in line with the Eastern than the Western tradition.

Take a simple Western sort of origami fold. Cut a strip about 3/4" wide from a blank sheet of 8 1/2" x 11" paper. Twist one end, then join it with the other end, and you have constructed a Möbius strip. (This is not merely a "thought-experiment," I suggest you actually make the strip!) Now take a pencil or pen and trace a line around the strip. When you have made a 360° revolution you will find yourself on the "back side" of the strip. Then completing another revolution, and you are back to the "beginning," all in one continuous process—a line as continuum. Call this tracing "Lineland." It is a linear, one-dimensional circle, which, from within its confines, simply repeats itself, *ad infinitum*. An additional completion of a trip around the strip along the line would be a simple repetition from a Linelander's perspective, for, locked within her world, she could not be aware of the "flip" of her universe in two-dimensional space—i.e., as you experienced when you traced a line on the strip, moving from "outside" to "inside," and back again.

Language is linearly generated along a one-dimensional time line also. But it is certainly no "Lineland," for there is a fundamental difference between the nature of language and that of the Linelander's limited world along the strip. If I repeat an utterance, say, "A rose is a rose is a rose," I am not simply tracing out three identical "circles," or "recursive loops." Memory comes into the picture: you remember the last re-iteration, "is a rose," which colors the preceding iterations, however slightly, and alters your expectations of future re-iterations. Consequently, the context to a degree changes. It is as if along the linear sentence on the flat strip, you wrote the Gertrude Stein line, "A rose is a rose is a rose," and with each re-iteration, your memory tells you you have "flipped" through three-dimensional space to experience the same utterance, "a rose," anew, which renders it a "difference that makes a difference." So the first instantiation of "rose" is *not* identical to the second one, and that one is different from the third one, even though to an almost infinitesimal degree. Unlike the Linelander, your memory, which includes three-dimensional space coupled with your perception of the one-dimensional unfolding of language along the two-dimensional strip in time, affords you a comprehensive—mediative in terms of Peirce's Thirdness—grasp. The signs of your world in general, with each re-iteration, are *not* what they were, they are always something different—discounting the inevitability of forgetfulness, of course.

The *not* I just wrote is not insignificant. It gives the ordinarily one-dimensional unfolding of linguistic sounds or marks a special, and somewhat unique, characteristic: language, we noted in Chapter Nine, can quite effectively say *ain't*, it explicitly contains the power of *negation*. If you take a quick trip around "Lineland," from *within*, you cannot say a second cycle is *not* different from the first one, which is an elementary exercise in linguistic practice. In other words, once again we see that language is not exclusively one-dimensional, for memory and context come into the picture. It is as if, given memory and awareness of context, we were outside Lineland. And, of course, we are. Were our Linelander to enjoy a form of memory, she could be aware of a certain happening *then*, a happening *now*, and she could look forward to certain happenings in the future. But, unlike us Realworlders, she could not survey massive segments of her world as a whole along the strip in terms of their "flip-flops" within that whole.

Now let us consider the two-dimensional characteristic of your strip. Call the entirety of the strip "Flatland." Draw a "Flatlander" on it, say, Ms. A. Triangle, something like this:

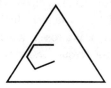

(glance ahead to Figure 12 if you wish). Imagine she travels along "Flatland" following the "road" you made consisting of the entirely of "Lineland." After you have journeyed 360°, notice that Ms. Triangle is now a mirror image of herself, that is, if you conceive of an infinitely thin mirror lying along the plane making up "Flatland." Now imagine she takes another 360° trip along the strip, and she has returned to the beginning. Or has she? Actually, limited to the two-dimensional plane, like the Linelander, she cannot actually know any beginning, ending, or center: she simply *is* where she *is* at the moment. She cannot really say she has completed one cycle, *not* two cycles, for she can't simply say one cycle *ain't* two, or three, or four . . . and so on. She is like a fish in water, simply *there*. Just as for the fish there is no possible universe that does *not* consist of water and nothing but water, so also for Ms. Triangle, there can *not* be any universe other than her two-dimensional world. Like our conception of the Linelander, from our imperious vantage in our three-dimensional "Sphereland," we can see exactly where she is, where she has been, and how many times she has traveled around the strip since we first became acquainted with her. But our view from "Sphereland" is another twist to the story. In order to introduce this story, let us dwell on the one- and two-dimensional worlds a few more moments.

Magritte can say his quite faithful depiction of a pipe is *not* a pipe by means of the caption underneath the image. It is a simple matter of using language. But can the two-dimensional painting by itself really say *ain't*? The question is somewhat problematic. Not only have many thinkers claimed pictures can't lie, they have proposed that they can't even *tell* the "truth." Plato and many of his Renaissance disciples believed paintings were mere illusions, deceptions. Positivists of the nineteenth century, and especially the "logical positivists" during our century, proposed that pictures are neither "true" nor "false," but simply nonpropositional, hence "nonsensical" or "meaningless." This is essentially Sol Worth's (1975) position when he writes "Pictures can't say ain't." Wendy Steiner (1982), we noted above, takes issue with this idea, arguing that pictures can quite effectively express negation, metastatements, and self-contradiction.

Steiner contends that many visual paradoxes constructed by Escher, the "Lewis Carroll of the visual arts," are ample demonstration of "the incompleteness of the fit between the Renaissance conventions of representation and the laws of the reality represented, between two-dimensional drawing and three-dimensional reality" (Steiner 1982:163). Escher's very lithograph entitled "Möbius strip" (1963) is a classical example. A Möbius lattice-strip is so constructed that we see ants on both "sides" making their way along the road to nowhere and everywhere. We can easily note that they are *not* going anywhere and at the same time they are going everywhere, and that there is *not* any inside or outside to the loop. But, of course, the ants are oblivious to all this: as far as they're concerned their journey is as natural as can be. Other effective Escher examples of negation are found in "Relativity," "High and Low," and comparable works illustrating a mix of dimensions, incompatible shapes, and incommensurable perspectives. Repeating our above observations, Escher uses multiple vanishing points to create the illusion of both up and down and back and forth and forward and backward within the same spatio-temporal setting. We can see that a stairway does *not* go up from one perspective and it does *not* go down from another perspective, though initial appearances suggest otherwise. In addition, a wall is *not* a wall but a floor, a patio is *not* below but above, a door does *not* open out but in, and vice versa. In each case, the artist's genius lies in his ability to combine discontinuous perspectives into a single, continuous spatial fabric.

In a roundabout way, pictures definitely *can* say *ain't*, though, of course, by use of channels other than words (symbols). The channels are spatial, not linguistic and temporal. They mix dimensions, not contradictory terms, as in the creation of paradoxes the likes of "This sentence is false." But in order for Escher to construct visual anomalies, he must entice his viewer into imagining that his figures on two-dimensional planes are three dimensional. They are like the "Necker cube" drawn on a flat sheet of paper, which we automatically see *as* a cube, even though we know full well that it is "really" no cube at all, but merely a combination of straight lines connected at various angles so as to give the impression of three-dimensionality (recall Figure 9 as a "hallway," as a "truncated pyramid," or as a mere "combination of lines on a sheet"). Yet it is a cube, *now* this way, *now* that way. And our experience through our linear time line affords awareness of change, of the cube's having been *that* way *then*, and *this* way *now*.

Of course, a binocular sort of vision affording the illusion of three-dimensionality was precisely the goal of Renaissance painting. We have the Cartesian coordinates, x and y, projected orthogonally in a third direction to yield another coordinate, z, to give the "vanishing point" in Figure 1. It seems purely spatial. Yet, almost invariably, time manages to seep in here also, either as a static "now" or depicted as a series of "nows." A three-dimensional "block" plus a roving time-line within it—the product of experience, of consciousness—provides for the possible implication of a fourth dimension. That implication came to the fore with works by the likes of Manet, Monet, Cézanne and others, as described above. And it was brought to a shrill pitch with the Cubist explosion.

The difference, I repeat, is that with Cubism, time as we think we know it apparently disappears altogether. Other than subjective, experienced time, there is no more than "abstract time."[4] In order to illustrate this phenomenon visually, take a look once again at your Möbius strip—or if you happen to have tossed it, quickly make another one. You now have a "Lineland," and a "Flatland" with its solitary inhabitant, Ms. A. Triangle. "Lineland" needs two dimensions for its full development along the strip, and "Flatland" needs three dimensions in order to incorporate the fold. It follows that we Realworlders, like our neighbors in their "lower" dimensions, need an extra dimension in order that our world may be properly constructed.[5] For example, we noted in Chapter Three that your left hand, and your left hand glove, are mirror images of their right-handed partners. A transformation of one into the other requires a series of "flips" through the next dimension, comparable to the flip of Ms. Triangle's Flatland in three-dimensional space. But attempting to conceptualize, and above all to visualize, a four-dimensional world can quickly place us in a pickle. So let's stick to Ms. Triangle's universe.

Flatten your Möbius strip so that it looks like Figure 12. Ideally, what you now have, if you discount the folds and simply take the squashed strip as a two-dimensional object, is what you see on the page of this book, clearly and simply. It is no longer a two-dimensional strip folded in three-dimensional space, but is now simply two-dimensional. Like the Necker cube, or a Cubist painting, it is merely a set of straight lines of various lengths connected at various angles so as hopefully to give the illusion of a three-dimensional object. (Or perhaps more clearly stated, it is like a flattened Borromean knot.)

Follow the straight arrows on your strip (they are in essence Ms. Triangle's entire universe). Begin at the bottom and move to the right, then upward and along the backside, then downward, and once again to the left. Now repeat the operation, and you have reached your starting point. In order to complete your journey, it was necessary to "burrow" from the "outside" to the "inside" and back again. But, taking the strip as it appears in Figure 12, there is no "outside/ inside," nor is there any "above/below," for everything is on a plane. You have simply followed a one-dimensional line from one "side" to the other of the plane, and your incursions into the "inside" of the strip and then "outside" again were no more than *imaginary*—i.e., they were atemporal, or better, they were in "abstract time," to which I referred above. They were *imaginary*, for there is no third dimension within which to make the "switch" from one plane to another.

Figure 12

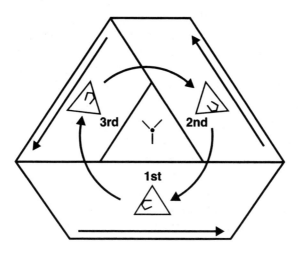

Now, follow Ms. Triangle's path in Figure 12 in the clockwise direction. This seems easy enough. She simply gyrates about a central point on the page, while rotating once in the process. However, in order to do so, it was necessary for her to "flip" herself into her mirror image in an *imaginary* third dimension. But this is equally as impossible as the straight line passing from "inside" to "outside" and back again since the strip is squashed: there is no third dimension. The upshot is that just as from our "higher" dimension we can see Ms. Triangle's pathetic limitations—though as far as she is concerned she can travel along her "Flatland" as freely as she pleases—so also we Realworlders in "Sphereland" are limited, since we have no experiential access to the *imaginary* realm of what is for us a "higher" fourth dimension. (Compare to the case of a grand master of conventional chess caught within the "bottomless chessboard," and our omniscient chess master's condescendingly gazing upon his hopelessly wandering about.)[6]

The problem with Ms. Triangle's "transcending" the world within which she is bound—or of our "transcending" our own three-dimensional system, for that matter—is remarkably demonstrated in Escher's "Dragon" (1952). The reptile is apparently trying to penetrate the two-dimensional plane within which it exists in Escher's work. It is attempting to stick its head under its wings and "burrow" into the other side of the sheet, then re-emerge in order to bite its own tail: an impossible task, for, inhabiting a "Flatland," there is for the dragon no such "outside." Computer scientist and musician Douglas Hofstadter writes of the dragon's heroic effort to "transcend" its sphere of existence. We the observers within "Sphereland," aware of the futility of it all, could try to aid the wretched beast. We could:

> tear it out of the book, fold it, cut holes in it, pass it through itself, and photograph the whole mess, so that it again becomes two-dimensional. And to that photograph, we could once again do the same trick. Each time, at the instant that it becomes two-dimensional—no matter how clearly we seem to have assimilated three dimensions inside two—it becomes vulnerable to being cut and folded again. (Hofstadter 1979:474)

All is to no avail. But, by the same token, just as the dragon is inextricably bound by its two-dimensional existence, so also are we by our three-dimensional living and breathing world.

III. We're in the Sign

"Now what has all this to do with signs?" I'm impatiently asked.

Well, take another gander at your strip, if you will. Call the first depiction of Ms. Triangle at the bottom a First, of Firstness. Call the depiction at the upper right a Second, and call the one at the upper left a Third. Passing from First to Second on the two-dimensional plane is simply a matter of rotation. But when proceeding from Second to Third, Ms. Triangle must somehow "flip" into her mirror image, and back again. Of course, as we now know quite well, she is ordinarily aware of no such "flip." As far as she is concerned, her travels take her along a continuous, harmonious, balanced, equilibrated, and symmetrical highway, without potholes, detours, speed-traps, congestions, or catastrophes. Only from our three-dimensional vantage can we see that she is actually "flip-flopping," with each gyration, from an *imaginary* "inside" to an *imaginary* "outside" and back again. It is as if her cadence were such that with each reiteration things were back to the same. But from our perspective, we see her in a syncopated, asymmetrical, offbeat, out-of-balance shuttle-step: 0 . . . ONE . . . Two . . . Three . . . n. (Ask the nearest horse if it is true that she runs with an asymmetrical gait and she will laugh at the question; as far as she is concerned, her ambulation is as smooth and natural as can be. Or ask a centipede how he is able to coordinate the movement of so many legs, and if he stops to think about it he will be paralyzed, for the natural continuum of his movements will be disrupted.)

The point is this. Our world—our "Sphereland"—is not as smooth, harmonious, balanced, and most particularly, as symmetrical, as we would like. Prigogine's "physics of complexity" and "chaos theory" have demonstrated this quite conclusively. But the relationship between symmetry and asymmetry is subtle. Peirce was living proof of this subtlety. Ambidextrous humans can switch from right- to left-handedness and back again with little effort, while most of us cannot do things except in an excessively asymmetrical way. Peirce was left-handed, which put him with about ten per cent of the population. And he was ambidextrous, a characteristic making him remarkably unique: his left-handed asymmetry was a mirror-image of our asymmetry, at the same time his ambidexterity gave his actions an element of symmetry. Perhaps because of this he claimed he saw things in an involuted way; perhaps not, I don't know.

Whatever the case, it seems quite likely that his sense of things and his thought were sort of "flipped" in comparison to most of his colleagues and associates.

Another example that might clarify my point is "dyslexia." "Dyslexic" individuals involuntarily and habitually "flip" the letters of the words they see, a characteristic that presents obvious difficulties in their ability to read. They might see "p" for "b," "b" for "d," "saw" for "was," or "evil" for "live." They might even transform "710" into "OIL." There is no consensus with respect to the cause of dyslexia or its precise nature. Most dyslexics are of average or above average intelligence, and some have trouble with hand-eye coordination. Whatever the cause and nature, it seems that they unwittingly tend to "flip" signs on a two-dimensional plane through three- and on occasion even four-dimensional space.[7] It might even afford them some special form of insight. It is like the person from a culture with many pyramids but no hallways or rectangular rooms who sees Figure 9 as a concave structure. She somehow "flips" the drawing into what it ordinarily would not be, and, caught within the "flip," she doesn't see it as a pyramid, as do the vast majority of her compatriots. In the case of the dyslexic person's inability to read, it is as if he were caught within the "flip" of the written sign and can't make his way back home: he thus sees the written signs before him in an awry fashion.

Whatever "flip" one is in, it often presents some handicaps, for sure, but it may also be capable of affording special insights. The number of creative individuals suffering from some impediment or other is remarkable. Whether their creative urge is largely due to an indomitable will, to strange demiurgic faculties their physical or psychological handicap offers, to environmental stimulation, or to sheer obstinacy, the fact seems to be that they have somehow overcome many of their drawbacks. Peirce must certainly be placed among this type of individual, especially in view of Brent's (1993) recent biography of the North American semiotician. (I must also concede that Peirce's idiosyncracies are also quite likely at least in small part due to the *fin de siècle* temper that prevailed during the last decades of his life.)

One of the many bizarre ideas floating around at the time was the notion of a fourth dimension. A number of mathematicians, philosophers, and various and sundry speculators and cranks, were toying with the idea of a fourth dimension as the zone where mystics dwell (it was "in the air"; Einstein was actually no prophet in the wilderness in this respect). I must hasten to add that

I allude to no such "otherworldliness" here. The reason I bring this issue up is that since, in order that there be three Peircean categories, there must be some principle holding them together, some sort of "fourth element." I refer once again to Peirce's numerous allusions to the concept of "nothingness," the field within which *semiosis* plays out its drama in "unbounded freedom," and which lies behind his categories (*CP*:6.203). Peirce was aware of the need for "nothingness" ("pre-Firstness") as that which makes possible the extraction of forms. The "nothing" of "nothingness" is utter vagueness, dimensionless freedom, chance, spontaneity. It is the undifferentiated, not merely "the notion of negation" or "emptiness." It is the primitive category prior to Firstness (origin), Secondness (otherness), and Thirdness (mediation). We have, I repeat, after Zero ("nothingness"), One, which is followed by Two, the split between *this* and *that*. Three, which brings the previously incompatible One and Two together, closes the circle, thus potentially reverting back to the continuity of the undifferentiated, of "nothingness" (*CP*:6.197-200).

This "nothingness," this "fourth element," I would suggest, is iconized in the *imaginary* "point"—the "node"—I constructed at the center of the squashed Möbius strip in Figure 12. It is necessary in proceeding from the more familiar triangular depiction of the sign as three binary relations in Figure 4 to that of a tripod connecting the three sign components at the central "knot" or "node" according to Figure 5. If you imagine the squashed Möbius strip in Figure 12 in terms of a *representamen* in the place of the First, an *object* in place of the Second, and an *interpretant* in place of the Third, all of them connected at the central "point," you are most likely beginning to tune in on the proper wave length. We have a point, a line, a plane, and a fold, all of which makes up the sign as a piece of origami art. If Figure 12 were construed in terms of a plane only, there would simply be a set of binary moves from First to Second to Third. When the "folds" are taken into account, however, the picture is infinitely enriched. This is a fundamental difference between the Renaissance illusion of three-dimensionality, of depth by the combination of binary Seconds, and Cubism's flattening the entire scene in order to present a more genuine picture of things from a multiperspectival grasp. In Shlain's (1991:193-94) words:

> The third dimension of depth had been glorified by the Renaissance painters. Modern painters, however, consistently introduced a flattening of perspective. Background and foreground were regularly

"scrunched up." Since Manet and continuing through the works of Cézanne, Gauguin, and van Gogh, artists increasingly preferred flattened perspective to illustrate depth. The Cubists severely compressed depth in their paintings, so the viewer's eye could not even penetrate it. In *Les Demoiselles d'Avignon* [*The Maidens of Avignon*], the work that began the Cubist movement, Picasso flattened his airless cramped canvas so completely that the viewer's eye could not peirce through to the background because there *was* no background.

Medieval art hypertrophied *qualisignification* in its tireless search for *legisignification*, the ultimate expression. And the artist became lost in the maze. Renaissance art provided depth in its hypertrophying *sinsignification*, but, ultimately, as the anguish-ridden philosopher Blaise Pascal (1623-1662) put it, the human individual was swallowed up in the awful gulf between the infinitesimally small and the infinitely large. Cubism flattened everything to a plane, somewhat commensurate with the Einsteinian flattening of time and space to a timeless succession of slices from the "block" universe. And yet, that desired omniscient grasp of the whole continued to elude the solitary semiotic agent, the artist, scientist, or writer, for, like Ms. Triangle, they all fell into the invisible interstices within the *plenum*: like time and space, they disappeared into the shadows. Pollock, Cage, Beckett, and others attempted to reach the timeless "nothingness" of pre-Firstness, that is, pre-*qualisignification*. But, virtually divorced from intellection, this exceedingly vague feel from "nowhere," from the "point," was capable actually of revealing very little.

Now, it seems, we must at long last concede that we are "within" the origami fold, "within" the stream of *semiosis*. But there is certain consolation in this concession: we are not alone. It is all a matter of the ongoing, incessantly repeating, obstinate push of the syncopated beat of Firstness-Secondness-Thirdness . . . *n*, which includes not isolated, autonomous individuals, but rather, the entire community of semiotic agents, and in fact, of the entire universe of signs.

IV. SIGNS, A BACKWARD GLANCE, AND LYING

"Now I insist," someone asserts quite emphatically, "that you get back to the nitty-gritty of the sign. After all, that's what you promised, isn't it? So, deliver."

Well, yes, I suppose it's about time. And time really is the issue. In spite of Cubism's attempt to do away with time altogether—and they were quite effective in their efforts—we simply cannot forget it. As we creep along our "world-line" in this vast four-dimensional space-time domain, we carry a massive burden of the past with us, however distorted it may be. And we cannot divorce our perception and conception of our world in any particular "now" from the whole of our memories and our expectations—which indelibly color whatever lies in store for us. In this sense our world—our "semiotically real" world as well as brute physical existence—is incessantly becoming something other than what it was. This is how things should be, since according to Peirce's conception, and the view emerging from the "sciences of complexity," the universe is an evolving, self-organizing whole: it lifts itself up by its own bootstraps. How, then, can I hope to account for this numbingly complex whole? If I remain faithful to my opening sentences in the Preface, I cannot expect to account for it. However, I am duty-bound at least to give it a try. So, once again begging your indulgence, consider the following.

Re-evoking Eco's (1976:6-7, 1984:177-82) dictum, semiotics, our human semiotics, *is the study of whatever can be used to lie.* But contrary to Eco, the sign is not simply something that "stands for" something else, something that is a "substitution for" something else, or something that "refers back to" something else in its absence, especially in the event that that "something else" was present at some time in the past. Rather, in light of the "interrelationist" theory I have suggested in this inquiry, the matter is quite different. To give a graphic illustration of what I have in mind, consider the sign according to Figure 5 to exist on a plane, with its "time-line," or better, its "time-flow," penetrating it and moving on into the future (Figure 13).[8] The singular plane represents no more than a single moment in the life of the sign. But actually, there is an indeterminate series of planes, each containing the sign in one of its myriad "translations" (i.e., like a "bottomless" set of sign slices, as a counterpart to our "bottomless chessboard"). Signs, within the temporal flow of *semiosis,*

267

in this sense enjoy myriad, and virtually unlimited, actualizations *for* their respective semiotic agents.

Figure 13

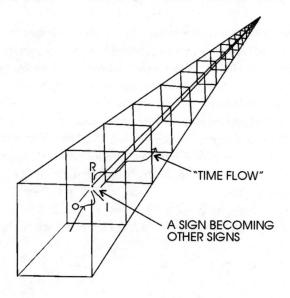

"TIME FLOW"

A SIGN BECOMING
OTHER SIGNS

From "within" their particular "time-flows," signs play loose and fast with our sensing, feeling, intuiting, and imagining faculties, and our reasoning and cognizing faculties. Consider, for example, an indexical sign and its object, *lightning* and *thunder*. They might be construed in terms of a simple relationship of contiguity, much in the sense of semiology. Things are not so simple, however, for the "semiotically real" world always manages to get into the act. And regarding time, there is a measurable temporal increment between the sign, *lightning*, and that to which it relates, *thunder*, which in the process becomes another sign. As a consequence, the signs can be conceived *by* some semiotic agent in terms of temporal causality: "*Lightning → Thunder.*" *Lightning* is the *representamen*, *thunder* the *object*, and the *interpretant* provides mediation between them bringing two otherwise isolated events together into what appears to be a "causal relation." The sign as such can be hardly more than an index, however. Language has not (yet) entered the picture. With the aid of language (i.e., symbolic signs), "*Lightning* → *Thunder*" can be put into a contrary to fact conditional: "If 'lightning' occurred, then 'thunder' would follow."[9]

In order to render the distinction between sign components more precise, "lightning" in and of itself is a conventional *representamen* whose *object* is *lightning*, and "thunder" is a *representamen* whose *object* is *thunder*. To this point the two signs remain unrelated. There are no necessary lines of "causality," but simple relation of sign to object. When the two symbolic signs are brought together by the sentence "If lightning occurred, then thunder would follow," lines of "causality" (or in the atemporal sense, of logical implication) are established, whether the actual events are present or not. Consequently, what has not (yet) occurred can become the object of a predication in order to bring what might occur, could occur, or must occur, into the realm of possible or necessary future events. And time has thus gained entry into the picture.

Without this dimension of time, everything would occur on a static set of disconnected signifying planes in Figure 13. It would be like a citizen of "Sphereland" flattened to a two-dimensional pancake—or in a Cubist painting—and forced to make his way through a disconnected set of worlds like that of Ms. Triangle. It would be like the omniscient chess master of her "bottomless chessboard" suddenly reduced to the timeless prison-house of an infinite set of two-dimensional boards totally unrelated to one another. When time and memory are properly included, in contrast, we are capable of looking at a plane from "this side" and the "other side." Within our three-dimensional existence we can see Ms. Triangle's "flips" along "Flatland" when passing from First to Second to Third. From "this side" of the plane in Figure 13, we are aware that a bolt of *lightning* came first and *thunder* followed on its heels at a later space-time slice. Memory of *thunder* occurring after *lightning* in times past has created expectations that the same will most likely occur now and in the future. Viewing the plane from the other side, in contrast, it is now *thunder* that relates to *lightning*. *Thunder* is the sign that there was *lightning* in the vicinity, which substantiates the complementary conditional, "If there were 'thunder,' then 'lightning' would have previously occurred."

In other words, memory now serves to link present signs to past signs whose interpretants become those very signs that emerged at a later time. "Thunder" affords a retrospective grasp of past signs that colors the interpretants of present signs. In another way of putting it, the complementary conditional, "If there were 'thunder,' then 'lightning' would have previously occurred," reverses the direction of the curved arrows in the flattened Möbius strip: they are now counterclockwise instead of clockwise, since the *object* (Second) and the *representamen* (First) have traded places—i.e., since we are now looking at the plane from the "back" side instead of the "front" side. This "relating back" is what makes Eco's lie possible. And this temporality is what makes our conception of *semiosis* human. We are never free of the past and we never cease forging the future as a result of our expectations. Otherwise, *semiosis* would hardly be more than a series of static slices out of the semiological salami.

Now, the whyfor of my quirkiness in this admittedly strange chapter is this. I have alluded to certain aspects of our world that remain untouchable by classical logic: time, left-right-handedness, change. Classical logic disallows the experience of temporal irreversibility, of change; it accepts only intellection. But in our everyday world of concrete living, virtually any activity requiring thought-signs, signs of the mind, the complementation and collaboration of the mind in the *semiosic* process, calls up both experience (Firstness) and intellect (Thirdness). This includes abstract and concrete, logical and translogical, *subsidiary* and *focal*, tacit and conscious, modes of knowing.

Take the notion of scale. In the abstract sense, scale is measured as a ratio. But to give the measure any genuine sort of meaning, there must be some consideration of that which is construed to be "real," the "semiotically real." This "semiotic reality" cannot be measured solely in abstract terms of ratio. The determination of scale in concrete terms of human sensibility, interaction, and meaning goes further, much further. It must relate to a "semiotically real" territory that is not reducible to mere ratio. For instance, a map can be calibrated by a ratio of 100 miles to the inch, which establishes its scale. But simply to state "One inch on the map represents 100 miles on the actual terrain" does not reveal the semiotic relation between map and the "real" and between map and its interpreter. The terms "one inch" and "100 miles" are there in the map. But they have no correlate with the actual territory in the sense of the map reader's feel for maps and that to which they relate. Above all, they contain no relation to the territory in the physical sense as experienced by the person *putting the map to use* (during a trip over the terrain by car, train, or bicycle, and experiencing the whole scene as it flows by). If the formal map-territory relations were fed into a computer, what is "in" the map would be what the computer "knows." But without concrete human experience regarding actual experience and physical interrelations, that "knowledge" would be virtually meaningless with respect to living and breathing human semiotic animals. The moral: abstract, formal "knowledge" (i.e., of virtually pure *legisignification*, Thirdness) is simply insufficient.

Yet this insufficiency is inherent in the very way we *put* numbers *to use*— and in the way we customarily *use* signs in general for that matter. In the realm of natural numbers, symmetry prevails. The string of ciphers marches in perfect order, on and on. If we want to include negative numbers, one side balances the other so as to retain symmetry. Positive numbers are non-negative and negative numbers are non-positive. One series is the inverse of the other, with 0 in between. What comes before the plane and what comes after are reversibly and symmetrically related; forward and backward, it's all the same, there is no time. However, in our concrete, temporal, irreversible world of everyday life, things are not so clean. An accountant might tell us that in a strictly formal sense, if out of the clear blue I give you $50.00, then your finances are plus $50.00 and mine are minus the same amount, no more, no less. Such abstraction, however, does not tell the whole tale: sooner or later Firstness and Secondness begin to exercise their force. No matter how altruistic I may be, I *feel* my loss, and no matter how indifferent you are to material wealth, your gain will be *sensed*. What arises, with respect to "semiotically real world" interactions, is *expected* gain or loss and *noticed* presence or absence. In other words, time and memory cannot be left out of the equation.

Formally, positive and negative terms merely imply parameters. In actual experience, in contrast, they imply gain and loss, presence and absence, here and there, inside and outside, then and now. A pentagon has five sides, a square five minus one equals four sides, a triangle four minus one equals three sides. Fair enough. Each geometrical figure stands straight and tall on its own as a positive value, while subtracting a side from it converts it into some other figure. If, however, a square is defined as a fence enclosing a ranch, then we have "positive" and "negative" in terms of how we *sense, feel, experience*, and *perceive* our "semiotic world." If a link in the fence is removed and ten head of cattle are stolen, the sensed "negative" value certainly becomes "real." There is a *noticed absence* of something that should be, could be, or otherwise would be, *present*. When we *feel* something should be somewhere at some time and it is not, we are often painfully aware of its absence. On the other hand, in the total *absence* of cattle-rustlers, all the livestock is *present* because that is what is *expected*. There is hardly any *expectation* of a portion of the *present* cattle becoming *absent* due to thieving. When we *expect* something to be *present*, and if it has always been *present*, we do not normally celebrate its *presence*. We do not constantly sing praises to the presence of earth, concrete, pavement, and floors underneath our feet to hold us up, but we *expect* support when entering a Boeing 707. We do not ordinarily notice the *presence* of oxygen entering our lungs when we inhale, but we would quickly *notice* its *absence* were the air pressure suddenly to decrease while we are in flight in the same Boeing 707.

It is, chiefly regarding human *semiosis*, *noticed* gain or loss, presence or absence, here or there, inside or outside, then or now, that creates *asymmetry*, *irreversibility*, between positive and negative in the "semiotically real" world of experience. And such awareness is included within *time*. Time is the flow that carries us along the river of *semiosis*, and *semiosis* is the river that carries time along in its flow. *Semiosis* enables us to make connections between objects, acts, and events along many and variegated asymmetrical, nonlinear pathways. In this regard, "nothingness," "0," really has nothing to do with time. Time contains the arrow in Figure 13 carrying signs—ourselves included—into their other, into other signs, incessantly, irremediably, irretrievably. In contrast to "nothingness," *noticed presence* and *noticed absence* are not possible without there previously existing, in time, their respective opposites. If *noticed presence* is acknowledgement of a set of things, in the sense of "set theory," even though these things may be only ciphers on paper representing numbers, then *noticed absence* corresponds to the "empty set," ø, not to pure "nothingness." A bowl full of fruit is acknowledged by the parent of a household as "full," regardless of whether there are ten apples and five oranges or the other way round. Either way, the set of items is as it should be. If at some point in time the bowl is found to be empty due to the prior presence of hungry young stomachs, the *absence* is *noticed*, and all the offspring are called in for an interrogation in order to determine who the culprit is. The "empty set" is acknowledgement that there is nothing whereas in another time and another place there could have, would have been, or should have been something. And if there is something rather than nothing, then that something is accompanied by acknowledgement, whether conscious or tacit, that there could have been, would have been, or should have been something else—or nothing at all—at another time and another place.

To repeat the definition with which I began the Preface: *semiotics* is the study of *semiosis*. And *semiosis* is, well, it's just *semiosis*. We make of it what we can, and get on with living.

NOTES

1   At this juncture I should point out that "randomness" and "chaos" (of "chaos theory") designate different phenomena. Very briefly—I cannot dwell on the issue here—chaos enjoys some underlying ordering principle, though we may not know what it is, while randomness does not. We can know a phenomenon is chaotic if we can discover that principle, but we cannot know without a shadow of a doubt if a phenomenon is truly random without tracing it out to its end, which exists at the infinite horizon, hence we cannot know it. The question—and a topic for future inquiry—becomes: Is so-called "purposeless art" the product of randomness (pre-*qualisignification*), or does it depict order-out-of-chaos (*qualisignification*)? (for further on "chaos theory," see Hall 1993).

2   In *For a New Novel* (1965) Robbe-Grillet had called for a nonreferential, completely literal, superrealist fiction, an "inhuman" work in which the character's eyes would "rest on things without indulgence" (Robbe-Grillet 1965:98). This disengaged view is close to Roland Barthes' (1972) "death of the author" and "objective literature," and in "minimalist" art, dance, and music in general. However, I should mention that after the 1960s and early 1970s there was a certain re-turn to subjectivity and intersubjectivity in language, art, and human relations (Battcock 1968). But consideration of that period remains beyond the scope of this volume.

3   I allude to the philosophy of science called "logical positivism," a last gasp attempt to salvage classical determinism that enjoyed its heyday from the 1920s through the 1950s.

4   This "abstract time" is strictly mathematical, specifically the product of the imaginary number $\sqrt{-1}$, which comes to bear in both quantum theory and relativity theory. For the relevance of this notion to semiotics as developed in this volume, you might wish to consult Merrell (1991, 1995a, 1995b).

5   See Gardner (1979) and Rucker (1984) for a layperson's discussion of the fourth-dimension in this regard.

6   The *imaginary* dimension allowing Ms. Triangle to "get" under the two-dimensional plane in order to "flip" into the other side is not entirely unlike the "role" of *imaginary* numbers used in what is termed an "Argand plane"—which can account for what I referred in note 59 as "abstract time." The "Argand plane," incorporating

√-1, has been used to account for our universe in both relativity theory and quantum mechanics. Limited time and space to not permit discussion of this intriguing phenomenon here (for further, see Kauffman and Varela 1980).

[7] One enticing explanation of dyslexia—which also brings Peirce to mind—suggests a problem of interhemispheric communication due to less asymmetry between the hemispheres than most of us enjoy (Hellige 1993).

[8] We must bear in mind, of course, that this "block" image of the "time-flow" of signs—ourselves included—is indelibly false to itself. It is Euclidean, patterning the Renaissance "vanishing point." Hence it is incapable of bearing genuine witness to the warps and folds, the woofs and the interlockings, of the convoluted, involuted, diverging, converging "time-flows" within non-Euclidean space and time dependent upon relative "frames of reference." Nonetheless, perhaps Figure 13 can at least afford a visual grasp, however vague, of the exceedingly complex process of *semiosis*.

[9] At the risk of appearing inordinately repetitive, here, once again, we have the essentials of Peirce's "pragmatic maxim."

REFERENCES

Barnes, Susan J. (1989). *The Rothko Chapel: An Act of Faith.* Austin: University of Texas Press.

Barthes, Roland. (1972). *Critical Essays.* Evanston: Northwestern University Press.

Beckett, Samuel. (1954). *Waiting for Godot.* New York: Grove (French edition, 1952).

———. (1958). *The Unnamable.* New York: Grove (French edition, 1953).

Brent, Joseph. (1993). *Charles Saunders Peirce: A Life.* Bloomington: Indiana University Press.

Cage, John. (1961). *Silence.* Middletown: Wesleyan University Press.

Eco, Umberto. (1976). *A Theory of Semiotics.* Bloomington: Indiana University Press.

———. (1984). *Semiotics and the Philosophy of Language.* Bloomington: Indiana University Press.

Gardner, Martin. (1979). *The Ambidextrous Universe: Mirror Asymmetry and Time-Reversed Worlds,* 2nd ed. New York: Charles Scribner's Sons.

Hall, Nina. (ed.) (1993). *Exploring Chaos: A Guide to the New Science of Disorder.* New York: W. W. Morton.

Hellige, Joseph R. (1993). *Hemispheric Asymmetry: What's Right and What's Left?* Cambridge: Harvard University Press.

Hofstadter, Douglas R. (1979). *Gödel, Escher, Bach: An Eternal Golden Braid.* New York: Basic Books.

CLOSING REMARKS

We think only in signs. These mental signs are of mixed nature;
the symbol-parts of them are called concepts . . . .
A symbol, once in being, spreads among peoples.
In use and in experience, its meaning grows.

–*Charles S. Peirce (1839-1914)*

TEN CLASSICS IN SEMIOTICS

Marcel Danesi
Donato Santeramo

In a volume such as this one, it is the customary practice to give the reader a list of "suggested readings." We have decided to break somewhat with this tradition and, instead, to offer the reader a list of ten works that reflect our own "top ten" favourites in semiotics. We apologize for leaving out works that other experts in the field consider important. The instructor will note that such names as St. Augustine, Derrida, Lévi-Strauss, Morris, Foucault, McLuhan, Bakhtin, Jakobson, Metz, Hjelmslev, Todorov, Kristeva, Baudrillard, Lyotard, Merrell, Deely, to mention but a handful, are missing from the selection. We encourage the instructor using this volume as a textbook to fill-in the gaps left by our selection with his or her own supplementary list.

Actually, choosing the ten most important publications of all time in the field of semiotics has turned out to be a much more difficult task than we envisaged when we first started thinking about drafting this final chapter. One of the first "methods" we used to test our preferences against those of other semioticians was to conduct a "probe" of bibliographies and reference sections in relevant articles and books. However, we soon came to the realization that what others cited as authoritative sources often did not match our own inclinations. So, the following selection of "top ten" works is not based on any "objective" criterion. It is a truly "personal" one. Note, moreover, that several of the books mentioned here have been extracted for inclusion in the readings section of this book.

Vico, Giambattista (1984). The New Science *(trans. Thomas G. Bergin and Max H. Fish) Ithaca: Cornell University Press [originally published in 1725 as* La scienza nuova*].*

In our view, this is the most important book on the mind ever written. Vico argued that the essential nature of mind could be unraveled by considering what its "modifications" reveal; i.e., by examining the symbols, languages, and all the uniquely human creations—myths, stories, works of art, scientific theories, etc.—that the mind has made possible and which have come to constitute "the world of civil society." Vico claimed that the imagination was the primary force that underlies the transformation of the world of sense into a world of reflection.

Peirce, Charles, S. (1931-58). Collected Papers of Charles Sanders Peirce, *ed. by Charles Hartshorne and Paul Weiss. Cambridge: Harvard University Press.*

One cannot be a "practicing semiotician" and not include the work of Charles Peirce among his or her "top ten" list. As we discussed in our opening remarks, his taxonomy of signs as *indexical, iconic*, and *symbolic* remains the basic framework within which to conduct semiotic research and within which to cultivate the entire field. Contemporary semiotic work would be unthinkable without its Peircean foundation.

Cassirer, Ernst (1924). The Philosophy of Symbolic Forms. *New Haven: Yale University Press, 1924. [English translation of:* Die Philosophie der symbolischen Formen, *3 vols. Berlin: Bruno Cassirer, 1923).*

With this work, Cassirer emphasized that myths and the culture-specific symbol systems they spawn underlie cognitive structures and processes. Like Vico before him, he pointed out that cultural symbologies and institutions sprang from an unconscious grammar of experience, whose categories were those of the imagination. The constituents of cultural symbolic codes are derived ultimately from sensorial experience. They are "constructed" by humans as conceptual tools for coming to grips with the more abstract concerns with which cultures must grapple.

Sebeok, Thomas A. (1979). The Sign and Its Masters. *Austin: University of Texas Press.*

This is a true modern classic that both "redefines" semiotics in biological terms and highlights the work of those semioticians who helped to lay down the theoretical and conceptual foundations of semiotics as a science. Although all species participate by instinct in the experiential universe, humans are particularly well-equipped with the capacity to model their sense impressions cognitively. It is when these mental transformations of our bodily experiences are codified into signs and sign systems that they become permanently transportable in the form of cognitive units, phenomenologically free from their physiological units of occurrence. The work of Sebeok on semiosis has made it possible to relate the world of bodily experience to the world of abstraction and thought, by having shown the latter to be a kind of evolutionary "outgrowth" of the former. In so doing, Sebeok has transformed semiotics into a life science, having taken it back, in effect, to its roots in medical biology. In other words, he has uprooted semiotics from the philosophical, linguistic, and hermeneutic terrain in which it has been cultivated for centuries and replanted it into the larger biological domain from where it sprang originally.

Eco, Umberto (1984). A Theory of Semiotics. *Bloomington: Indiana University Press.*

Eco's work has made it saliently obvious that sign systems are connected inextricably to the contexts (personal and social) in which they are anchored. Interpretation, therefore, is a by-product of psychological and social structures that contribute substantially to the form and even contents of the interpretation process. Semiotics is perceived by Eco to be the science that studies this fundamental process.

Langer, Susanne K. (1942). Philosophy in a New Key. *Cambridge: Harvard University Press.*

One of the most important lessons to be learned from Langer is, in our view, that at the most primary level of mind we apprehend the world through "feeling," i.e., we "feel" that the world has a structure. She calls this the "presentational" form of cognition. This is present in all thinking in such a way that it is even more "ordered" than language and logic. Linguistic and logical categories are derivatives of bodily experience.

Saussure, Ferdinand de (1916). Cours de linguistique générale. *Paris: Payot.*

It goes without saying that without Saussure's definition of the sign as a relational process between a signifier and a signified the modern study of semiotic phenomena might not have taken the course that it has. Saussure was among the first to note that signification was both related to, but not necessarily dependent upon, communication.

Greimas, Aljirdas J. (1966). Stuctural Semantics. *Lincoln: University of Nebraska Press.*

This work has helped shape the idea that there is a propensity in the human species to take the "bits and pieces" of meaning inherent in basic sign-making processes and project them onto a series of what would otherwise be perceived to be random actions. The result is a "narrated" universe that makes sense primarily in terms of its own symbolic-narrative structures.

Barthes, Roland (1957). Mythologies. *Paris: Seuil.*

This is one of the first publications to apply semiotics to the study of cultural behaviour. Barthes drew the attention of semioticians to the value of studying common, cultural events (wrestling, strip-teasing, etc.) as modern mythological reifications. He thus inspired the first semiotic works analyzing the relation of "pop culture" to deeply embedded signifying processes.

Lakoff, George and Johnson, Mark (1980). Metaphors We Live By. *Chicago: University of Chicago Press.*

This important work argues persuasively that our most common concepts are forged via metaphor. Lakoff and Johnson show this by simply taking concepts apart and revealing their underlying metaphorical structure. Although the main claims made by Lakoff and Johnson are not new to anyone who has read Vico, they have "shaken up" the world of contemporary language study. Lakoff and Johnson have shown how common concepts, ranging all the way from love to justice, are grounded in metaphor, and since communication is based in large part on the same conceptual system that we use in thinking and acting, that language is an important source of evidence of what that system is like.

FOLLOW-UP ACTIVITIES AND QUESTIONS FOR DISCUSSION

CHAPTER 1: TZVETAN TODOROV

Follow-up Activities:

1. Make a list of all the definitions of sign found in this chapter.

2. Choose the one that you think is the most understandable one, giving reasons why.

3. Summarize St. Augustine's theory of signs, giving examples of its validity with examples of your own.

Questions for Discussion:

4. Can you come up with any words in English or any other language you know that support the "naturalist" perspective espoused by various ancient Greek philosophers that words were originally forged to be imitative of the things they refer to?

5. Discuss St. Augustine's contention that the phenomenon of signs in human life is a manifestation of human spirituality. Do you agree?

6. St. Augustine distinguished between signification, the production and understanding of signs, communication, and their use in actual social life. How do you think the two dimensions are interconnected? Do you think that signs exist for purposes other than communication? If so, what are those purposes?

CHAPTER 2: CHARLES S. PEIRCE

Follow-up Activities:

1. Define *qualisign*, *sinsign*, and *legisign* in your own way, giving examples from everyday language and/or other forms of communication.

2. Define *rheme*, *dicisign*, and *argument* in your own way, giving examples from everyday language and/or other forms of communication.

3. Define *icon*, *index*, and *symbol* in your own way, giving examples from everyday language and/or other forms of communication.

Questions for Discussion:

4. Do you agree with Peirce that iconicity is the most basic form of signification (the making and use of signs) in the human species? Give reasons why you do or do not agree.

5. Can you find examples of Firstness (iconicity), Secondness (indexicality), and Thirdness (symbolism) as being sequential in the development of cognition and representation in the human child? In other words, can you think of any evidence in the literature on child development that shows a natural sequence of Firstness-to-Secondness-to-Thirdness forms of thinking and communicating?

6. Discuss Peirce's contention that semiotics is a doctrine. What do you think this means? Compare it with other doctrines. After reading this chapter, how

would you define semiotics (as a science, as part of philosophy, as part of logic, etc.)?

CHAPTER 3: FERDINAND DE SAUSSURE

Follow-up Activities:

1. Define *signifier* and *signified*, giving examples of each.

2. Summarize Saussure's characterization of *language* and *speech*.

3. Can you see any points of contact between Peirce's definition of sign and Saussure's?

Questions for Discussion:

4. Do you agree with Saussure's contention that, with few exceptions, signs are arbitrary: i.e., that there is no iconic bond between signifier and signified?

5. Is it possible to integrate Peircean semiotic theory with Saussurean? In what ways?

6. Is it possible to have signifiers without signifieds, or vice versa (e.g,. nonsense words)? If so, what would this imply for semiotic theory?

CHAPTER 4: RICK OSBORN

Follow-up Activities:

1. Explain the difference between the "strong" version of the Whorfian hypothesis and its "weak" version.

2. Explain the difference between "linguistic relativity" and "linguistic determinism."

3. Can you give examples of your own that argue in favour of the Whorfian hypothesis?

Questions for Discussion:

4. Do you believe that abstract concepts are impossible without language? Defend your answer; in this way you will enter first-hand into the intricacies and pitfalls of the Whorfian hypothesis.

5. Do you think that sexist language shapes attitudes towards the affected sex? Again, defend your answer, so that you can come to understand the difficulty of resolving the debate on the Whorfian hypothesis.

6. An area that is often considered a goldmine for the debate on the Whorfian hypothesis is colour terminology. What is a colour? Do you think that those speaking different languages with different colour terms see different "colours?"

CHAPTER 5: GEORGE LAKOFF AND MARK JOHNSON

Follow-up Activities:

1. How do Lakoff and Johnson define *concept*?

2. Can you give more expressions that derive from the "argument is war" concept?

3. Can you come up with the metaphorical ways of conceptualizing "love," "justice," "hope"? Here are a few examples of the "love is a sweetness" concept to help you get started: She's so sweet; This is my sweetheart; Hi honey, how are you?

Questions for Discussion:

4. After having read this chapter, do you think that all abstract thought is metaphorical in nature or origin? Explain, illustrate, and defend your point of view.

5. What are "ideas"? Provide a catalogue of the metaphorical concepts that refer to ideas: e.g., "ideas are plants" (This idea is growing on me; Your idea bears no fruits; Your idea has many ramifications). Now, do you think that all knowledge is forged by metaphor? Defend your position.

6. The sentence "Colourless green ideas sleep furiously" has become a famous one in linguistics, since it was used by the influential linguist Noam Chomsky in his 1957 book *Syntactic Structures* to make the case that it "meant nothing" although it had the "structure" of a sentence. But, since then, research has shown that people will find a metaphorical meaning for such sentences, known technically as anomalous strings. What does it mean to you? And why do you think it creates a meaning? Can there be any well-formed utterance without a meaning that can be attached to it? Here's another example: "Mindless thoughts eat only vegetables." Does it mean anything? What? Why?

CHAPTER 6: PAUL PERRON

Follow-up Activities:

1. Explain the concept of *narrative grammar* in your own words.

2. Explain the idea of *generative trajectory* in your own words.

3. What is a "grammar of modality"?

Questions for Discussion:

4. Can you give a Greimasian analysis of your favourite short story?

5. Why do you think people tell and enjoy stories, from simple tales to complex novels?

6. What differences, if any, do you see between drama and narrative, poetry and narrative? Do other forms of expression—music, painting, etc.—also have narrative form? Explain your answer providing illustrations.

Chapter 7: Susanne K. Langer

Follow-up Activities:

1. Summarize in your own words the difference between *presentational* and *discursive* forms.

2. Give examples of presentational forms.

3. Give examples of discursive forms.

Questions for Discussion:

4. What is visual art? Explain your answer utilizing the discursive vs. presentational dichotomy.

5. What is musical art? Once again, explain your answer utilizing the discursive vs. presentational dichotomy.

6. We often say that this work of art or that one is "beautiful." What does this mean?

Chapter 8: Stanley J. Grenz

Follow-up Activities:

1. Define *postmodernism* in your own words.

2. Define *postmodernity* in your own words. What's the difference between *postmodernism* and *postmodernity*?

3. Give a brief historical summary of the origins and development of postmodernism.

Questions for Discussion:

4. Give examples of postmodern forms of visual art. Why are they postmodern?

5. Do you agree with Grenz that film-making is the foundation for postmodern culture? Explain your answer.

6. What do you think will come after postmodernism in our culture, if history is indeed a dynamic process, constantly evolving and changing?

CHAPTER 9: MARCEL DANESI

Follow-up Activities:

1. Take an ad from a lifestyle magazine. What are the features of the ad that stand out? Why is the ad effective?

2. Compare a print ad with a television commercial.

3. Relate your analysis to Danesi's chapter.

Questions for Discussion:

4. Do you think that advertising shapes world view?

5. How is meaning generated by ads and commercials?

6. Do you think that we are living in an "advertising culture"?

CHAPTER 10: ROCCO CAPOZZI

Follow-up Activities:

1. Get a copy of Eco's *Name of the Rose* and read it.

2. Get a copy of the film version of the novel. Which one did you like better? Why?

3. Relate your answer to Grenz's chapter, and especially to his ideas about film-making.

Questions for Discussion:

4. Why do you think that *The Name of the Rose* became a best-seller?

5. What do you think is the main theme of the novel?

6. Who determines what the meaning of a novel, or any work of art for that matter, is?

CHAPTER 11: FLOYD MERRELL

Follow-up Activities:

1. Get a copy of Edwin A. Abbot's novel *Flatland* and read it. Discuss it in class.

2. What does Merrell mean by "We're in the sign"?

3. What is lying, in semiotic terms?

Questions for Discussion:

4. Expressions such as vantage point, point of view, standpoint, etc. reveal a visual basis to abstraction. Do you think the sense of sight has become a crucial one for the making of knowledge?

5. In what sense do you think that semiotics offers a vantage point from which to view and understand human beings?

6. Now that you have gone through 11 readings in semiotics, can you define semiotics in your own terms? How would you explain what semiotics is and does to someone who knows nothing about it?